I0822005

Critical Perspectives on Canadian Theatre in English

General Editor Ric Knowles

2005

Aboriginal Drama and Theatre
ed. Rob Appleford
volume one 978-0-88754-792-8

African-Canadian Theatre
ed. Maureen Moynagh
volume two 978-0-88754-794-2

Judith Thompson
ed. Ric Knowles
volume three 978-0-88754-796-6

2006

Feminist Theatre and Performance
ed. Susan Bennett
volume four 978-0-88754-798-0

George F. Walker
ed. Harry Lane
volume five 978-0-88754-800-0

Theatre in British Columbia
ed. Ginny Ratsoy
volume six 978-0-88754-802-4

2007

Queer Theatre
ed. Rosalind Kerr
volume seven 978-0-88754-804-8

Environmental and Site-Specific Theatre
ed. Andrew Houston
volume eight 978-0-88754-806-2

Space and the Geographies of Theatre
ed. Michael McKinnie
volume nine 978-0-88754-808-6

2008

Sharon Pollock
ed. Sherrill Grace & Michelle La Flamme
volume ten 978-0-88754-751-5

Theatre in Alberta
ed. Anne Nothof
volume eleven 978-0-88754-753-9

Collective Creation, Collaboration and Devising
ed. Bruce Barton
volume twelve 978-0-88754-755-3

2009

Theatre Histories
ed. Alan Filewod
volume thirteen 978-0-88754-831-4

"Ethnic," Multicultural and Intercultural Theatre
ed. Ric Knowles & Ingrid Mündel
volume fourteen 978-0-88754-832-1

Design and Scenography
ed. Natalie Rewa
volume fifteen 978-0-88754-833-8

2010

Theatre in Atlantic Canada
ed. Linda Burnett
volume sixteen 978-0-88754-890-1

Popular Political Theatre and Performance
ed. Julie Salverson
volume seventeen 978-0-88754-891-8

Canadian Shakespeare
ed. Susan Knutson
volume eighteen 978-0-88754-893-2

416-703-0013 • orders@playwrightscanada.com • www.playwrightscanada.com

Design and Scenography

Critical Perspectives on Canadian Theatre in English

volume fifteen

Critical Perspectives on Canadian Theatre in English

volume fifteen

Design and Scenography

Edited by
Natalie Rewa

Playwrights Canada Press
Toronto • Canada

Playwrights Canada Press
215 Spadina Avenue, Suite 230, Toronto, Ontario CANADA M5T 2C7
416-703-0013 fax 416-408-3402
orders@playwrightscanada.com • www.playwrightscanada.com

The publisher acknowledges the support of the Canadian taxpayers through the Government of Canada Book Publishing Industry Development Program, the Canada Council for the Arts, the Ontario Arts Council, and the Ontario Media Development Corporation.

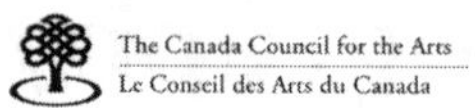

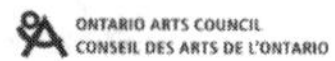

Cover image: Jin-me Yoon, between departure and arrival, 1996/1997.
Partial installation view, Art Gallery of Ontario.
Video projection, video montage on monitor, photographic mylar scroll, clocks with 3-D lettering, audio. Dimensions variable.
Courtesy of the artist and Catriona Jeffries Gallery, Vancouver.
Production Editor/Cover Design: JLArt

Library and Archives Canada Cataloguing in Publication

Design and scenography / Natalie Rewa, ed.

(Critical perspectives on Canadian theatre in English 15)
Includes bibliographical references.
ISBN 978-0-88754-833-8

1. Theaters--Stage-setting and scenery--Canada.
I. Rewa, Natalie, 1956- II. Series: Critical perspectives on Canadian theatre in English 15

PN2087.C3T54 2009 792.02'50971 C2009-901468-8

First edition: May 2009
Printed and bound by Hignell Printing at Winnipeg, Canada.

For Tetiana Rewa

З подякую за материнську любов, і любов до театру

Table of Contents

General Editor's Preface

Critical Perspectives on Canadian Theatre in English was launched in 2005 with the intention of making the best critical and scholarly work in the field readily available to teachers, students and scholars of Canadian drama and theatre. It set out, in individual volumes, chronologically to trace the histories of scholarship and criticism on individual playwrights, geographical regions, theatrical genres, themes and cultural communities. Over its first three years the series published nine volumes, collecting work on Aboriginal Theatre, African-Canadian Theatre, playwrights Judith Thompson and George F. Walker, Feminist Theatre, Queer Theatre, Theatre in British Columbia, Environmental and Site-Specific Theatre, and Space and the Geographies of Theatre. I am very proud of this achievement, proud that these volumes have already been widely cited in subsequent scholarship, and proud that, although this is primarily a reprint series, essays newly commissioned for individual volumes have been nominated for and have won scholarly awards.

As the series continues, so do its original objectives. Each volume is edited and introduced by an expert in the field who has selected a representative sampling of the most important critical work on her or his subject since circa 1970, ordered chronologically according to the original dates of publication. Each volume also includes an introduction by the volume editor, surveying the field and its criticism, and a list of suggested further readings which recommends good work that could not otherwise be included. Where appropriate, the volume editors commission new essays on their subjects, particularly when these new essays fill in gaps in representation and attempt to correct historical injustices and imbalances, particularly those concerning marginalized communities. The volume topics have also been chosen to shed light on historically marginalized communities and work, while individual volumes have resisted the ghettoization of such work by relegating it to special topic volumes alone.

Volumes 10 through 15 carry on the work of the first nine volumes. They continue to address the work of individual playwrights, including Sharon Pollock, of geographical regions including Alberta, of genres including Collective, Collaborative and Devised Theatre, and of marginalized communities, here focusing on "Ethnic," Multicultural and Intercultural Theatre. They also strike out in different directions, assembling a history of the criticism of Design in Canadian theatre, and reflecting on the multiple histories of Canada's theatre histories.

It is my hope that this series, in conjunction with the publications of Playwrights Canada Press, Talonbooks and other Canadian play publishers, will facilitate the teaching of Canadian drama and theatre in schools and universities for years to come. I hope by making available and accessible comprehensive introductions to some of the field's most provocative figures and issues, that they will contribute to the flourishing of courses on a variety of aspects of Canadian drama and theatre in classrooms across the country. And I hope that they will honour the work of some of the scholar/pioneers of a field that is still, excitingly, young.

Ric Knowles

Acknowledgements

My sincere and heartfelt thanks are first to the many authors, journal editors and photographers who have generously participated by granting copyright for their work to be reprinted, and on one occasion before the article appeared in print. My special debt of gratitude is to Ric Knowles and the editors at Playwrights Canada Press for their vision of this series and for their support of the design of this volume in particular, with so many images. My thanks go to Marianne VanderDussen who assisted with the preparation of collection and for her spirit of collaboration. To Michael J. Sidnell, my thanks are for steadfast support.

All the essays are published with the permission of the copyright holder. Original publication information is: Herman Voaden and Lowrie Warrener. "*Symphony*: A Drama of Motion and Light For a New Theatre." *A Vision of Canada: Herman Voaden's Works 1928–1945.* Ed. Anton Wagner. Toronto: Simon and Pierre (1993): 133–138; 141–143; 145–148; 152–155. Permission is granted by Anton Wagner, Literary Executor of the Herman Voaden Estate; Reid Gilbert. "'And then we saw you fly over there and land!': Metadramatic Design in the Stage Work of Morris Panych and Ken MacDonald." *Theatre History in Canada/L'Histoire du théâtre au Canada* 11.2 (1990): 134–147; Michèle White. "VideoCabaret and the Subversion of 'Scenography.'" *Canadian Theatre Review* 70 (1992): 45–49; Natalie Rewa. "Astrid Janson's Design for Performance." *Australasian Drama Studies* 29 (1996): 85–99; Ronald Fedoruk. "The Cosmopolitan Classroom." *Canadian Theatre Review* 91 (1997): 5–8; Allan Watts. "Discipline Makes Better Art: Michael J. Whitfield Talks About Repertory and Opera Lighting." *Canadian Theatre Review* 107 (2001): 32–36; Ana Cappelluto and Edward Little. "Seeing the Light: Montreal's Axel Morgenthaler." *Canadian Theatre Review* 107 (2001): 37–42; Rahul Varma. "Robert Lepage's *Zulu Time:* A Colonialist Fantasy." *alt.theatre* 2.4 (2003): 4–5, 15; Anna Friz. "The Loudspeaker as Instrument: The Soundworks of Nancy Tobin." *Musicworks* 88 (2004): 42–51; Jerrard Smith. "Collaboration and Confluence: A Multidisciplinary Approach to Environmental Scenography." *Scenography International* 10 (2008); Michael Devine. "Keileydography: The Symphonic Theatre of Jillian Keiley." *Canadian Theatre Review* 128 (2006): 31–36; Dany Lyne. "Acceptance speech at the 2006 Siminovitch Prize in Theatre Honouring Designers." Siminovitch Prize.com (2006); Camellia Koo. "The Box: What Happens When You Place the Audience and/or a Performer Inside an 8'x 8' Box." Pure Research, Report. Nightswimmingtheatre.ca (2007); Kathleen Irwin. "The Bus Project: Technologies, Spectators and Locational Practices." *Theatre Research in Canada/Recherches Théâtrales au Canada* 29.1 (2008): 93–109; Natalie Rewa. "Michael

Levine: Tracing the Moments of Scenographic Dramaturgy" is published here for the first time.

Gilbert and Irwin are reprinted by permission of the authors and *Theatre Research in Canada/Recherches théâtrales au Canada,* c/o the Graduate Centre for the Study of Drama, University of Toronto, 214 College Street, 3rd floor, Toronto, Ontario M5T 2Z9. Tel, 416-978-7984; fax 416-971-1378. Email: tric.rtac@utoronto.ca, web: www.lib.unb.ca/Texts/TRIC.

Koo is reprinted with the permission of www.nightswimmingtheatre.com.
Lyne is published with the permission of www.siminovitchprize.com.
Smith is published with the permission of www.scenography-international.com.

Photos

All images from pages 61–76 are published from the following sources:

1. Sketch by Herman Voaden. Scenario for First Movement of *Symphony.* Credit: York University Libraries, Clara Thomas Archives & Special Collections, Herman Voaden fonds F0440, image ASC04916.
2. Sketch by Lowrie Warrener, possibly for the Fifth Movement of *Symphony* (1930). Credit: York University Libraries, Clara Thomas Archives & Special Collections, Herman Voaden fonds F0440, image ASC04917.
3. Sketch by Lowrie Warrener on reverse side of first page of Second Movement of annotated draft of *Symphony* (1930). Credit: York University Libraries, Clara Thomas Archives & Special Collections, Herman Voaden fonds F0440, image ASC04901.
4. *7 Stories,* by Morris Panych, Arts Club, Seymour Street, Vancouver, 1989. Credit: Ken MacDonald.
5. *7 Stories* by Morris Panych, Arts Club, Granville Island, Vancouver, 2004. Credit: Ken MacDonald.
6. *7 Stories* by Morris Panych, Arts Club, Granville Island, Vancouver, 2004 Architectural details and painting (close up) Credit: Ken MacDonald.
7. Deanne Taylor in *The Patty Rehearst Story.* By Deanne Taylor. Hummer Sisters. 85 St. Nicholas Street (1976), Frank's Place (later Ydessa Gallery) 1976, The Kitchen Centre for Music and Video, New York (1978). Credit: Rick Shiomi.
8. Deanne Taylor as Sister DeeDee in *The History of the Village of the Small Huts, Part 1, New France.* By Michael Hollingsworth, Theatre Passe Muraille, 1985. Credit: Rick Shiomi.

9. Ontario Culture and Sports: One of eleven installations for the Ontario Pavillion for Expo '86 (Vancouver). Projections on Plexiglas tubes. Credit: Barry Jones.

10. *Jacob Two-Two*, Projections and costumes. Young People's Theatre (Lorraine Kimsa Theatre for Young People) 1989. Credit: Michael Cooper.

11. *The History of the Village of the Small Huts: The Great War*. VideoCabaret, 1993. Seen here in back row: Janet Burke, Alan Bridle, Mackenzie Gray. Front row: Hugo Dann, Cliff Saunders. Credit: Michael Cooper.

12. *The Rez Sisters* by Tomson Highway. University of British Columbia, 2007. The set design was by Parjad Sharifi (Iran), lighting design by Chris Littman (USA), costume design by Jay Havens (Canada). Seen here from L-R Yoshi Bancroft, Sarah Afful, Hilary Fillier, Cecile Roslin, Maura Halloran, Kate Hilderman, Kim Harvey, (Top) Tracy Olson. Credit: Tim Matheson.

13. *La Vie qui bat*. Choreography Ginette Laurin, musical direction Walter Baudreau. O Vertigo Danse/Société de musique contemporaine du Québec. Salle Pierre Mercure, Montreal, 1999. Credit: Axel Morgenthaler.

14. *Lulu, le Chant Souterain*. Composer Alain Thibault and libretto by Yan Muckle. Chants Libre, l'Usine C, Montreal, 2000. Credit: Axel Morgenthaler.

15. *Don Juan*. By Felix Gray. Chants Libre, Théâtre St.-Denis, Montreal, 2004. Credit: Axel Morgenthaler.

16. *Concerto grosso pour corps et surface métallique*. Choreography by Danièle Desnoyers. Carré des Lombes, 1999. Credit: Nancy Tobin.

17. "The Funeral Procession." *Ra* by R. Murray Schafer. Patria Music/Theatre Projects. Holland Festival, Leiden, 1985. Credit: F. Falkenhagen.

18. *The Palace of the Cinnabar Phoenix* by R. Murray Schafer. Patria Music/Theatre Projects. Haliburton Forest and Wildlife Reserve, 2006. Credit: Risheng Wang.

19. Asterion site map. Credit: Jerrard Smith.

20. "The 2' x 2' grid" for *Jesus Christ Superstar*. By Andrew Lloyd Webber and Tim Rice. Direction by Jillian Keiley. Musical Direction by Petrina Bromley. Artistic Fraud, 1998. Credit: Jillian Keiley.

21. *Jesus Christ Superstar*. By Andrew Lloyd Webber and Tim Rice, 1998. Credit: Jeff Melbourne. Courtesy of Artistic Fraud.

22. *The Bus Project*. Sketches for the kiosk by John Reichert.

23. *The Bus Project*. The kiosk located in the Regina STC Bus Depot, designed and constructed by John Reichert, 2004. Credit: Kathleen Irwin.

24. *Candide*. By Leonard Bernstein. Directed by Robert Carsen. Théâtre du Châtelet, Paris, 2006. Credit: Courtesy of Michael Levine.

25. *Candide.* Preliminary sketches by Michael Levine. Artist's sketchbook. Credit: Courtesy of Michael Levine.
26. *Madame Butterfly.* By Giacomo Puccini. Directed by Anthony Minghella. ENO (English National Opera), London, 2005. Credit: Courtesy of Michael Levine.

Introduction: Critical Perspectives on Design and Scenography in Canada

by Natalie Rewa

Design and *scenography* are yoked together in the title for this volume so as to emphasize their distinctness and their complementarity. Even more important is the interaction between the perspectives and activities that these two terms connote: a powerful current in the creative energies represented in this volume, albeit a mostly unconscious one.

As the familiar term that appears in programs and is usually applied to sets, costumes, lighting and sound, *design* attributes processes and their products to individuals within a creative team. These designers are listed in sequence after the director so as to confirm a hierarchy in the organization of the theatre, or at least the production. This segregation of facets of design that are usually highly integrated also draws attention away from the architectonics of the visual and aural narration of the performance—that is, its *scenography.*

Scenography emphasizes the "graphic" dimensions of the materiality of the performance—their eventfulness. Moreover, the *scenography* is what comprises all the design categories—sets, costumes, lights and sound—modulating the focus of attention onto the spatial dynamics, the active presence of the performers in the given spaces, and the choices of materials which have entered the interpretative and creative vocabulary of the production. Insofar as the creative work of the designers is dramaturgical, rather than primarily decorative or representational, and articulates vocabularies for the synaesthetic dialogue with the spectators, *scenography* has become (once more) the usual term of choice.[1] The British designer Pamela Howard[2] advocates the term *scenography* to describe the work of designers in production because, she argues, it acknowledges not only the artistic research and design process, which contribute to the conceptualization of the *mise en scène,* but it also draws attention to the ongoing and active scenographic communication with the spectators (Howard 125). The development of an environment for performance and the choices of design elements become key terms in the vocabulary and structure of dialogue between stage and spectators. So while this volume foregrounds creative expertise focused on any one area of production design it also tries to make clear how designers shape performance; and how the consciousness of this more comprehensive creativity has developed in Canada. Much more than a matter of mere terminology, then, these two terms mark the not-unstressful dynamics of the creative motives and energies that have gone into the materiality of stage presentation in the periods and places represented in this volume.

Camellia Koo's contribution to this volume speaks to the widening scope of the designer's function in production. It is the report of a well-known young designer on her residency in Nightswimming's program of Pure Research in 2005.[3] It has been included as an insight into scenographic research into the dynamics of performer-spectator responses to a stage-object. In her experiment an 8'x8' box becomes a "relational object" (Bouriaud 26) used to provoke and develop human encounters. Koo documents a series of games in which the participants—actors, producers and graduate students—remake, or recharacterize the box according to its appearance and their immediate responses to being in it, or observing it. The final segment in the report extends the research to an installation of the box at the Audience Re/Location TURN LEFT HERE FESTIVAL at Buddies in Bad Times Theatre 1–2 March 2007, where it served to facilitate spectatorial relationships to immigration. Clearly, scenography in Canada has long since liberated itself from the paddock of stage decoration.

In 1979, Tom Doherty noted in his preface to the catalogue for the Canadian Exhibition to the Prague Quadrennial for that year: "Twenty five years ago, theatrical activity in Canada was dominated by touring productions of Broadway plays. There were only a handful of professional companies using Canadian talent and staging at least some original work." He associates the rise of the professional designer in Canada with the establishment of theatre companies and the construction of theatre buildings across the country during this period. By the time of the exhibit in 1979, the Associated Designers of Canada (ADC) had been in existence for fourteen years and its membership, claimed Doherty, had risen to "roughly a hundred."[4] Two years later, in 1981, Quebec designers formed their own organization, L'Association des professionnels des arts de la scène du Québec (APASQ), to meet the needs of designers working under contractual arrangements different from those in the rest of Canada. The contributions to this volume bear witness to that development of a community of professional designers in Canada.

In the period before the founding of the ADC and L'APASQ such writing as there was about theatre design was often in the form of advice, appearing in such journals as *Curtain Call* (1929–1941) or *Callboard* (1949–1995). Substantial discussion of design (as distinct from reviews) arrived with *Performing Arts in Canada* (1961) and was continued in *Scene Changes* (1973), *Canadian Theatre Review* (1974), *Canadian Drama* (1975), *Theatrum* (1985), *Theatre History in Canada/Histoire du Théâtre au Canada* (1980), and more recently *alt.theatre* (1998). A noticeable development through the 1970s, in interviews with designers and commentaries on their work, was the sense of a fresh understanding of design as a production element not confined to décor and decoration.[5] There was also a progressive diversification of perspectives on design as other theatre practitioners, critics and even scholars joined in the discussion.[6]

In this volume several broad areas of concern may be discerned. A main one is the kinds of understanding and modes of collaboration between creative artists that do or might obtain in theatrical production, whether in accordance with a specific mandate or the conventions of interaction between collaborators. Another is, of course, the exploration of approaches to design for theatrical presentation or performance by individual designers working in their designated fields. Then there is the more specifically Canadian preoccupation with designing with an awareness of cultural and regional diversity. And, to pick out another shared concern, there is discussion of the manipulation of the materials or technologies which have entered into the design vocabulary and that, by their ephemerality, may have been forgotten. By way of introducing the contributions, I group them in relation to these prominent concerns.

Collaborative efforts…

Some of the earliest Canadian approaches to scenography, in the sense noted, were by the playwright Herman Voaden. In the composition of *Symphony: A Drama of Motion and Light for a New Theatre* in 1930[7] his collaborator was Lowrie Warrener, a painter and sculptor, and the resulting scenario marked the culmination of their work together over two years. Influenced by the canvases of the Group of Seven and by F.B. Housser's *The Group of Seven: A Canadian Art Movement*, Voaden invited Lowrie Warrener to join him in the creation of a "painter's ballet." Their brief was the complex search for modes of expression for a "picture drama" and Voaden recalls the process as an uneasy relationship of writerly with painterly. In a note to Violet Kilpatrick he described the work in progress as a "Canadian rhythmic-dance-colour-music-light-pantomime drama, without need for dialogue or poetry or libretto." The sketches by Voaden and Warrener show their contrasting approaches—Voaden working through the scenario horizontally by way of a ground plan and thinking through locations while Warrener's visual and volumetric imprint[8] fills the space with an overwhelming presence of the mountains. In five movements Voaden and Warrener created a rhythmic pattern in the scenario, notably in the locationally specific episodes of the first, third and fifth movements, in which the presences of man and woman narratively dominate. Excerpted here are the second and fourth movements that Voaden denotes as originating from Warrener's conception of a stage: the second movement, "The Northern Wilderness," describes a luminously-intense environment and the fourth, under the more interpretive title "The Prairie Farm," plays out the life forces of earth and sky as six choral groups of figures. The scenario and the commentary offer a particularly rich sense of scenographic invention as a negotiation of the visual, aural, spatial and rhythmical.[9]

Scrolling forward to present times, the interview with Michael Levine included here considers four specific models of a designer's collaborative dramaturgy. He tells how discussions between director and designer provide him with distinct templates for creating the scenography, and his remarks attest to diverse approaches to rehearsing and designing. He had to develop modes of working with the late Anthony Minghella who wished to continue the processes of discovery in the rehearsal hall while he was directing *Madame Butterfly* for the English National Opera (ENO, 2005) as well as with Japanese and British cast who devised *The Elephant Vanishes* (Théâtre Complicité, 2003) in a workshop. Levine's collaborations with the Canadian Robert

Carsen, who directs operatic productions in great houses abroad but not in this country,[10] now amount to almost two dozen productions; on this occasion he considers how, working together, they conceived bold productions of *Candide* (Châtelet, 2006) and *The Coronation of Poppea* (Glynbourne, 2008) with a notable emphasis on the exploiting of the potentialities of advanced theatre technology.

Several other examples of such collaboration are documented in this volume. Reid Gilbert's account of the partnership of Morris Panych and Ken MacDonald between 1983 and 1990 maps their "writing" for the stage as a dramatological scenography. He argues that their "palpable presence of themselves as agents of creation" recasts both the performance and spectating of it by invoking wholly new codes of analysis of the visual and the textual. Gilbert traces the crucial crossovers of creative presence between the collaborators and their distancing of still-recognizable conventions of the stage through four seminal productions. Gilbert observes the explosion of character from the multiple personae of composer/musician and performer in *Last Call.* The scenography traps the spectators between conventions of westerns and television variety shows when balloons drop from the ceiling as the murder of one figure is narrowly averted and the duo launches into a lullaby. He considers the reconfigurations of Shakespeare in *The Haunted House Hamlet*, a site-specific ambulatory presentation at the Tamahous Theatre in Vancouver and le Monument National in Montreal, and in a *Comedy of Errors* laced with intertexts of Hollywood westerns among other cultural forms. He analyzes MacDonald's Magritte-like painted stage wall in *7 Stories*, with its 18" wide ledge as the spatial counterpart to Panych's existential angst-ridden text. Here we are able to feature images of a remount in 2004 of *7 Stories* at the Arts Club on Granville Island in Vancouver. MacDonald's reworking of the design increases the building's list and supplies architectural details that further complicate the rear-view mirror vision of the initial design.

My own study of the first two decades of Astrid Janson's work is motivated by further consideration of her signature scenography of freestanding scenery and her use of diverse, unusual materials first seen when she was the resident designer at Toronto Workshop Productions in the 1970s. Janson's inventive attention to the human figures, the puppets and the spatial configurations in the black box space of the Alexander Street theatre (now home to Buddies in Bad Times) embodied the social and artistic mandate of TWP. The essay traces her work in dance, television and in other theatres as a study of analogues to the early work in theatres that had very different mandates and audiences such as the Royal Winnipeg Ballet, the London Grand Theatre, Young People's Theatre (the current Lorraine Kimsa Theatre for Young People), the Tom Patterson Theatre at the Stratford Festival, CBC dramas and in the installations for the Canadian pavilion at Expo '86. Her ongoing collaboration as costume designer with VideoCabaret has maintained a politically probing visual imprint in these productions.

The roles of resident designers in two other examples in this volume also assume the fundamentally performative contributions of visual and aural design contributions. The historical mock-epic projects of VideoCabaret conceived by Deanne Taylor and Michael Hollingsworth, and the *Patria* cycle by composer R. Murray Schafer and his collaborators have made major contributions to scenography in Canada. Michèle White links the emergence of Videocab's McLuhanesque, technologically-infused aesthetic and performance ethos to a rejection of high art and to resignifiying concepts of "scenography." VideoCab's aesthetic has roots not only in live video art and gallery installation but also in the Caribbean carnivalesque, made familiar in Toronto as the lavishly-costumed annual Caribana parade. White notes how the artistic politics of the founding artists attracted collaborators whose experience was not necessarily in theatre but whose ear for the sound bite, or eye for the photo-op contributed greatly to the forging of an incisive cabaret style.

When Jerrard Smith describes his near 25-year association with R. Murray Schafer in designing eleven parts of the *Patria* cycle it is as one who has revelled in the complexity of accommodating performance to unusual spaces and their scenic and acoustic assets and peculiarities. Smith notes how each distinct design for the installments of the *Patria* cycle embodies Schafer's rejection of "stale art"—the easily recognizable and commodified—and with access, electrical supply and the given scenery, acoustics and characteristics of such diverse locations as Union Station, the wilderness of Banff and the Haliburton Forest maintain the composer's call for "difficulty" in performance. Smith's brief has included the development of safe, but not facile, circumstances for performance in found venues. From an understanding of the transformative and ritualistic nature of Schafer's theatre he presents poignant and practical issues in his essay about the complex demands on a designer of such theatre and the framework for training designers for it. And he discusses the process of building a community of volunteers to mount the productions as integral elements to the scenography. He notes the necessities of looking at space not as a Brookian vacancy but as a landscape designer might, or an architect or museum display designer, and this distinct approach is documented in the image of the floating stage for the production of *The Palace of the Cinnabar Phoenix* and the map of the labyrinth for one of the *Asterion* installments. These are, of necessity, organic encounters with the place for creators and spectators alike.

A final model of collaboration included here, and one that is distinctive in its use of design, is presented by Michael Devine in his study of Jillian Keiley's forging of "kaleidography"—a mathematically-based staging process. Devine offers a two-part argument that first situates Keiley's arrival, development and experimentation in the "roiling waters of St. John's theatre scene" and then shows how Keiley's familiarity with such modernist experiments as eurythmics by Émile Jaques-Dalcroze, Vsevolod Meyerhold's biomechanics and Edward Gordon Craig's precise choreography enable her to "compose" as a tightly scored analogue to symphonic music. A score for each performer that accounts for each unit of time and the segmentation of individualized movements on a precise grid of the stage floor constitute the framework of a fusion of choreography and costuming into a scenographic entity. Devine traces Keiley's employment of this seemingly rigid structure over several productions, demonstrating its flexible theatricality. A chart from the production of *Jesus Christ Superstar* (1998) tracing the path of each performer to a unifying tableau provides a glimpse of how the "individual" scores come together as a construction of colour and light in performance.

To design from diversity

An important thread in the critical discussion of design for the theatre is appreciation of demographic transformation in Canada, and its implications. Here, the consciousness of Canadian diversity enters the discussion in several different ways. Essays by Ron Fedoruk, Rahul Varma, and Kathleen Irwin sweep away vestiges of a nostalgic image of that Canada of two founding cultures that never was. Fedoruk finds that the reality of international students in the design program at the University of British Columbia requires him to re-open questions of curriculum and teaching methods. He contrasts training in design that goes hand in hand with the training of painters, sculptors and architects with the strong literary bent of training of students in Canada. That the formations of international students entering the UBC program tend to be visual rather than textual must be a significant factor in re-shaping the UBC curriculum. He argues for a reconfiguration of design programs which would reconsider current assumptions and take into account different trajectories of training so as to negotiate more deliberately between designer dramaturgy based in text and one based in in physical forms and spatiality. Distinct cultures of design and scenography come into view as he recognizes the traditions that are played out by his students and how they read texts with a view to production.[11] For this volume he has added a postscript to his article of almost a decade ago: he concludes that there is an even stronger imperative to re-examine design curricula in order to address not only the "vast diversity of cultures already represented in the Canadian mosaic," but also to acknowledge the "landed immigrants… and recently naturalized Canadian students" who do not appear as part of the international statistics," but whose presence affects the way plays are designed. By way of example he offers an image of a 2007 production of Tomson Highway's *The Rez Sisters*, designed by Parjad Sharifi from Iran, with costumes by Jay Haven of Canada and lighting by Chris Littman of the United States as an intercultural dialogue in which the staged rez becomes a visual and spatial encounter of cultures.

Rahul Varma reads the multi-media scenography of Robert Lepage's *Zulu Time* as a case of cultural colonization of the East. He contends that this dramaturgy of the visual expresses unacceptable racist attitudes altogether at odds with a multi-racial and multi-cultural society. In the Lepagian "apocalyptic burst of technology" (ExMachina) Varma detects a deracination of culture that implicitly denies lived realities in the interest of its own phantasmagoria of technologies.

Kathleen Irwin, like Fedoruk, from the west, considers whether the scenographic narratization of great demographic diversity is realizable in forms other than merely the representational. Her account of *The Bus Project* demonstrates the political activism in the "shifting and expanding role of the site-specific scenographer" (Irwin 38) and, like Jerrard Smith, she investigates the cultural textualities of found space as a landscape for performance. Challenging scenography that excludes the everyday, her exploration of psychogeography in *The Bus Project* leads her to the conviction that a changed understanding of the community of spectators can be played out on a screen and within the migratory locus of bus depots in Regina and Saskatoon. Her insight into scenographic modes of registering realities of migration and diversity that, by their very magnitude seem too unwieldy for the stage, constitutes a shift in perspective in response to rather intractable design issues.

Specific vocabularies...

The artistic vocabularies of design and scenography are the concern in several of the contributions to this volume. Three of them consider the materiality of design directly though the materials in question are not the tangibles of sets and costume but the ephemera of light and sound. An interview with Michael Whitfield, a study of Nancy Tobin's sound art and another of Axel Morgenthaler's lighting probe these once familiar areas of design.

Whitfield's conversation with Allan Watts is a window on the work of a lighting designer who works internationally from his base at the Stratford Shakespeare Festival, to which he has been attached since 1974. At Stratford he became Head of Lighting in succession to Gil Wechsler, the American lighting designer who regularized Tyrone Guthrie's original lighting concept while maintaining the outlines of the original approach. Since the Stratford Festival is the only theatre in Canada which, from its founding, has specifically envisioned lighting design as part of its mandate, Whitfield's perspective on lighting design is central to the critical perspectives gathered in this volume. Initially conceived outside the conventions governing commercial lighting—that is, eschewing highly individualized lighting design for each show—the Festival's theatres maintain their own aesthetic structures for lighting design according to the particular stage configuration of each and the general repertoire. So Whitfield's account of the artistic remit of lighting designers at the Festival within the given working parameters is a critical example.[12] Whitfield's observations on his own work at the Festival or elsewhere and on his interaction with the artistic collaborators on each production—whether it be opera, ballet or spoken word theatre—have a more general resonance in terms of the possibilities for dialogue between artists using their distinct vocabularies.

Ana Cappelluto and Edward Little, in their profile of Axel Morgenthaler, present a light artist who not only works in theatre but has been commissioned for urban installations. Cappelluto and Little describe Morgenthaler as a *concepteur visuel* who treats light as if it were a solid material. He prefers to design sets and lighting together and so access directly the synaesthetic energies of the two modes of perception, leaving the exact origins of the effects imperceptible. From a review of his lighting for dance, film and theatre emerges Morgenthaler's case for the development of software which would enable productive involvement of the lighting designer in the scenography overall despite the tight time restraints of North American rehearsal schedules.

The third essay in this grouping takes up sound design that uses amplifying devices to originate sound rather than simply broadcast it. Anna Friz notes how Nancy Tobin's early experience as a DJ led her to discover and develop an aptitude for the manipulation of sound for performance and she goes on to consider how Tobin's designs manufacture sound for dancers in a like manner. Speakers hidden: her design makes them the acoustic analogue to the visible lights—either hanging above the stage, or transforming the dance floor into an instrument played by the dancers through their choreography. Conceiving of each sound design "kind of like inventing a tradition," she invites her collaborators to learn to think in hertz so that they can together "highlight listening in a socially relevant context."

Coda...

The contribution by Dany Lyne marks a significant change in the critical response to design and scenography. Her acceptance speech for the prestigious Elinore & Lou Siminovitch Prize on October 24, 2006 is a definitive moment in the decolonization of designers within the theatre industry in Canada.[13] Her bracing forthrightness cuts to the realities of being a designer in Canada, arriving at mid-career on the brink of burnout from pressures of maintaining a gruelling schedule of simultaneous contracts in order to survive financially. While articulating the exhilaration of creative work, she emphasizes the pragmatic difficulties of maintaining a studio, the need for creative exploration and the implications of the contractual obligations governing how she works. Her speech broke a silence and pushed back against the divisive isolation to which the design community is vulnerable by inspiring working groups of designers to meet and communicate, to discuss working conditions and contracts, and to enhance the visibility of design and scenography in Canadian theatre.

Notes

1 The visual theorist W.J.T. Mitchell specifically excludes performance from his discussion but it is nevertheless helpful to consider his working premise: "to put our relation to the work of art in question, to make the *relationality* of image and beholder the field of investigation... what does the picture want from me or 'us' or from 'them' or from whomever" (Mitchell 49). Such an approach will also enable a perspective on scenography as a dynamic experiential engagement between creation and reception in the theatre.

[2] Pamela Howard was the first director of the annual Scenofest, an International Festival of Scenography established in 1994 by the International Organization of Scenographers and Theatre Technicians (Organisation Internationale des Scénographes et technicians de Théatre-OISTAT). She is Professor Emeritus of Scenography at Central Saint Martin's College of Art and Design in London, England.

[3] The company provides space, money and resources for studio-based research into provocative theatrical questions of form and performance. "Pure Research" is designed to foster theatrical experiments which are not linked to a particular project.

[4] The enhancement of professional status within the theatre has always been evident in articles about the ADC and in many interviews. In 1982 Tom Doherty explained that the mandate of ADC is in tandem with efforts by Actors' Equity and the Guild of Canadian Playwrights, but that the recognition of design "as a profession is a very recent development" (Doherty, "Recognizing" 41).

[5] Mary Kerr's photo essay and reflections on the choices she made in her design for *Mandragola* at the Vancouver Playhouse in 1974 was a first for this kind of documentation (with ample photos) of the work of a designer. Eight years later Susan Benson added wryly in an interview with Brian Arnott that there was an overall lack of awareness of how design operated in performance and that "what starts out as a creative team effort sometimes develops into a kind of shopping list from the director, merely demanding extra props and costumes without discussing the intent behind them" (Arnott 31).

[6] Ric Knowles's study of the two distinct approaches to *A Midsummer Night's Dream* in 1976 and 1977 by Robin Phillips at the Stratford Festival reveal how Susan Benson's costumes provided substantial visual architectonics for the productions (see Knowles, "Robin").

[7] For an account of Voaden's writing of the play see Wagner.

[8] In his sketch, probably for the fifth movement "The Mountains."

[9] Voaden's intense engagement with the technology of the theatre in his projected Theatre of Beauty contrasts starkly with the critical imperatives of the workers' theatre of the 1930s. While its leaders enlisted a strong and vibrant visual component in its posters and publications such as its magazine *Masses* (1932–1934) they held a self-proclaimed "puritanical attitude" to the stage. David A. Hogg, in the first issue of *Masses* advocated a Workers' Theatre that would reject conventions of the commercial stage in favour of "crude Elizabethan surroundings, without the aid of curtain or stage scenery or special lighting, [that] should be able to stage soul-gripping plays" emphasizing the choreographic display of the human presence.

[10] Carsen and Levine also collaborated on *Mario and the Magician*—a libretto by Rodney Anderson and music by Harry Somers. The Canadian Opera Company premiered this opera in the Elgin Theatre in 1992.

[11] Ric Knowles in his exploration of lighting manuals "from the perspective of a director and materialist critic rather from a position *within* the discourses of professional lighting design." (Knowles, "Looking" 5) reveals how these textbooks imprint students in the hierarchy of theatre creation, often leaving the student of lighting design at a loss to deal with designing for productions in a diverse Canada (Knowles, "Looking" 8).

[12] The non-illusionistic space pressures artists at the Festival Theatre into working differently than in a proscenium arch theatre. Tanya Moiseiwitch's conception of a thrust stage has bearing on all artists since it is equally demanding on directors and actors, and as Ric Knowles traces it demands a strong and focused attitude to design which is fundamentally dramaturgical given the intimacy with the audience that also forestalls naturalism (Knowles, "Legacy" 41).

[13] Further exploration of the status of the designer and specifically women designers is available in a PACT study by Rebecca Burton.

Works Cited

Arnott, Brian. "Artists Not Craftspeople." *Canadian Theatre Review* 33 (1982): 30–39.

Bourriaud, Nicolas. *Relational Aesthetics.* Dijon-Quetigny: Les Presses du réel, 2006.

Burton, Rebecca. *Adding it Up: The Status of Women in Canadian Theatre.* Canada Council for the Arts, 2006.

Doherty, Tom. "Preface." *Theatre Design Explorations/Scénographie au Canada.* Ed. Therese Beaupre. Associated Designers of Canada, 1979. np.

———. "Recognizing the Designer." *Canadian Theatre Review* 33 (1982): 40–43.

ExMachina. http://lacaserne.net/index2.php/theatre/zulu_time/. Accessed 25 January 2009.

Hogg, David A. "Theatre Of Actualities." *Masses* 1.1 (1932). np.

Howard, Pamela. *What is Scenography?* London: Routledge, 2002.

Irwin, Kathleen. "The Site's the Thing: The Shifting and Expanding Role of the Site Specific Scenographer." *Canadian Theatre Review* 126 (2006): 38–41.

Kerr, Mary. "*Mandragola*: A Designer's Portfolio." *Canadian Theatre Review* 2 (1974): 34–39.

Knowles, Ric(hard Paul). "The Legacy of the Festival Stage." *Canadian Theatre Review* 54 (1988): 39–45.

———. "Looking for Enlightened Lighting: The Discourses of Lighting Design, Training and Practice." *Canadian Theatre Review* 107 (2001): 5–10.

———. "Robin Phillips' Strange and Wondrous *Dream*." *Theatre History in Canada* 9.1 (1988): 38–58.

Mitchell, W.J.T. *What Do Pictures Want?: The Lives and Loves of Images.* Chicago: U of Chicago P, 2005.

Wagner, Anton. "'A Country of the Soul': Herman Voaden, Lowrie Warrener and the Writing of *Symphony*." *Space and the Geographies of the Theatre.* Ed. Michael McKinnie. Toronto: Playwrights Canada, 2007. 28–44.

from Symphony: A Drama of Motion and Light for a New Theatre [1]

by Herman A. Voaden and Lowrie Warrener

"*Symphony*," by Herman Voaden [2]

I had hoped to make my first trip across Canada in the late summer of 1929 when Gordon Alderson, Lowrie Warrener and I returned from San Francisco and Seattle. But we were short of money and pressed for time. So we drove home by the better roads of the Northern States. I promised myself "the happiest of trips" the following summer. In the winter and spring of 1930 I planned the bigger adventure. John Murray Gibbon, General Publicity Agent for the Canadian Pacific Railway, was providing free passage across Canada for artists in return for one of their paintings. [3] I wrote him, asking if I could cross Canada with Lowrie Warrener. He gave us passes. We were to write a "painter's ballet." This was *Symphony: A Drama of Motion and Light for a New Theatre.*

I could not wait till the summer for this "happiest of trips." During the fall of 1929 I read F.B. Housser's *The Group of Seven: A Canadian Art Movement* and met Housser and several members of the Group. In December I wrote *Northern Song* in which the painter Keith dreams of northern lands "charted more magnificently." My excitement and eager desire to see Algoma and the north shore of Lake Superior were at such a pitch that when the Christmas holidays came I took the train to Nipigon and back, stopping at Port Coldwell, where the Group had painted, for several days.

I told the story first in my introduction to *Wilderness* when it was printed by John Flood in *Boréal* in 1978 and in *The Developing Mosaic* [ed. Anton Wagner] in 1980. I was recalling from memory what happened some fifty years before, and my account of events and people both in the Agawa Canyon and on the North Shore was inaccurate. There were more passengers in the café car through the Algoma wilderness than a trapper and the conductor, and I spent several days at Port Coldwell. It was not a passing glimpse of the harbour from the train.

Lowrie Warrener and I left on June 17, 1930 for our trans-continental journey. What eager excitement as we saw the "wider margins"—the North Shore, the prairies, the mountains, the sea! *Symphony* was written in those summer days of intensive creative excitement. It is a unique collaboration between a painter and a playwright. Lowrie, an artist, saw everything pictorially. I, as dramatist, had a play craftsman's sense of shape and development. And I felt, in a measure, responsible for the success of the venture. I had made the commitment to John Murray Gibbon and was determined to carry it through to a successful conclusion. So I continually urged Lowrie to press on with the task—perhaps too urgently for his sensitive spirit at times. The bust which he did of me in Billie Lang's studio in Winnipeg in early August before we went on to Port Coldwell shows this resentment on his part. The bust is larger than life size, and while the upper half and eyes are true to the young Voaden, the nose, mouth and chin are stylized and Neanderthal in treatment (Flood 15).[4]

The writing of *Symphony* marked the end of my two-year collaboration with Lowrie Warrener. That autumn I went to the Graduate School of Drama at Yale University. Our relationship was not that of patron and artist. We were *both* artists. True, I bought his sketches and an earlier sculpture, "Absinthe" (Flood 15) and the big portrait bust of me—because I liked them and wanted them. But we were co-workers, co-creators, never more so than in *Symphony*.

An essential point must be made. We intended *Symphony* to be a *play*! As late as July 29 in that summer of 1930, it was to be the work of an artist and dramatist, a "picture drama." But at Glenn Hughes' playwriting course in San Francisco in the summer of 1929 where I wrote *Northern Storm* we were required—as in all playwriting text books—to write a scenario. So we wrote a scenario, *Symphony*. "You see, I didn't want to actually start work on the dialogue till the structure and organization was fairly definite in our minds and clearly stated" (Voaden, "Train" 5). Writing about the prairie scene, for which we had completed a "fine framework," I said that we were using "words and chanting and music" to accompany and intensify the movements of figures and forms and colours ("Train" 5).

Then came the moment of truth. On August 12 I wrote Violet Kilpatrick "the play may finally work out as a Canadian rhythmic-dance-colour-music-light-pantomime drama, without need for dialogue or poetry or libretto, requiring only more careful restatement and a musical score to be complete. At times I think it is very impressive." Two days later this was confirmed. There was to be no dialogue. And the practical Voaden has his reason for the decision. "As such we are sure to finish it."

And so the picture drama became a painter's ballet. It was a natural and right decision. For me the play was not the thing—certainly not the realistic play. My love of music, dance and painting was as great as my love of theatre. *Symphony* was a precursor of *Rocks*. And Lowrie Warrener was not prepared to write a play, nor interested in doing so—even a picture drama. So we wrote *his* kind of drama, wordless, close to dance, music and painting—a painter's ballet.

In truth it had been a painter's ballet from the beginning. We dreamed of it, planned it, wrote it as a painter's ballet. But we clung to the belief that it was the scenario for a picture drama till, late, we ourselves realized the truth.

I want to pay tribute to Lowrie Warrener whose contribution, as will be apparent, was as great as mine in creating it. I am happy that *Symphony* was published in *Canadian Drama* (Voaden and Warrener) before his death, that I was able to share with him the modest publication fee, and that he knew he had a prime role in writing an important early Canadian theatre work.

from *Symphony: A Drama of Motion and Light For a New Theatre*
by Herman A. Voaden and Lowrie Warrener[5]

Requirements: Symphony orchestra; trained ballet; ample and well-equipped stage with exceptional lighting facilities.

Symphony is in Five Movements, each to be introduced by an Orchestra Prologue and a Story Recitative which shall be sung by Chorus, or solo voice, or spoken.

Music and choreography to be created.

There is no dialogue.

Story

First Movement: A Large Eastern City. The central figure, called Man, is disappointed in love and almost crushed in the maelstrom of the city's frenzied greed. Alone of its victims, he escapes, beaten and broken.

Second Movement: The Northern Wilderness. Man is confronted with the vast silence and terror of the wilderness, whither he has taken himself in flight. He conquers his fears, achieving a new strength and courage.

Third Movement: Fishing Village on a Northern Lake. A fisherman now, married and with one child, Man meets the central personal tragedy of his life, the death of his wife.

Fourth Movement: A Prairie Farm. His pilgrimage has brought Man to the prairie, where as a farmer the more impersonal tragedy of his life is enacted… the failure of his crops through drought and hail. He is now past middle age.

Fifth Movement: The Mountains. In a lonely, austere, and remote world, the early experiences of Man's life are summarized. The final mystical experience of his death brings the play to a close of prophetic serenity.

Excerpts

Second Movement: The Northern Wilderness
Orchestral Prologue
Recitative

The foreground is low swamp area, a tangle of dark depressing undergrowth. The rocks that flow up to the ridge in the background are not visible at first.

The form of Man can be dimly discerned in the undergrowth. At first he is still, like a wounded, frightened animal. The music is low, fearful and expectant. Then he begins to move, crawling on his hands and knees, fighting with wet slimy branches, and finally rising and struggling to push his way through them. His efforts are of no avail. He becomes more hopelessly entangled in them, and stumbles and lies still, exhausted.

Once again he rouses himself and beats his way to one side of the stage, only to become confused and return to the identical spot from which he had started. Then terror seizes him. The music grows more nervous and ominous. He looks slowly in every direction like a hunted man, eyes distended and hands clutching the branches about him. His fear numbs him and holds him immovable and rigid. He stands in a flood of light, wide-eyed, staring, a ragged and dishevelled figure. The light about him diffuses into solid dark free forms that bend and seem to hang threateningly over him. Long lanes and tunnels wind vaguely through and around these forms, leading to complete darkness in the wings and rear. Shadowy black shapes slink out of the gloom and weave and glide in a dance that brings them always back to the central figure of fear. Grey shapes are also seen, luminous in the darkness. As shadows and forms twist and glide vague lights appear and disappear, enhancing the effect of weird terror as seen in the face of Man. Phosphorescent gleams as of the eyes of animals are seen, and forms of beasts hurry through the gloom. The music alternately swells in volume and dies down to an ominous moan, growing and fading with Man's fear. Swift shadows as of night swoop across the stage, and the eerie night sounds of the birds and creatures of the woods are suggested in the orchestration.

Finally the sounds and motions of the night build up to a climax of intensity and movement. The wind comes up, the tree forms sway into more grotesque and menacing attitudes, and the whole north takes on motion. Then Man's inner imagination transforms the shapes and figures that terrorize him into huge overpowering shapes that close in upon him, soft and yielding. As he resists and rejects them they change into other shapes and move and writhe about him. They rush against him and appear to smother him, then scatter for a new attack upon the senses. The music mounts to a still higher pitch of intensity and reaches a climax as Man, unable to stand the strain any longer, stretches himself to his full height in a last gesture of defiance and courage, and slumps heavily to the ground.

Silence for a moment. The dark shadows and forms have ceased to move. The music begins again in an altered mood of resignation and stillness, even serenity. Utterly exhausted, man lies in a small area of light in the centre of the foreground. Calmness dissolves his fear and restores his sanity and the light upon him grows in warmth, refuelling his vitality and lending him new vigour and energy. The trees and forms about him appear in a new guise of friendliness. His tenseness is broken and he is drawn out of his paralysis. The music is steadily more confident and hopeful. Emerging from behind a dark cloud, the moon is seen over the high ground above him, revealing rhythmic, friendly surfaces of rock a little distance from him. Reaching these, he walks slowly and calmly up their gradual slope, as if drawn by their lifting and intimate levels. Reaching the ridge, he is silhouetted in the clear light of the sky; the moon throws his shadow back to mingle with the darkness of the night and the twisted fear forms he has left behind him. The music is strong and almost exultant.

For a moment he stands at the summit, regarding the scene before him. In its sturdiness his figure resembles one of the dark wind-blown jack pines that crown the ridge. Finally he moves out of sight down the other side of the hill. The moon bathes the entire ridge in a mysterious sheen of silver-grey light.

• • •

Fourth Movement: A Prairie Farm
Orchestral Prologue
Recitative

The prairie stretches far away to the horizon, a great brown fallow field in the foreground. In the sky is the last greyness of winter. Man, dressed as a farmer, enters and scans the horizon as though looking for something. He stands numbed with cold, waiting. The music is low and unsympathetic, but becomes bolder and more kindly as the sky gradually lightens and warmth takes the place of cold. Man's body moves and takes on added life. As the warmth grows he turns and slowly walks toward the wings, coming back with a sack of grain. He stops in the centre to pour some into a small sowing sack around his neck, and then starts to sow, his motions taking the form of a ritual and accompanied by music in the same spirit. A frenzied thankfulness is apparent in his actions. When he is finished he surveys his work with satisfaction; lightly tossing the grain bag over his back, he strides off with a gambler's air of confidence.

The grains, light green figures, move in from the wings and dance about, in a rising and falling motion to the accompaniment of a nervous chant in the music, which grows gradually louder and more vibrant as light gusts of wind blow by. The grains cower motionless and still. Sales agents, grotesque figures, slowly appear upon the stage and as the clouds grow heavier they begin to dance, their dance and the music becoming more boisterous. Light gusts of rain blow over the grain figures. They receive them joyfully. The agents retreat off stage. The clouds grow heavier. The winds, light grey forms, start weaving through the crowd, to a new happy rhythm in the music. The grains move in unison with them. Clouds disappear from the sky, and the winds blow more slowly; finally they fade into the wings. The grains have reached an upright position.

Sluggish brown sun figures appear. The grains stand still. The suns swell into a consuming heat, and the heat waves form a twisting train about the grain figures. The fear forms move rapidly on the edge of the mass. The winds begin to break through the line of fear forms, rushing at the heat waves to start them moving. The heat waves slowly push their way through the grains and off the stage, leaving them drooped as if in pain. The winds follow close and as they dance through the grains and after the heat waves the grains revive and move or sway from side to side, growing in height. Dark clouds appear and throw ominous shadows over the waving grains. The fear forms are seen along the edge of the stage, swaying back and forth. Clouds grow heavier, and the agents flow into the stage. The music is ominous. The farmer hurries from the wings and stands in a protecting attitude in front of the grains. The clouds become darker and the agents wax more blatant and gloating. The fear forms push through the grains and surround the farmer, spreading out and joining hands with the agents to dance madly around both the farmer and grains.

When the dancing and music have reached a pitch of fanatical hysteria, dead silence falls. The grains stand upright and the farmer is tense. The fear forms twist and writhe and the agents stand sullenly. Then the winds dance airily on to the stage to light music, followed by a few drops of rain that form a slight mist. The agents disappear from the stage and the fear forms seem to shrink and fade into the wings. The farmer droops into an attitude of thankfulness and the grains start a slow-weaving, growing, rhythmic dance to music.

The sun creeps up and mist rises as the heat increases. The heat waves again move slowly in front of the grains making them wilt a little and droop. Once more the fear forms crowd upon the stage as the heat waves grow and converge into a sluggish mass, gloating and sweating in front of the grains.

The farmer struggles up and down in front of the grains with the fear forms leading, following, and passing him. Then the winds appear and crowd up against the grains from the rear, pushing them and the farmer and the fear forms against the mass of heat waves. The fear forms and the farmer make way for the grains, who try to pass the heat waves. The winds slowly leave the stage, and the grains droop and stumble and fall in a heap on the edge of the stage.

The winds appear from the wings again and lightly dance around the sluggish heat mass, starting it moving slowly. The grains revive a little, and the winds gradually push the heat waves to the far side of the stage.

The winds grow more active and sweep the heat waves off the stage. Then they rush back, dancing in and out among the grains who rise, join hands, and dance joyously with the winds. The winds leave them, and the grains continue to dance, stretching up and up until their arms seem to be beckoning to the rain god above them. The music swells up, aiding them, and light drops of rain descend upon them. They dance with all the gaiety of youth. The farmer kneels in an attitude of thankfulness.

Then the rain becomes colder and the grains dance more slowly, as though numbed. The agents swarm upon the stage, followed by the fear forms. As the grains stop dancing the fear forms and the agents dance madly in varying rhythms to music, in and out among them. Finally the rain gives way to hail and the farmer is seized with terror. The grains are battered down mercilessly, and the fear forms and agents dance in a wild and gloating spirit to the accompaniment of frenzied music.

After a moment the hail turns to rain and the dance ceases, the music assuming a more quiet rhythm. The agents leave the stage, followed more slowly by the fear forms. The grains painfully revive and the farmer leaves the stage slowly. The rain lessens and stops, and the sun begins to shine with a dry intense warmth.

The heat waves come in from the wings and surround the grains. The grains stand motionless. The heat waves close in relentlessly. The farmer rushes back and breaks through to the grain, followed by the fear forms who begin to dance to the sluggish intense heat rhythms of the music. The heat waves press closer yet. They move sluggishly, crowding and wilting the grain, numbing even the dance of the fear forms. The grains wilt and fall in a drooping mass behind the farmer, who stands resigned. Finally the heat waves close in and obliterate the grains entirely.

The stage darkens. Lights come up showing the grains, motionless and brown on the ground, with the heat waves fading into the wings and the farmer standing hopeless, looking as though the blood had been dried up in him and he had become a part of the grains. Lights go out and come up on a bare stage, with the farmer standing, in a drooping crucified posture, with a yellow light playing about him. On all sides of him the great dry plains stretch away endlessly.

Observations by Herman Voaden

Second Movement

I played a considerable part in planning and writing the first Movement. But the Second Movement was Lowrie Warrener's almost completely. It is the true painter's ballet we set out to create. He developed the approaches we used in the next three movements, peopling the stage with strange, moving shapes, shadowy forms, and patterns of changing music, colour and light. Lowrie had been lost in the northern wilderness—in the Killarny area. He often talked about it; it was one of the strange, fearful experiences of his life. He wrote the first draft of the movement in pencil, on three old sheets of brown paper. Then we started to work over it.

The Movement is clearly shaped. The first part ends with the huge overpowering shapes closing in on Man, moving and writhing about him, and with music of mounting intensity. The second part is serene. The trees and forms now appear in "a new guise of friendliness." Even the "rhythmic" surfaces leading up to the ridge before Man are "friendly." It is a sign of how much our friends in the Group of Seven meant to us that Man's sturdy, triumphant figure resembled "one of the dark windblown jack pines that crown the ridge."

Fourth Movement

During the Depression the southern prairies were hardest hit. As we came down the Crow's Nest Pass in the dawn to the flat yellow bleached fields, we thought we saw a crucified Christ arising from them. Our destination was the town of Ogema, sixty miles south of Regina, where Ed Kilpatrick, Violet's uncle, lived. He was town clerk, Sunday School teacher, baker, pillar of the church. We were with his family until July 29.

There was an empty shack on the prairie, perhaps a mile from the village, and there we went each day, taking a lunch, and staying till the dinner hour. There we wrote the "fine framework" for the prairie Movement, and Lowrie worked out the scenario for the Second Movement, in which he was lost in the wilderness. We completed the prairie Movement in Port Coldwell shortly after we arrived there.

The toll of the Depression was a grim fact of life in Ogema. There was no unemployment insurance, no welfare in those years. Ed Kilpatrick quietly saw to it that there was food and help for those in need in the town. Stories of crop failure through hail and heat were everywhere. I have a clipping, "Cyclonic Storms Hit Grain Area" which we had when we wrote the Movement. "Hailstones… cut standing grain down over a large area, stretching all the way from Amisk, Alta., to Brandon, Man." (*Vancouver Province*).

In the complicated Movement that we devised (again, with Lowrie Warrener making the major input) there were six groups of forms or figures. Those on the side of the farmer were the green grain figures and the winds—light grey forms. The evil ones were the sluggish sun figures, the heat waves, the fear forms, and the grotesque sales agents, profiting from selling insurance against crop failure.

In the first paragraph Man is alone—the sower—a sack of grain on his shoulder. He is almost a biblical figure, or one reminiscent of Millet's "The Reaper." We were not concerned with the anachronism of sowing "a great brown fallow field" in the Canadian West by hand.

The second paragraph has a musical ABA form. The grain figures dance nervously. Gusts of wind threaten a storm; the sales agents dance boisterously. Instead of a storm, light rain falls. The agents retreat, and to a happy rhythm in the music, winds and grains move in unison. In the rest of the Movement there are three crises in which the evil forces almost destroy the grain. In the final moment, after they have succeeded, the farmer is standing "in a drooping crucified posture," with a yellow light playing about him as it played about the coffin in the Third Movement.

Lowrie Warrener believed the stage should be able to create any picture, and I was willing to try. The Movement begins with the prairie stretching "far away to the horizon" and ends with "the great dry plains stretch away endlessly."

The Movement is complicated, at times repetitive. I wrote as Lowrie dictated. The result lacks the dramatic shape—the steady build to a climax, which I should have insisted we achieve. Then, as now, I had a sense of wonder at the seemingly endless sequence of vividly changing pictures we were creating.

Our original manuscript of *Symphony* shows the great hopes and big plans we had for it. We believed it was a unique work, and called for nothing less than a "symphony orchestra, trained ballet, ample and well equipped stage with exceptional lighting facilities" to produce it. It required a much bigger stage than mine, and forces I could not command—orchestra and ballet. And we needed a composer.

One whom I approached was Sir Ernest MacMillan. On July 6, 1932 I wrote to Violet Kilpatrick reporting that "I saw MacMillan today—youthful, quiet, clear-eyed. He read *Symphony* rapidly, exclaiming once or twice in praise. "'Well done,' he said when he put it up. He would like to do the music—but it is a year's work and he is *very* busy. He kept the script. In any case the interview was keen and interesting. We had much in common—our youth—our idealism. It was all worthwhile."

I wrote to or spoke with many other leading musicians, composers, producers and influential people hoping to persuade them to produce *Symphony*. There was interest in the work, but the production problems were so formidable, and the cost so great, that no one would attempt it. *Symphony* remains unproduced to this day.

(1930, 1982)

Notes

1 This introduction and the scenario of *Symphony* are included in this volume as an example of the vision for a scenographic theatre that Herman Voaden would call "symphonic expressionism." For a comprehensive discussion of the writing of the play see Wagner.

2 Herman Voaden prepared this introduction to the scenario for the publication of the collection of his plays, *A Vision of Canada*, in 1993.

3 This was a tradition, written into the Railway Act, that went back to William Van Horne's time. Possibly Canada's greatest art collector, he commissioned artists to paint the scenery along the railway as it crossed the mountains (Voaden's note in original—ed.).

4 This sculpture was shown and won Honorable Mention at the Canadian National Exhibition gallery in September of 1930 (Voaden's note in original—ed.).

5 Lowrie Warrener had come to the composition of this scenario having enjoyed some acclaim as a theatre designer. His set for *Antony and Cleopatra* directed by Carol Aikins at Hart House was praised. John Flood features images of it (Flood 14) and describes it: "the predominant colours were silver and black; there were movable panels upstage and the soldiers made their entrances from behind a star in the centre stage, other characters from the wings" (13). His designs for four one-act plays developed an Adolphe Appia or Edward Gordon-like flexibility of elements: drapes, pylons, stairs, platforms, archways, and screens (Flood 13). This design was influenced by the work that Warrener had encountered in Antwerp and Paris where he had spent two years after graduating from the Ontario College of Art in 1924.

Works Cited

Flood, John. "Lowrie Warrener." *Northward Journal* 25 (1982): 11–28.

Vancouver Province, July 8, 1930.

Voaden, Herman. "Symphony." Voaden, *Vision* 134–36.

———. "Train just out of Regina," Letter to Violet Kilpatrick. July 29, 1930. Herman Voaden fonds. York University Archives and Special Collections. Box 1991-020/033, Files 4 & 5.

———. *A Vision of Canada*. Ed. Anton Wagner. Toronto; Simon and Pierre, 1993.

——— and Lowrie Warrener. *Symphony: A Drama of Motion and Light for a New Theatre. Canadian Drama/L'Art dramatique canadien* 8.1 (1982): 74–83.

Wagner, Anton. "'A Country of the Soul': Herman Voaden and Lowrie Warrener and the Writing of *Symphony*." *Space and the Geographies of Theatre*. Ed. Michael McKinnie. Toronto; Playwrights Canada, 2007.

Editorial Note

For sketches by Voaden and Warrener, see illustrations 1–3 (61–62).

"And then we saw you fly over there and land!": Metadramatic Design in the Stage Work of Morris Panych and Ken MacDonald

by Reid Gilbert

In *The Mask in Place: Essays on Fiction in North America*, George Bowering suggests that historiographic metafictions now demand an interplay between reader and writer which does not leave the reader "in the dark waiting for the stage lights to be lit upon the scene for you and left there for your imagined occupation" (Bowering 30). In a similar assertion, Linda Hutcheon notes that "As in the Bakhtinian carnival, in the postmodernist novel there are no footlights separating art and audience" (Hutcheon 63).

These comments seem to betray a significant misunderstanding of the process of drama, a failure to recognize an essential characteristic of the genre. In "Marginalizing Drama: Bakhtin's Theory of Genre," Jennifer Wise also reacts against the application of what she calls "the anti-literary energies of theatrical culture to the novel" while withdrawing "them theoretically from the theatre itself." She points out that "it is not the absence of *footlights* that distinguishes novels from plays but the absence of bodies," those of "the actors who perform them" and of "the spectators who attend them" (Wise 19). Indeed, as Keir Elam has noted, far from separating audience and text, the theatre has always presented "in the form of *discours,* a network of 'pragmatic' utterances or *énonciations* rather than a series of abstracted *énoncés*" (Elam 144). Even theatre critics have sometimes ignored the multiple sets of relationships (often momentary) among text and audience, intertext and audience, actor and audience, text and actor, intertext and actor, subtext, mode and convention which set up a complex semiotic structure among the participants in the illusion on stage. Richard Hornby contends that "the principal fallacy in realistic dramatic theory was in its assigning a passive role to drama. The ingenuousness of this theory is the same as that of the traditional naive view of language.... Drama has an operative function similar to that of language. Rather than mirroring life passively, drama is instead a means of thinking about life, a way of organizing and categorizing it" (Hornby 25–26). Émile Benveniste has pointed out that an "utterance is performative [only] in that it *denominates* the act performed," not because "it can modify the situation of the individual, but in that is *by itself* an act" (Benveniste 237). In drama, performative language combines with action and *deixis* in a complex system.

In the process of organization, however, the audience—as, indeed, the playwright and designers of any production—all employ established references, literary, historiographic, religious and cultural allusions, archetypes, and a shared understanding of the process of drama itself, of the conventional devices which allow the suspension of disbelief. Modern audiences, raised on film and video, superimpose another set of referents on those implicit in the form, although contemporary viewers may often be unaware of the codes already in place. It is, of course, this complicated overlapping of physical and literary texts and the active role of the viewer which constitute metadrama, illustrating what Elam calls Benveniste's classic distinction between *histoire* and *discours*, "the 'subjective' mode geared to the present, which indicates the interlocutors and their speaking situation" (144). A subjective response to speaker and situation is not only evident, but is always demanded in the stage work of Morris Panych and his frequent collaborator, Ken MacDonald.

Panych and MacDonald have produced a varied body of work, appearing together as writers and actors, and working individually (but often on the same production) as director, production designer and musical director. At times, they have shared the creative process with other writers and directors; at other times, they have created the entire production themselves. These artistic activities are usually seen as distinct, but, in this continuing partnership, mutual approaches consistently surface, even when the team is working with others. Because they work on different aspects of the design and production of their shows but with a common vision, their collaborations present a rich source for the study of the necessary interplay among production specialists. But, more important, their work also demonstrates the intricate relationship between the illusion created and the act of creation. Their work shows a conscious manipulation of dramatic text and stage effect to produce an array "of pragmatic utterances," to create what Elam calls a "dramatological approach" rather than one "dedicated to *sjuzet* and *fabula* alone" (144).

Through their work, from their early collaborative writing and acting in *Last Call: A Post Nuclear Cabaret* to their involvement in the Tamahnous *Haunted House Hamlet*, to their popular Arts Club (summer 1989) production of *7 Stories* (which opened at Tarragon Theatre in February 1991) to their partnership in the design, textual emendation, and direction of the Arts Club's 1989 production of Shakespeare's *Comedy of Errors*, to their adaptation of *The Beggar's Opera* at Studio 58, Panych and MacDonald have consistently played with the barriers of illusion and have superimposed upon the narratives they present the palpable presence of themselves as agents of creation and of the stage as a metadramatic process.

In *Last Call*, the audience is required to work with Panych both as writer and as highly physical actor to create a number of different *personae* and two contradictory endings. The last two survivors of the nuclear holocaust find one another and stumble into a theatre where the victimizer Bartholomew Gross (himself dying of radiation sickness) forces the weaker Eddie Morose (blinded by the blast) to play the piano in a grotesque cabaret. Thus a device which shapes the action also allowed MacDonald (who played Morose in the original productions) to sing his own songs and direct the music while highlighting Panych as performer. It also instructs the audience to anticipate both the form of the "two-hander" (which is faithfully observed) and of the lounge act (which is satirized). The theatrical form grows out of the inciting action, then, in a way it does not, for example, in John Gray's *Billy Bishop Goes to War* where the audience must immediately recognize the one-man convention and move imaginatively beyond it. In *Last Call*, the audience does not move beyond the form but is always reminded of it, so that the form itself becomes a metaphor and the audience comes to understand the anti-nuclear message intellectually long after it has perceived the implications of the theme in the convention itself, in the desperate pun of a one-man show—and a tacky one, at that—starring the one dying man left on the planet.

More interesting, however, is the duping of the audience by a double ending. The audience has been instructed to respond within two theatrical conventions it understands and which Panych develops in a parallel design. Gross is able to dominate Morose because he has found a gun, a grim symbol of the aggression which has led the world to this disaster. As Gross sings, "The man with the word may have otherwise heard/but the one with the gun is GOD" (26). Beyond this rather obvious symbolism, however, the gun also prompts the audience's familiarity with the conventions of the Western and Gangster movie. As Hornby has observed, American "nuclear policy is shaped by the archetype of the Western gunfight, in which the hero must allow the villain to draw his gun first, but must then draw his own gun quickly enough to kill the villain before he can effectively fire" (26). To protect himself, Morose sings Gross to sleep and then steals the gun, hiding the bullets. But this "first-strike" allows Gross to counterfeit betrayal ("Trying to kill me, Morose?... I'm aware of your potential violence"[52]), permitting him to retaliate and kill his companion, halving the world's population and sealing the fate of humankind.

The audience is aware of (and is actively synthesizing) two sets of theatrical conventions. It recognizes the expectations of this attitude to war, and is, therefore, trapped between anticipating the proper ending for the Western shootout (which it realizes must also end the species) and hoping for an ending more in keeping with the protocols of the lounge act which run alongside. This desire is even stronger in the television audience trained, as it is, to expect happy resolutions in variety shows. In the play, the action seems to end with the strongly coded lullaby, and an apparent reconciliation between the two men; in the TV version, the cabaret resolution is exaggerated into singing and dancing with balloons falling from the ceiling. But the lullaby has a Western theme ("Close your eyes, rest your head—And the coyotes will sing of the dead" [52]) which prompts the audience to recall the Western intertext and its set of expectations which have not been satisfied. And in the TV razzmatazz, the audience lacks a sense of theatrical completion even while it is elated; it knows that the froth of a cabaret is artificial and too insubstantial for the issues in discussion. Therefore, it is prepared for Gross's abrupt cancellation of the euphoria—"On the other hand, I think we've managed to simplify things just a bit.... I think it's just a bit naive. A bit contrived"—and for the second, dark ending in which Gross does kill his partner. The ending now reveals a second, cynical theme, suggesting that the audience's own expectations, born not of reasoned analysis, but of allegiance to theatrical forms, may necessitate the end of the human race: the historiographic implications are striking. The audience has not simply witnessed a prophetic *histoire*, but has assimilated units of text and action which, all taken together, constitute the play and the fate of the world.

In the CBC television version of *Last Call* this "network of 'pragmatic' utterances" continues, but is overlaid with another set of intertexts in which the contemporary audience's familiarity with video technique creates a further segmentation of the action and a continual shift in and out of illusion.[1] Gross drags around cameras, filming himself, so that the audience watches the play being created in a high-tech "play-within-a-play," one of the traditional properties of metadrama. Indeed, in order to act out the second ending, Gross rewinds the video tape to the juncture point, revealing that the action we have been watching is recorded—that it is not real life and can be reprocessed at will. In this revelation, the double ending takes on an even more sinister importance. After the shooting, Morose is dead and Gross vanishes from the monitors as the frame freezes; the audience and electronic machinery, however, are still present, sharing a theatrical world devoid of humanity. As long as the tape runs, the world continues, but if it should stop, what will be the fate of the audience watching? Here, dialogue does not merely refer deictically to the action (to borrow Honzl) nor even entirely constitute it (Elam 157), the only action and the dramatic reality is reduced to an electronic one, a robotic world peopled only by the audience which has outlived the last two humans and which will continue to exist within this context only as long as the video tape runs. In this version of the play, discourse has become electronic, and visual rather than vocal, and has also come to be all that there is. At the instant the programme goes off the air, the audience experiences not the end of an *histoire*, but the process of its own annihilation; stripped of any proairetic value, the final *énonciation* is a horrifying vision of an entirely theatrical apocalypse.

The Tamanhous Theatre production of *Haunted House Hamlet*, written by Peter Eliot Weiss during Morris Panych's tenure as Artistic Director of the company and starring Panych as Hamlet in its original production in 1986 and in the one which travelled to Montreal's Festival of the Americas in 1987, is an entirely metadramatic adaptation of Shakespeare's play. A new Prologue presents a young burglar breaking into a haunted house where he finds the corpses of Shakespeare's characters. These come to life and begin to act out Shakespeare's play while, simultaneously, the story of the young man unfolds as he interacts with the plot of *Hamlet*.[2]

As with John Krizanc's *Tamara*, the performance takes place not in one auditorium but throughout a large, multi-roomed production space (Tamahnous House in Vancouver, Le Monument National in Montreal). After the Prologue, audience members move at their own volition, following characters from scene to scene and, depending on their choices, watch the Shakespearean play, or the discovery of the Shakespearean plot by the young burglar, or an entirely different play of their own devising. Random selection, of course, dictates that no two theatregoers see the same play, although the whole audience is drawn together at the end of the first half and at the conclusion. These collective moments resolve the new drama while remaining true to the Shakespearean plot. Nonetheless, the effect is to deconstruct the Shakespearean play and, despite many spectators' best attempts to follow Hamlet and the main story line, the simultaneous arrangement of scenes prevents a strictly chronological viewing. It is amusing to watch some audience members running from scene to scene, synopsis in hand, trying to "catch" the big set speeches they remember from traditional productions, trying to piece together a traditional plot in the face of this production's aggressive segmentation of the text into myriad semiotic units arranged along endless axes and in dozens of indexical directions.

The white hangings and shrouds of Ken MacDonald's set reflect the decomposition of the mouldering Shakespearean characters, but also instantly cue the audience to the patterns of the horror movie, as does the title. The effect is to decentre the Hamlet story by foregrounding the conventions of gothic horror. And yet, because of its familiarity, the Shakespearean play continues to intrude, causing very complex, binary oppositions. One is reminded of Levi-Strauss's model of myth; to the degree that Shakespeare's "sweet prince" has become a literary myth, he lives in this production, but the *Hamlet* one knows at its conclusion is a new myth with new allusions and a different numinosity. Terry Eagleton's summary of Levi-Strauss fits this production exactly: "Myths have a quasi-objective collective existence, unfold their own 'concrete logic' with supreme disregard for the vagaries of individual thought, and reduce any particular consciousness to a mere function of themselves" (Eagleton 104).

The set also deconstructs the original story and establishes the multiple vantage points from which the audience hears the new *discours*. As the audience arranges itself around rooms, stairways and landings, each viewer sees the play from her own perspective; for each, certain characters become important because of proximity or lose some of their credibility because contact destroys the theatrical illusion. Because the audience moves, the etiquette of the playhouse is suspended. As a result, audience members come and go, and look around as well as at the performers, so that other spectators may enter the dramatic unit with which a viewer is interacting at any moment. If another Hamlet character moving to his next scene also strays into the frame, the *sjuzet* becomes extraordinarily complex and, at times, bewildering to a viewer intent on sifting out the *fabula* she remembers as Shakespeare's storyline: the conception reminds its viewers at all times that they are watching a play abstracted from a play—not simply a play, nor real life, nor a historical event from Elsinore or Elizabethan London—and that they are engaged in a dramatological process.

In production, the most striking aspect of Panych's highly popular play, *7 Stories*, is MacDonald's set. It grew from a collaborative planning stage in the writing and from purely practical restrictions of the venue, at the Arts Club Seymour Street stage. Faced with a need to erect an apartment building at least eight stories high on a stage with an eighteen-foot ceiling, MacDonald found a solution inspired by Magritte, which also perfectly concretizes the point of the play (MacDonald). The surrealistic style invites the juxtaposition of incongruous vignettes, suggesting on a visual level the inner poetic meaning which resonates through a collection of stories which, on the surface, seem like individual satires of contemporary manners.

As in *Last Call*, the set of *7 Stories* provides the dramatic device needed to bring on and off the stories and, because of both its naturalistic representation of a tall building, and its simultaneous lack of realism as it blends into sky, allows the suggestive ending in which reality fuses into fantasy.

At the opening, a Chaplinesque Man dressed in suit, bowler and umbrella is revealed on the seventh-floor ledge of a building, apparently contemplating suicide. Just as he seems to "come to… a resolution [to jump]… the window next to him flies open" and a woman leans out, screaming "Let GO of me!!! Let GO!!"(5). Hers is the first of the seven stories, each presented by characters speaking through the seven windows arranged across the set. The characters each interact with the Man, and sometimes with each other from window to window in a series of separate enunciations each establishing particular deixis. Each reveals the essential self-centredness of these modern lives: a couple who sham violence to enliven their stale marriage, a hilariously paranoid psychiatrist, a con man, a religious fanatic, partygoers who have hundreds of friends but prefer their sweaters, an impossibly sensitive decorator who sums up the shallowness of these lives: "Consensus? A thousand people all shouting 'beige! beige!'? And who asks the all-important question, 'Which beige?'" (64).

The final window discloses a cynical personal nurse who "hates old people" (82) and a marvellously otherworldly old lady who sums up her philosophy of life in a timely story about trying to stop a similar suicide in Paris:

> We hadn't walked halfway across [le Pont Neuf] when he started to climb over the side of the bridge. I didn't know what to say. So I blurted out the only thing in French that I'd ever learned: "Le pamplemousse est sur la table." I don't even know what it means. But he responded very positively. He thought about it for a moment, and then smiled…. Whatever it was I said, it seemed to be something for him to hang his hat onto. (95)

Armed with this new credo which, the old lady points out, "has a certain—preciseness," the Man is moved by her call for him simply to surrender, to "fly away." He leaps into space not to suicide, but to flow into his own imaginings, into the irrational world of Magritte. Panych says the play is an attempt for him to come to grips with his major problem as a writer: his inability to free himself from intellectual questions and just "fly away" (MacDonald). It is also another example of the way Panych-MacDonald collaborations segment action into separate stories and strip theatrical illusion even as they use it.

The ending in which the Man flies, his umbrella open to the wind, depends on the audience's accepting the two possibilities of the set with its architectural solidity and its airy transparency; it also depends on intertexts of the Charlie Chaplin tramp and even, perhaps, on an allusion to Mary Poppins. Lighting effects assist the illusion that the Man is flying into space and landing on the building opposite. There, windows open to reveal four new characters.

The audience must accept that the set now represents the other building, and must participate, as Kripke suggests is possible in theatre, by accepting the verbal "stipulation" of a possible world which cannot be "discovered" (Kripke 266–67). But this suspension of disbelief is immediately attacked by the next segment of dialogue in which the four commentators attempt to figure out the "message" of the play:

> 2: We saw you talk to that old lady.
> 4: To all those people.
> 2: We saw the whole thing from beginning to end.
> 3: And then we saw you fly over here and land!
> 4: There's just one thing…
> 2: We don't get it.
> 1: What's the flying supposed to represent? Is it an existential statement or what?
> 2: It's a Jungian thing, isn't it?
> 3: I don't agree. I think it's political…
> —
> 3: There's a suggestion of mass revolt.
> —
> 1: I detect strong religious overtones.
> —
> 4: I think it's just weird. (98–99)

These speeches are strongly metadramatic examples of what Hornby calls "self-reference," where the play directly calls attention to itself as a play. These four characters exist within the main play as neighbours, exist within a separate play-within-the play, and simultaneously pull the audience out of the illusion both by becoming its representatives in asking questions and by satirizing the whole play in mock literary analysis.

The man ignores this interrogation and returns to the main play, flying back to the first ledge. But, surely, the inner play to which the man returns is not the same as it was before he flew away. Hornby says that in "the theatre… the world of dramatic illusion stays put. The stage itself provides it with a frame of coherence [and it is] unified by the very nature of its relationship to [the audience]" (111), but in *7 Stories* the imagination of the audience is stretched to accommodate more than one relationship to the Man and to the fiction. Hornby goes on to suggest that "a play may lack rational coherence, but, if it engages us, it always has an intuitive coherence." This "intuitive coherence" is essentially dramatological and it is the only explanation of the ending of *7 Stories.* The Man realizes "I have to forget… try… to forget everything… and wait… just wait for the wind again…" (102), and the audience also realizes that it understands this wind and that it can come to us all, but that an understanding of the wind is non-rational, theatrical, intuitive.

Immediately this is perceived, voices of the police arrive in a blackout to break up the crowd gathered to witness the suicide, a crowd which now includes the audience, for unlike the neighbours it has, of course, entered the dramatic world by surrendering its need for rational explanation. "Alright, Ladies and Gentlemen—break it up.... Everything will be fine... so let's just disperse... and go home. Show's over" (102).

What is important is that the audience has come to this understanding not by believing the fiction into which it has moved, but by seeing it as fiction, by seeing the show as a show which is now "over," by engaging in the process of drama which is "a means of thinking about life, a way of organizing and categorizing it."

Morris Panych and Ken MacDonald continue to adapt classic text in complex, metadramatic productions. Their treatment of *The Beggar's Opera* condensed the original, but also filled the stage with fantastic machines interpreting eighteenth-century occupations in electronic terms and added new layers to Gay's already tangled *mise en scène.* It further displayed the interwoven enunciations which made so intriguing their adaptation of Shakespeare's *Comedy of Errors* for the Arts Club Main Stage. The Shakespearean production will serve to illustrate the dramaturgy of both.

In it, Panych and MacDonald work together to create a very complex visual and histrionic segmentation of the original play, employing intertexts of the American cowboy myth, the Hollywood western movie, TV versions of the western film, and the audience's own contemporary preconceptions about Shakespearean drama.

The adaptation—which entails the new setting, appropriate bits of local dialogue, new business and an added song—is situated in a frontier town, à la Dodge City. The two Antipholus brothers become a cowboy hero imitating John Wayne's walk and speech pattern, and a filmic western bully. The two Dromio brothers become cliché frontier sidekicks. Aegeon, the merchant, easily became a travelling drummer; the Courtesan, Miss Kitty from *Gunsmoke.* This sounds contrived and, indeed, the audience approached the show with some trepidation. But in production the conception worked brilliantly—and with considerable popular success. It works because the audience is immediately confronted with the theatricality of a two-level set and is immediately engaged in recognizing and sorting out an array of sometimes complementary and sometimes opposing semiotic units in accent, costume, characterization, added songs, and set.

The rustic main street is faithfully reproduced, but at stage rear a clearly artificial moon rises and lowers on visible ropes; cutout cactuses are moved in and out of position; a row of steer skulls form footlights.[3] The Abbey of Ephesus is replaced by an Oprey House Theatre, centre stage, whose playbill announces a travelling production of *Comedy of Errors* and establishes that the magic in this world is not religious but theatrical. As we shall see, this emendation of the text becomes pivotal.

More important than these somewhat Brechtian touches which seek to distance the viewer is the overall treatment of stage and auditorium that both distances and lures. The thrust stage is given an artificial proscenium and, outside it, a loge, stage left. At the opening, the figure of Aemelia appears in the box not as Abbess of Ephesus, but as an Elizabethan theatregoer, wearing the traditional costume the audience expects in Shakespeare and carrying an enormous folio. Opening the book, she blows out a great cloud of dust; the audience laughs, exposing its secret opinion that Shakespeare is, after all, somewhat musty, and setting in motion the central hermeneutic code by revealing that this is, after all, a story, that it will now unfold and that some resolution will occur. The audience is invited to participate by watching the drama progress even as the stage theatregoer herself watches from her loge.

A very particular deixis is established among this character, the audience and the actors on stage. Of course this use of audience on the stage is, itself, an Elizabethan technique, but few in the popular audience know it. What they see is a play-within-a-play unfolding with their collective permission that it be set in the West, that it be funny, and that it not be sacred text from the Bard of Avon.

At the conclusion of the play, however, Panych catches the audience which has come to accept the theatregoer as mediator between its world and that of the stage action. At the resolution, the theatregoer comes on from inside the Oprey Theatre, becoming, at once, the audience's representative on stage, the wife of Aegeon and the Director of the Theatre *qua* Abbess. She leads the sets of twins and the women off through the Oprey Theatre door. A curtain falls (for the first time) and suddenly the audience finds itself inside this Oprey Theatre; the loge becomes correctly placed and historically correct for a nineteenth century auditorium and the revelation of identity becomes a scene in *The Comedy of Errors* advertised for that Oprey Theatre that night. More: the twins who have emerged onto this stage in dim lighting are suddenly revealed as a surprise pair of actors when the "real" twins enter from the rear of the auditorium and come forward, mount the stage and greet their doubles, now seen as the "actors" in the Oprey production: the audience is thoroughly tricked.[4]

The conclusion arrives but in a complex layering of perception: the play the audience thought to be a game of Western icons laid over Shakespeare becomes a real Western in that its characters are no longer *dramatis personae* but fellow audience members. In contrast, the theatregoer and her fellow spectators are suddenly seen as the real actors in the Road Show production—which makes the audience also into actors. Inside the Shakespearean play, the hermeneutic code discloses itself in a traditional comic revelation and, as audience, the spectators experience the pleasant sense of closure which audiences of this play have enjoyed since 1594.

Inside Panych and MacDonald's play, however, the spectators find no closure because they are now actors in an avowedly artificial production which will move on. The "real" twins have not actually found their brothers because they have found only other actors. But in the Temple of the Theatre (and now the substitution of a Theatre for an Abbey becomes powerful) the brothers are reunited, since all are actors (as are the spectators) and all is theatrical. The music, the set, the emendations to the text, the acting styles, and the concluding *peripeteia* all rely on the collaboration—indeed, the complicity—of the audience with the design team: the audience must radically alter all indexical relationships including its own most personal sense of the I, the here and the now. To view this production is to participate in the active deconstruction and reconstruction for which Barthes argues in *S/Z.*

Panych and MacDonald appear to have succeeded in creating a dramatic text which escapes closure even as it leaves its audience comfortably satisfied with Shakespeare's denouement. If this is true, then Panych and MacDonald are working in a truly postmodern drama, one which escapes the narratological forms of fiction to exist purely as theatre.

(1990)

Notes

[1] For further discussion of the TV version, see also Miller 340-43.

[2] For additional commentary on the adaptation, see Weiss.

[3] Interestingly, all recent sets by MacDonald feature obvious footlights—an unconscious reply to Bakhtin, perhaps.

[4] In a remounted, travelling production which toured through fall 1990, the proscenium, curtain and loge were eliminated. The Shakespearean theatregoer/Director/Abbess walked mysteriously onto the stage to blow away the dust from the folio and wandered across the stage to mark Act divisions and to enter the action at the end. This staging, made necessary by tour conditions, significantly reduced the effect of the ending, making less powerful the layering I discuss.

Works Cited

Barthes, Roland. *S/Z.* Trans. Richard Miller. New York: Hill, 1974.

Benveniste, Émile. *Problems of General Linguistics.* Trans. Mary Elizabeth Meek. Coral Gables, FA: U of Miami P, 1971.

Bowering, George. *The Mask in Place: Essays on Fiction in North America.* Winnipeg: Turnstone, 1982.

Eagleton, Terry. *Literary Theory: An Introduction.* Minneapolis: U of Minnesota P, 1983.

Elam, Keir. *The Semiotics of Theatre and Drama.* London: Methuen, 1980.

Hornby, Richard. *Drama, Metadrama, and Perception.* Lewisburg: Buchnell UP, 1986.

Hutcheon, Linda. *The Canadian Postmodern: A Study of Contemporary English-Canadian Fiction.* Toronto: U of Toronto P, 1988.

Kripke, Saul. "Naming and Necessity." *Semantics of Natural Language.* Ed. Davidson and Harman. Dordrecht: Reidel 1972. 253–355.

MacDonald, Ken. Interview with the author. 6 April 1990.

Miller, Mary Jane. *Turn Up the Contrast.* Vancouver: CBC and U of British Columbia P, 1987.

Panych, Morris. Interview with the author. 6 April 1990.

———. *Last Call: A Post-Nuclear Cabaret.* Madeira Park: Harbour, 1983.

———. *7 Stories.* Vancouver: Talonbooks, 1990.

Weiss, Peter Eliot. "Rewriting Hamlet." *Canadian Theatre Review* 54 (1988); 18–23.

Wise, Jennifer. "Marginalizing Drama: Bakhtin's Theory of Genre." *Essays in Theatre* 8.1 (1989): 15–22.

Editorial Note

For photos of the set for *7 Stories* (1989 and 2004), see illustrations 4–6 (63–64).

VideoCabaret and the Subversion of "Scenography"

by Michèle White

A basic working definition of VideoCabaret International, the brainchild of Deanne Taylor, Michael Hollingsworth, and company, might be that it marries elements of high-tech minimalism with theatrical extravaganza within a poverty aesthetic that says "we find it on the streets."

Its genesis may be found in the highly theatrical pieces of performance art that came out of the basement of the galleries, A Space in Toronto and the Western Front in Vancouver, in the seventies and resulted in the first incarnation of the Hummer Sisters, the performance art group to which Taylor belongs. The art of the time was off the walls, half performance and half graphic. As Deanne Taylor describes it, "we were more theatrically located than anyone else at A Space at the time. We wanted to work with performance and text, music and video, to think visually and put it in front of people. It wasn't avoiding the gallery scene *per se* or anti-disciplinarian in intent, it was just multi-media, multi-dimensional in nature."[1] Perhaps what existed was a good example of what Leo Steinberg terms "inter-art traffic" (Steinberg 21).

There are now much closer associations between various forms of alternate, popular, and high art theatre which are embodied in groups like VideoCabaret and in the performance art movement. Arguably VideoCabaret, which has its origins in a Dada sensibility to the degree that Performance does, shares much of the same territory and agenda even though the latter is categorized as visual art and the former as theatre.

When Michael Hollingsworth returned to Toronto after a period of exile, disenfranchised from the established theatre community, he was looking for an alternate venue which was not so easily definable in terms of existing practice in the city. Hollingsworth wanted to draw on sources from the live rock and roll world to Marshall McLuhan while still working with text.

The Hummers were interested in the cabaret format and the idea of performance in a place where there could be interaction with the audience, where people could drink and smoke without being told in which direction to look and what to see. Their other major interest, video technology, became subject as well as means through the first VideoCabaret production, *The Patty Rehearst Story*, where the role of media was a significant part of the story. Hollingsworth learned to write for video—both prerecorded and performed live on stage.

VideoCabaret International, from these various beginnings, now describes itself as the oldest of the small alternative theatre companies and celebrated its fifteenth season in the spring of 1991.

Since 1985, two distinct streams have developed within the company. Michael Hollingsworth embarked upon the mega-cycle of his plays, *The History of the Village of the Small Huts*, which has involved the core company in its multiple incarnations over these years. At the same time, Deanne Taylor was translating her deep love for the Trinidad Carnival tradition into the Toronto Caribana experience through the Island to Island parade group she founded. And Taylor has written, developed, directed, and produced her opera about reproduction, *2nd Nature*, in Toronto at The Theatre Centre in 1990 and Theatre Passe Muraille in the fall of 1991.

The scenographic progression from VideoCabaret's *Patty Rehearst* through to the Histories and *2nd Nature* is based in the two component parts inherent in the company's title. Technology as both form and content and the audience as participant provide the foundation for the majority of their work.

The work begins with what will be seen rather than what will be heard. The performance area for *2nd Nature* included 19 small arches with video screens inset and one large screen set back from the main stage. The video was produced live to allow spontaneity in the actors' performances (in two hours of production there is only one prerecorded image). Video artists put props, models and maquettes on turntables or on their bodies, lined up the cameras, lit and shot the images. Simultaneously, a colour artist set colourization codes and manipulated effects during each scene through switchers he controlled. There were interactive moments between the video and the performers such as when the performers playing spermatozoa were backed up by a sea of video spermatozoa on their way to fertilize the ova. And there were performance moments when the video dominated before attention switched back to the performers. The childbirth at the end of Act One began with the actor playing Volo, then the focus moved to a psychedelic explosion on the video monitors accompanied by voice-over and the sound from the band, before returning to the actor.

Visually the presentation of *2ndNature* has moved away from what Taylor affectionately calls "the everything out there for everyone to see, the big tech mess approach" of classic VideoCabaret where the performance space reflects the mechanics of production. In the first version of *2nd Nature* the video production occurred behind the audience. Taylor wanted to try out a system in which there was a greater degree of focus on the stage alone. Now she is starting to return the mechanics of the visual experience to the audience, to envelop them more in the total performance process which includes music creation through the band and video creation through the video artists. In the second production of *2nd Nature*, they are still too peripheral for what Taylor eventually thinks should happen. The *2nd Nature* set ranged over the full horizontal potential of the theatre's stage and presented multiple vertical levels for performance. Ultimately, she feels the stage itself might return to the more compact black box concept, although in this context she sees a white box (110 monitors in a white room which can all go to black thereby creating the black box. The physical production elements would then be drawn into the immediate space around the box and clearly available to the audience.

The physical nature of the performance space and its capacity to embrace the audience reflect the cabaret atmosphere which the company strives to achieve. This becomes more and more difficult to accomplish as VideoCabaret feels compelled to reach a bigger audience. The intimacy of the Cameron House, the Queen Street West bar which is their headquarters, Lee's Palace, or the other "nightclub" venues which have normally been VideoCabaret's "theatres," will inevitably be lost. The two recent projects, the *Histories* and *2nd Nature*, are the VideoCabaret productions most mimetic of conventional theatre productions and which, in fact, parody traditional theatre formats and require conventional theatre spaces. These productions acknowledge that, in a time of economic downturn, both the funding bodies and the company's own sense of responsibility demand a broadening of the audience base.

The company has worked with very little financial backing since its inception. Hollingsworth refers to "economic necessities that become an aesthetic principle" in a half-joking way but in fact a poverty aesthetic informs a great deal of the group's work. The aesthetic sensibility which has driven VideoCabaret's work over these years has come out of their marginalized financial situation as much as anything else because the materials and the imprimatur that the establishment, the cultural agencies and institutions provide has been largely absent.

The *Histories* by Michael Hollingsworth, the Hummer projects and Deanne Taylor's opera, *2nd Nature*, are a conscious process of self-referencing: a kind of personal growth for this primarily self-educated, self-defined art network which is recasting itself constantly against the high art establishment. VideoCabaret and its associated artists make their art out of what is around them, however limited the physical resources may be, partly out of necessity and partly out of the drive that motivates most contemporary art practice—the search for identity. The set for *2nd Nature* included corrugated cardboard arches, columns and vegetation, and crinkled tin-foil clouds. Taylor says that a third staging of the play would be done using costumes created from piles of coloured clothing bought at the Goodwill store. In redeveloping the costumes between the two productions, Taylor wanted to move from the consciously fantastical to a street-wise look. Taylor says: "Before they were more queenly and princessly and not so fifties evening gown glam." But the crinolines and pom-poms are paired with sneakers and Spandex to mock satirically the costumed musical or operetta. It's a kind of post-punk *Iolanthe* fairy visualization, which mixes eras and styles with all of the panache of a "borderline Queen Street band, dressed-up-dressed-down."

This kind of visual play calls into question the privileged status of establishment theatre and its production values, and the privileged nature of the audience it attracts. Addressing issues of privilege and the patriarchy began with the Hummer Sisters' retro-feminist visual strategy. "We were collectors of rhinestones and rubber lace, very interested in our mothers' aesthetic. We were four women in a theatre group who started by decorating a room for the audience and who had no budget for costume." Very self-consciously they arranged leopardskin throws around the space and dressed up or masqueraded in curlers and crinolines—"girl stuff"—over black jeans and T-shirts, within a post-feminist aesthetic which strove to revalue "feminine" artifacts.

This feminist focus on claiming "decoration" or "art" as appropriate means for making alternative theatre provides an impetus for Taylor's involvement in the Carnival parade tradition of Trinidad. This is the legacy of a culture with a very sophisticated apprehension of the visual aesthetic, where people learn to interpret "text" through purely visual means. In *2nd Nature*, Taylor wanted to draw into a theatrical setting the visual world of Carnival and, by extension, Caribana. It is an attempt to recreate the whole realm of a Carnival band within the structure of a mock-opera. Taylor has translated the visual hierarchy of the band into the character structure of *2nd Nature.* A band refers to a distinct parade group, one of many, which may typically include 100 floor members in a section wearing relatively simple, cheap costumes led by an individual or character whose more developed costume relates to the floor members' costumes but also to the band leaders, the king and queen. The king and queen costumes are much more elaborate physically and thematically.

The bands portray whole realms of human experience—historical, political, fictional, fantastical, sexual—within the masquerade form (which has antecedents in Greek and Elizabethan drama) but all through purely visual means and without language. Taylor had seen 2000 costumed people in a band on the road implying the gigantic end of a metaphor. She had also seen smaller bands accomplish the same end in a more compact way and felt she could translate this into the VideoCabaret idiom, in a kind of living cross-cultural experiment, where the visual experience is valued more richly than within our culture.

In *2nd Nature*, the character Volo (representing the ego, the voluntary functions, the mind) is equivalent to the Carnival band king. She wears silvery white and maintains a cool and regal aloofness until her catharsis in Act Two. Auto, keeper of the glands, immune system, and hormones, becomes the queen. She wears black but also armbands and a lotus-shaped headdress that contain all the colours of the other characters. The lower powers, or individual characters in charge of different realms, are represented through the characters Cardia (the cardiovascular system) red and black, Gusta (the intestinal system) orange and yellow, Doc (the immune system) blue and green, and Ovary (the reproductive system) pink with hot pink polka-dots. The floor members are replicated by the twenty video monitors as a sort of Greek chorus amplifying, through visual imagery, both concrete and abstract, the on-stage action.

The Carnival influence led her to pattern and colour coding for costumes. She wanted a strong connection between the black for Auto and the white for Volo; "the way the underworld and overworld aspects of Carnival come together as light and dark is a very strong theme in *2nd Nature.*" Primary colour and patterns were assigned to the organ sisters, the back-up singers' characters, and Ovary was given "a hot pink radical upsetting polka-dot look because she's the wild card, joker in the deck." This coding allows for greater identification of the characters and for the quick re-identification of the second generation of the same characters in the second act when the performers exchange roles.

As Dara Rowland put it in *Artviews*:

> Taylor found a strong link between visual and literary creation in the concept behind the masquerade characters and the logic which guides their presentation. In parade, these characters have only a moment to present a lasting visual impression and to communicate their message musically. In designing a band (a distinct thematic group within the entire parade), a designer/producer simplifies ideology and narrative, and employs the elements of colour, construction, shape, form and imagery which best relate the theme. For Taylor, whose writing draws its strength from such immediate strategies, the seamless fusion of the politically activated artistic expression in Carnival reflected her own metaphorical wordplay. (21)

If VideoCabaret is theatre for those who want to see video, hear music, and have a visual experience, then the role of the scenographer, in this context, takes on different dimensions. In the first place, VideoCabaret designers weren't scenographers in the traditional sense of set, costume, and lighting artists but more often video artists working on video production and installation aspects in collaboration with the Hummers. Also the conventional practice of the director imposing an interpretation of a text on a body of people involved in separate processes is antithetic to the VideoCabaret practice. Instead the emphasis is on the ensemble, on company development of material, the "tribe" process of evolving the works where the text is not separate from the visualization. The work begins with what will be seen rather than what will be heard. It is an aesthetic in which the practitioners can continue to investigate themselves as artists through individual productions integrating music and text and costume and imagery with a long process of development. Scripts get two or three workshops of a week or more with the designers involved at the inception. The visual imagery of the characters and the evolution of the performance space goes through a process of constant dialogue, involving everyone. The process is a replacement of the romantic value system that rewards genius, originality, and individuality with a post-modem one that values the common experience of the collective.

VideoCabaret works with contemporary and immediate issues as subject matter through an evolutionary process. Its self-referencing, parodic processes reflect the present state of the arts and amplify the voice of a community. In the final parts of Hollingsworth's *Histories*, which is the next major company project, it has the potential to expand into the high-tech video field it has claimed but within the scale of larger productions and space. It has a visual aesthetic which both allows for spontaneity and the possibility of survival through reduced means. (If need be, its product could be distributed through the video format in the future, bypassing the live theatre process.) VideoCabaret should be and is a company with gravitational pull for those disenfranchised from the traditional theatre world. And it's the kind of company which will continue to mirror, albeit subversively, ourselves to ourselves.

(1992)

Notes

[1] Quotations from Deanne Taylor and Michael Hollingsworth are from interviews the date and time of which are unrecoverable—ed.

Works Cited

Rowland, Dara. "VideoCabaret." *Artviews.* 13.2 (1987); 16–21.

Steinberg, Leo. "The Glorious Company." *Art and About Art.* Ed. Jean Lipman and Richard Marshall. New York: Dutton, 1978. 8–31.

Editorial Note

For photos from *The Patty Rehearst Story* and *The History of the Village of the Small Huts, Part 1, New France,* see illustrations 7–8 (65).

Astrid Janson's Design for Performance

by Natalie Rewa

Astrid Janson began her professional career with the 1972–73 season of the Toronto Dance Theatre for which she designed nine productions. Since then she has designed for all the major performance media—theatre, dance, opera, television and film. She has also completed such projects as an eleven-set installation of Ontario history for the province's pavilion at Expo '86 in Vancouver; and four hundred costumes for the Conklin and Garrett's Antique Carnival for the Calgary Stampede in 1978. She has designed for small alternative theatres, for the major regional theatres and for the Stratford and Shaw Festivals, scarcely pausing in her work over more than twenty years, while bearing and raising her two children.[1]

Characteristic of Janson's work is an acute attention to the sculptural qualities of free-standing scenery and to the silhouettes of costume as they interact with the light, qualities that contribute to an intense theatricality. Her scenography often deliberately situates itself between visual art and environmental installation, in that "intermediate position of the theatre—between the moving, continuous world and the still discrete world of the visual arts" (Lotman 51). What might, at first, appear to be static forms, dominating the stage area, become performative by creating opportunities for dynamic lighting and choreography. Such qualities make her stage structures inextricable parts of the performance. In all her designs there is the strong appreciation for the fact of an uncurtained stage, so that the initial "gestalt" of the exposed set is transformed as a performance environment in which all the elements conspire to modify the spectators' understanding of stage representation.

Janson's sculptural attitude to design is probably not unrelated to the fact that much of her work has been in theatre spaces in Toronto that have been adapted to performance from other uses. These venues, claimed for the theatre by Toronto's alternative theatre movement of the 1970s, effectively changed the relationship between the spectators and the performers and asserted a distinct professional presence in the face of the large commercial touring productions. One such space was the former hardware store acquired by Toronto Workshop Productions.[2] At TWP, Toronto's first political theatre since the workers' theatres of the 1930s,[3] Janson was made particularly conscious of the distinctiveness of the alternative theatre ethos and economy. As the resident designer from 1973 to 1977, and as a freelancer for another five years, she designed a number of notable productions.[4] Other theatres for which Janson has designed have similar architectural histories: the Tarragon (established 1971) had been an electronics factory; what became in 1977 the home of the Young People's Theatre had been built as a garage and stable for the Toronto Street Railway Company in the late nineteenth century; the Toronto Free Theatre (established 1971) created two theatres in what had originally been a functioning gas works; and the Centaur Theatre, located in old Montreal,[5] after its renovations in 1974 enjoyed two performance spaces in what had formerly been the Montreal Stock Exchange. The stages of the Shaw Festival built in 1973[6] and the Grand Theatre in London, Ontario (which was originally a Masonic temple dating from the nineteenth century) called for different design strategies from Janson; as, again, did the studios of the Canadian Broadcasting Corporation where she was a designer between 1975 and 1984. It has been under such varied architectural circumstances that she has developed her command of performance design.

In 1979, Tom Doherty characterized Janson's scenography as "kinetic" in the exhibition catalogue produced by the Associated Designers of Canada which accompanied the exhibits to the Prague Quadrennial (qtd. in "Preface"). In the same publication Janson's own comments amplified Doherty's:

> When working in converted spaces—renovated warehouses, churches, factories—where seating is seldom more than 350, I try to meet the challenge that these limitations present by originating a design which embraces the entire space, including the audience. This is what I attempted to do with *Les Canadiens* and *Esmerelda and the Hunchback of Notre Dame*, and the two designs represent different treatments of the same space. Both design concepts reflect my belief that form without function is worthless. This is not to deny the aesthetics of design, but rather to attempt to bind the aesthetics to the action on stage; to discover an integral stage form which captures the heartbeat of the work.
>
> In *The Hunchback*, two small ladders and a wheel, the only elements added to the basic set, became everything: gallows, table, seating, pillory. In full view of the audience, the actors manipulated the mechanical part of the set to create scene changes. There was a sense of magic about the production as the set continually and unexpectedly took on new faces. The openness of the changes was exciting for the audience. While an intermission may be convenient for refreshments and relaxation, it is not the time for scenery changes…
>
> Often a design concept will nurture and help give shape to the production. In *The Hunchback*, the mechanical nature of the set and the use of the puppets meant that performers inter-acted with the set in a very important way. In *Les Canadiens* the skateboard track helped create both the speed and distance necessary in an interpretation of the game of hockey within a limited space. (Artist's Statement)

Janson's designs for the first two productions of Rick Salutin's play, *Les Canadiens*, are particularly interesting for the way in which she realized the playwright's metaphorical and literal representation of ice hockey as the premise for an exploration of historical and cultural tensions between French and English Canadians, figured as the Toronto Maple Leafs and the Montreal Canadiens. For the production in Montreal, at the Centaur Theatre in the Spring of 1977, Janson transformed the stage into the Montreal Forum, home of the Canadiens.[7] Her design cast the spectators as fans and used a backdrop of abstract images representing tiers of imagined spectators facing the real ones. This other crowd was created using two layers of cloth on which Janson painted concentric circles to suggest faces and which during crucial moments in the action was made to appear animated by light striking the backdrop as the layers of fabric were slid in opposite directions.

For the production in Toronto, at TWP in the fall of 1977, Janson continued with her experimentation and on this occasion physically transformed the auditorium into a miniature version of the Montreal Forum, with TWP's bleacher seating constituting one end of the "rink." Replacing the two-dimensional anonymous spectators of the Montreal backdrop were life-sized puppets (among them a playful likeness of the playwright himself) seated in the upper reaches of the "stands" opposite the audience. The image of the hockey game was completed by the roller skates and skateboards used on the "ramps" encircling the "rink." In Toronto, of course, the production had a further resonance of "Hockey Night in Canada,"[8] since Maple Leaf Gardens, home of Toronto Maple Leafs, is only about a block away from TWP's former theatre.

For Beverly and Raymond Pannell's *Refugees*, a co-operative production by Toronto Workshop Productions (TWP) and Co-Opera Theatre in the fall of 1979, Janson once again created a highly dynamic environment for the performers.[9] For this story of two Jewish families emigrating from Europe to Canada between 1930 and 1975 she created an unspecific and inhospitable "temporary waiting space" out of 1,200 plastic milk crates. She chose the crates not only as strong blocks from which to construct the architecture of the set and the floor of the stage and for their trampoline-like spring,[10] but also for their great potential for lighting effects. She anticipated a lighting design that would cast shadows through the grids of the base and sides of the crates if lighting instruments were to be placed inside them.

Another fascinating experiment that Janson conducted while at TWP was with the use of freestanding scenery. In several productions in her second—1974–75—season at TWP she created settings by means of movable screens, a few key set pieces and multiple-use props that were manipulated by the actors. This kind of scenery was employed in the award-winning group-devised production of *Ten Lost Years* (1974), which was based on memoirs of the Depression in Canada. But for the set[11] of *You Can't Get Here From There*, Jack Winter's theatrical critique of the Canadian government's response to the coup in Chile, Janson did something quite different. She challenged theatrical conventions with a literal "box" dominating the stage. Two walls of this cube were transparent (constructed from lucite) and could pivot to allow entry, the other two sides were stationary and opaque and, like the floor, covered in white carpet. The scenography was a strongly signifying contribution to the work. It presented images of Canadian participation as successive frames of Chilean experience. It was a "huge display case or store window into which the Chilean refugees could peer, but only rarely penetrate" (Carson 136). Janson made further use of the front panels of the cube as a screen on which documentary images of the Chilean disaster were projected: tanks in the streets and dissidents rounded up in a soccer stadium. The juxtaposition of the immediate theatrical event with the documentary images created a powerful visual dynamic between the actors and the narratising slides.

Janson's projections onto the lucite walls of the cube were a conscious rejection of stage painting. Instead of solidifying space (Mallet) as painting does, she defined it by means of light and the textures of the surrounding materials. Projections were also key elements in her designs for Theatre Compact's production of Hugh Leonard's *Da* in May 1976 and for *Summer '76*, Jack Winter's play about the Olympics, produced by TWP shortly afterward. For *Da*, Janson's design animated a kitchen set by projecting images onto a backdrop sky of giant balloons. For Winter's play, she projected images of former Olympic contests onto an imposing structure modelled on the Olympic stadium in Montreal, the immense arm for the retractable roof soaring up from the stage floor to extend over the heads of the spectators. But perhaps her most dynamic use of slides was in the production *The Mac Paps* (1980), the play by George Luscombe and Larry Cox about the involvement of the Mackenzie-Papineau Battalion in the Spanish Civil War. For this work, Janson devised a stunning and disturbing sequence in which blood-spattered images of war were alternated with slides of Picasso's *Guernica*. The "screen" in this case was a wall made of elastic strips stretched taut. When the actors passed through the wall they distorted the images (Janson, Interview).

When she came to design for the proscenium arch theatres of the main stage of the Shaw Festival or the Grand Theatre in London, Ontario, Janson adapted her concept of "filling the space, but not filling it completely" (Whittaker) which had been so successful at TWP. The result was a quite different kind of scenography. For the production of *The Cherry Orchard* at the Shaw Festival in the summer of 1980 Janson's composition of the stage picture was dominated by lace "banners" which were suspended above the stage floor from the grid at various depths of the stage. This design presented the spectators with distinct visual textures as specific combinations of different kinds of lace were lowered to denote each act. (Scene changes between the acts consisted of raising some banners and the lowering of others, an operation that could be completed quickly and with stunning results.) When lit, the lace had the potential to project intricate and beautiful gobos on the floor and cyclorama. The stage floor was left unencumbered by individual pieces of furniture. Instead, Janson designed a platform which could be manoeuvred to the forefront of the stage, where a couch and a bookcase suggested the nursery. This scenery provided several distinct entrances to the main acting area, since an actor could be seen on stage well before becoming an active figure in a scene. On occasion, the banners served as "corridors" to the main performance area. In effect, by their position and height, and by the light cast on them, the banners could open the expanse of the stage to the attention of the spectators or reduce their consciousness of it.

Janson's rejection of painted scenery has remained constant throughout her career, but the use of paint in her designs has on at several occasions created startling effects. For Lorca's *Blood Wedding*, produced at the Banff Centre for the Arts in 1988,[12] Janson designed a backdrop that was painted during the performance. Paint was applied to the backdrop from nozzles located along its top edge and the excess dripped into a trough at the base, so that after the curtain call, spectators looked across an empty stage to the abstract patterns in glistening fresh paint—the residual spatial inscription of the tragic event.

When Janson designed at the Grand Theatre in London between 1988 and 1995, she took advantage of the proscenium arch to frame several interesting painterly effects. In the production of Sharon Pollock's *Blood Relations* (1989) the staircase to the second floor and its supporting structure was conceived of as a free-standing almost scaffold-like set. It was painted red, a shade that was reminiscent of Victorian interior design, and also vaguely of raw meat. A spectator's initial correlation of colour and material seemed to be confirmed when aspects of the furniture were explored more specifically: the upholstery and legs of the settee, and chairs, all had a visual nuance of being constructed of raw flesh and bone. The overall effect was neither blatant nor accusatory of Lizzie Borden, but rather akin to the ambiguities engendered by Jana Sterbak's use of fresh meat for her sculpture "Vanitas: Flesh Dress for an Albino Anorectic,"[13] which asked spectators in galleries to consider the way their perspective sees fashion. She also used the distantiation of the proscenium to create *trompe l'oeil* effects in a production of A.R. Gurney's *The Dining Room* in 1992. For the dining room itself Janson created an almost surreal impression of a two-dimensional picture for the opening tableau. This initial effect, obtained largely through the lighting, was a painterly and hyperrealistic "study" in blue, with light glinting off the silver of the sconces and the candlesticks as visual relief.

Recent productions designed by Janson demonstrate her poetic sense of theatrical space. Both O'Neill's *Long Day's Journey into Night* and *The Stillborn Lover* by Timothy Findley were performed in the [Stratford Festival's] Tom Patterson Theatre[14] in 1995.[15] The theatre offers a challenge to designers: it is a forty-foot long thrust stage with seating for 496 spectators. Janson's designs for this peculiar space revelled in creating two distinct spatial rhythms. For *Long Day's Journey into Night* Janson's set had as its focal point a wide staircase to the second floor, upstage centre. The staircase was framed by a "hall" using scrim walls on which were delicately stencilled wallpaper patterns. The staircase remained lit throughout the performance, so that it was never totally out of the audience's field of vision. The second storey of the house was suggested by two squares of cloth, located above the hallway of the staircase. They seemed to be pinned to the theatre's girders, but since they were hung just beneath the lighting instruments they too could be gently lit. The stage was essentially bare with the exception of a seating area, defined by a old Persian rug on which stood a wicker table and four chairs, about one third of the way down the thrust. The periphery of the room was lightly indicated by furniture (a flowerbox, a magazine rack and a bench) placed along the downstage edges of the stage. By a sort of magic realism of the design, the Tyrones seemed to be suspended in the parlour, between the exit to the garden (located downstage) and the staircase (upstage) ascending to the second floor. Janson had stretched the room onto the "frame" of the stage—a distortion corresponding to that of the lives of the inhabitants and effected without radical transformations.

The treatment of this same performance space for *The Stillborn Lover* was entirely distinct. The setting is a house in Ottawa overlooking the river to which a career diplomat and his wife, who suffers from Alzheimer's syndrome, have been recalled from their Moscow posting. Janson chose to represent this house in terms of Juliet Riordon's memories of a better time—when the Riordons first met and married in Japan during the war. A series of wall-less platforms, laid out along the length of the thrust stage in various configurations and heights to suggest discrete rooms, compartmentalized the space, with those upstage enclosed by Japanese paper-like walls. In this design the openness of the playing area was interrupted by the edges of the platforms, which became smaller bare stages, redolent of the Japan evoked by Juliet's kimono and her memories. Even a function of the hanamichi, or entrance ramp, of the Japanese theatre was enabled by the structure of the platforms and their use.

The great American designer Robert Edmond Jones averred that "In the last analysis, the designing of stage scenery is not the problem of an architect or a painter or a sculptor or even a musician, but of a poet" (Jones, qtd. in Langer 77). Janson lives up to this demand in that her designs are always conceived as working, like poetry, in time rather than as static constructions—as implicated in the action rather than as its spatial context.

Between 1975 and 1984 Janson worked in the costume design department of the Canadian Broadcasting Corporation (CBC) as well as continuing to design for the theatres as a freelancer. She was at the CBC during a significant period when the Corporation was committed to the development of distinctly Canadian programming, whether it was for a drama, sitcoms or variety programs.[16] Amongst other ventures, the CBC broadcast in-studio performances of productions from the Stratford and Shaw Festivals,[17] developed television series and produced individual scripts written by Canadian playwrights and adapted the work of Canadian novelists.[18] And for these nationalistic initiatives it drew on the talents of artists who had begun in the alternative theatres, Astrid Janson among them.

Janson's work never lost its theatricality as she adapted it to television but retained to an extraordinary degree the vibrancy and excitement of her stage designs. Costumes for CBC variety programming became one of Janson's signatures, demonstrating how clearly she understood the role of costumes in mediating live performance through television. Among the programs for which she designed costumes were *Ladies' Night* (1978) and *Anne Murray in Jamaica* (1980), two showcase programs for Anne Murray, and *Let's Save Canada Hour* (1979), featuring satirist Don Harron and monologuist Yves Deschamps. For *Dream Weaver* (1980),[19] Janson created sixteen glittering sequined costumes for the figure skating champion Toller Cranston, his guests and a chorus of eight disco dancers. *Dancin' Man* (1980) was a showcase for Jeff Hyslop in which he danced ballet, broadway, tap and jazz with exponents of these forms as his guest stars—Karen Kain, Frank Augustyn, Honi Coles and Ann Reinking. Janson designed costumes for each of these dance forms and the costumes for the choruses in this program made a startling contrast to Hyslop's black trousers and white shirt. Wittiest, perhaps, were the designs for the Broadway chorus of men and women, which offered images of Egypt and the pharaohs as the counterpart to lyrics about a chorus dwarfed by the presence of the "star." The chorus of peons were clothed in gold and lapis coloured lamé cloth: the female costume was a blue bandeau with striped dance shorts and front skirt, with a tall gold cylindrical hat, complete with a dramatically poised blue serpent; the male chorus's gold-coloured loincloths were decorated with large gold medallions and they wore a more modest version of Hyslop's pharaoh's headcloth. Janson's appreciation for the exigencies of each style of choreography was evident, in these last two shows, not only in the weight, movement and colour of fabrics but also in the choice of detail which could be highlighted by the camera.[20]

While at the CBC Janson also designed several long-running programs, including *King of Kensington*, a situation comedy about a family who live in a culturally distinctive downtown neighbourhood of Toronto. Janson established the series in the imagination of the viewers by the lead character's maroon high-school football jacket, emblematic of his nostalgia for youthful athletic glory. For a variety program hosted by country singer Tommy Hunter she also designed an original costume, an appliqué shirt and blue jeans that got Hunter out of a suit and contributed to a more relaxed atmosphere on *Tommy Hunter Country* and thus to a more informal relationship between Hunter and his guests. In its time this costume constituted a new, contemporary image for country entertainment on home screens.

In 1980 Janson became one of the design team for the premiere of *Home Fires*, a serial[21] following the life of the Lowe family in Canada during the Second World War. Costumes for this series are evidence of Janson's insights into naturalistic costuming. Whereas in the early episodes the costumes were derived from the peacetime economy and concepts of femininity, later episodes suggested a sensitive frugality to the War effort. Episode 17, "Operation Rescue," is a good example of the performance of fashion. In it, Hannah Lowe and her volunteer committee work to get a shipload of Jewish children out of Vichy France to Canada. Hannah wore a white blouse with inserts of lace in the collar and a sensible box-pleated skirt, in significant contrast with the starched shirts worn by Dr. Lowe in his clinic and also with the party dresses which appeared later in the same program.

Janson's appreciation of the performative potential of television costumes is particularly evident in *Clowns* (1980) and an operatic version of Sheridan's *The Rivals*[22] (1981). In both shows the costumes leaned towards stage theatricality. In *Clowns*, a love story set in a circus company and performed as a musical, Janson's costumes emphasized the fantasy, departing from the circus motif most tellingly in a sequence in which the costume itself came alive. When the pregnancy fairy arrived through a lace heart archway, in a voluminous dress that resembled a pink cloud made of chiffon, the initial image was of a Valentine's Day greeting come to life, which was further encouraged by a soft-focus lens of the camera. Janson's costume for the jilted clown worked the same way, extending a rosy "what if?" scenario of pregnancy. But the fantasy turned into a nightmarish vision when the pregnant clown's costume inflated at a stroke of the fairy's wand, to the point where the pregnancy overwhelmed her and she toppled over.

In the studio production of *The Rivals* the costumes capitalized on the parodic mise en scène by John Coulson which brought together, on the small screen, the image of opera chorus on the stage with the chorus of dancers and singers on a grand staircase reminiscent of Busby Berkeley's Hollywood extravaganzas. White wigs and silvery satin breeches or pseudo military uniforms constitute the costumes for the male chorus which performs as back-up to Lydia Languish singing about her *ennui* and during the courtship by Sir Anthony of Mrs. Malaprop.

The production revels in the potentialities of in-studio performance with plenty of close-ups. The dresses are all perceptibly wider than authenticity might dictate. The *pièce de résistance* of the costuming is, as one might imagine, Mrs. Malaprop's get-up for the scene in the park when letters are passed. She is resplendent in a costume equivalent to her linguistic idiosyncrasies, an exaggeration of all the elements found in the other costumes—a headdress, constructed of a silvery white ribbon stiffened into the shape of a three-masted galleon under full sail, riding the waves of her wig. Her frock is yet wider than any of the other females and constructed with such solidity that the farthingale resembles a shelf with scalloped edges, or something akin to a baker's tiered banquet confection.

Such costume work for studio production appears to have influenced Janson's work for live performance in a most fascinating way. In much of her work through the eighties and early nineties Janson emphasized the sculpting of costumes in counterpoint with the architectonics of setting. This shift in focus in the scenography is intriguing for its coincidence with Janson's designs for dance, opera and musicals during the same period. There is a reorientation, through costume, to the humanness of the performer, as in *The Firebird* danced by the Royal Winnipeg Ballet during the 1981–82 season, *Cabaret* produced by the Centrestage Theatre Company in 1983, *The Grace of Mary Traverse* at the Toronto Free Theatre during the 1986–87 season, the opera *Rusalka* produced by the Opera Company of Philadelphia in November 1988, and *The Wizard of Oz* produced by Marlene Smith at the Elgin theatre during the season of 1989–90. For the Royal Winnipeg Ballet's *The Firebird* (1982) the costumes were closer to second skins than costumes. Janson abandoned the traditionally delicate costumes for classical ballet in favour of large wings, scales and leprous skin transforming the dancers into the creatures of the ballet's narrative and its choreography. The costumes embodied the themes of the ballet itself, so that the dancers and their costumes became inextricably linked rather than decoratively interpretative. Janson later also applied this concept of second skin as costume for the opera *Rusalka* (1988), performed by the Opera Company of Philadelphia. The application of dance-like costumes to opera was a bold choice which insisted on the singer's presence within the visual tableau, as well as the musical expression. Here, instead of the robes and flowing velvets of other productions of opera, Janson created spandex and velour costumes which were teamed with enormous headdresses for such characters as the lizard.

Through this period Janson enjoyed the way in which distance could meld the real with the unreal and in *Cabaret* (1983)[23] human figures took the stage with life-sized soft puppets which had very strong reminiscences of Georg Grosz's drawings dating from the twenties and thirties. Janson's most fascinating experiment bringing together human form with setting occurred in *The Wizard of Oz* (1989–90) where performers "wore" the set in certain scenes, as for example the brown lamé "evening gown" as tree trunk and green voluminous "coiffure-hat" of the chorus to create the forest.[24] The cinematic realism of the film starring Judy Garland was eradicated in favour of a theatricality that included scaffolding for the castle for the Wicked Witch, in the tradition of Popova's constructivist experiments with Meyerhold.[25]

For the production *The Grace of Mary Traverse*[26] Janson realized Timberlake Wertenbaker's feminist probing of superficial nostalgia for the seventeenth century. Janson's costume for Mary Traverse, for example, was particularly memorable in the way that her overskirts were of black tulle exposing the undergarments so that they became the symbolic focus.[27] And Janson made the audience privy to the mechanics of a theatrical pregnancy by simply tying a pregnancy pillow under the skirt. This arrangement also figured a predatory society with the suggestion of a spider carrying a pouch of eggs. Similarly imbedded in the silhouette of the other costumes were images of other creatures (goats and serpents) which became apparent the more the spectators observed the costumes. The descent into the underworld was no less pronounced, if ambiguously presented, in Janson's conception of a large sweeping curved ramp, providing both ascent out of the struggle and a descent to the lower depths.

Janson's most striking costumes are those for the productions of VideoCabaret, of which she has designed seven in the last three years. The company has developed a cartoon-like style of performance for its satirical presentation of Canadian history and politics. VideoCabaret's shows are presented as a succession of short quick scenes, staged in a black box. Most recently the shows have been produced at the Theatre Centre, once a Legion Hall and seating only about two hundred. There VideoCabaret creates a "videoscreen" as the conceit for the stage, a black frame and a scrim, through which the spectators watch the stage action. Janson's costumes often dwarf actors and construct larger-than-life silhouettes.[28] For example, in the series of Michael Hollingsworth's historical plays, *Village of the Small Huts, The Great War,* Janson's costume mimicked the design of military uniforms but grossly parodied them in the material used for construction. The olive green jackets were made from a shiny laminate fabric and were sewn to pad out the actor; the military medals turned out, on close inspection, to be bottle caps and plastic fruits, the checkered suit of Prime Minister Mackenzie King was created from a silver and black lamé fabric altogether appropriate for the theatrical revenant of a devotee of the spiritualist séance.

For the *VoxPop* cabarets held to coincide with contemporary political events—the federal election in 1993 and the Quebec Referendum in 1994—Janson's parodies of the news anchors' and reporters' "chic" was unabashed. And her unapologetic and carnivalesque use of Canadian Maple Leaf fabric for the costumes was a wonderfully sane response to Canadian political fever and the sick-room atmosphere that attends it. In these instances, Janson's ability to summarize a character's importance to the sketch/scene comes through very clearly.

Janson is fascinated with the choice of materials used in the scenography based on how they might be sculpted physically and by the lighting. This attention to materiality within the *mise en scène* focuses on the properties of the materials used in construction and their interaction with at least one other element (solidity to sustain weight, or opacity, transparency or the ability reflect light, for example) to encourage the spectator's active interpretation of the total composition. Much of the effect that Janson develops by her designs relies on the distance between the performance and the spectators for the kind of detail which can contribute to the performativity of the seemingly static materials. While discrete items or materials may be recognized it is the way which they are used that takes precedence in the "process" of the performance. Janson's scenography changes and functions "in time" as much as "in place," matching the process of performance of the human element.

Janson's insights into the relationship between the scale of the design within the particular performance space and the kind of performance (theatre, dance opera or television) focuses on the human performing artist. The particular performativity expected from the dancer, singer, or actor's body becomes a major component in her designs; Janson's sets and costumes take up questions of the premise for fictionality and potential choreography rather than serve simple contextualization. It is not that the figure is contextualized by the design, but rather that the figure is part of it, of the total visual composition, often inextricably linked into the interpretation. Janson's choice for free-standing scenery, or fabric for the costumes, is based on how they can repeat motifs from another element of the performance and thereby contribute to spatial rhythms. The human figure is not suspended between the art form and theatricality; rather the visual space becomes continuously performative.

(1996)

Notes

1. Janson has rarely slowed down; even during her two pregnancies and maternity leaves she continued to work. In August 1981 her son was born and in January 1984 her daughter. During each of her pregnancies she designed at least four shows.

2. In his history of Toronto Workshop Productions Neil Carson provides a useful description of the transformation of the hardware store at 12 Alexander Street in

downtown Toronto into the new home of Toronto Workshop Productions during the winter of 1966–67. The space was redesigned by Gerald Robinson who had already had experience designing small theatres. (He had designed the Colonnade Theatre, a pocket theatre in a downtown boutique complex.) Using a similar concept to his already successful Colonnade theatre, Robinson designed a versatile theatre for TWP:

> an open stage backed by two levels of dressing rooms on one side and a costume room on the other. In front of the stage would be a steeply raked set of bleacher-like seats with the ends bent around the thrust stage. Two control booths were to be built into the upper corners of the auditorium from which sound and light operators would have a full view of the stage. In what had once been a windowed showroom at the front of the building, the architect had designed a box-office, two public washrooms, and an administrative office for the theatre staff. (Carson 77).

3 Toronto Workshop Productions was one of Canada's most dynamic political theatres of the seventies. George Luscombe the artistic director and *metteur en scene* of most of the productions for which Janson designed was heavily influenced by the traditions of the group theatres and more specifically by Joan Littlewood's Theatre Workshop. He had been a member of the Workshop between 1952 and 1956, before returning to Canada to establish TWP in collaboration with other like-minded Canadian theatre artists.

4 Some of Janson's notable designs were for Toronto Workshop Productions *Ten Lost Years* (1974), which the company took on Canadian (1975) and European (1976) tours; *Captain of Kopenick* (1975); *Summer '76* (1975; revived in 1976 and taken on the European tour in 1976); *Esmerelda and the Hunchback of Notre Dame* (1978–79); *Refugees* (1979) and *The Mac Paps* (1980).

5 The company leased space in the auditorium but in 1974 the company bought the building and renovated it according to the designs of Montreal architect Victor Prus.

6 At its founding the Shaw Festival was first housed in rented premises on the second floor of the Court House. A decade later the Festival Theatre designed by Ronald J. Thom opened.

7 *Les Canadiens* was performed at the Centaur Theatre in Montreal from 10 February to 6 March 1976 and directed by Guy Sprung; George Luscombe directed the Toronto production which ran from 20 October to 19 November 1977 at TWP. Astrid Janson designed both productions.

8 The name of the radio and television weekly broadcasts of the hockey games by the Canadian Broadcasting Corporation.

9 This production was nominated for a Dora Mavor Moore Award for set design.

[10] The floor was characterized as a trampoline by Marilyn Lightstone, who performed in the production. See Collins.

[11] This original set was destroyed by fire in the theatre on the night of 4 November 1974. The production did open several months later on 31 December in the Alexander Street space.

[12] The production was part of the summer masterclass with director Michael Alfreds and later toured across Canada during the fall of 1988. The tour was a showcase for the actors and the set from the Banff production was not included.

[13] Jana Sterbak's sculpture was a dress created totally out of slabs of meat sewn into an elegant sleeveless day dress. The sculpture was exhibited in galleries with the decomposition of the material of construction strongly challenging the aesthetics of the object itself.

[14] The Tom Patterson Theatre was once the arena of the local community centre.

[15] *Long Day's Journey into Night* was part of both the 1994 and 1995 seasons. *The Stillborn Lover* was part of the 1995 season.

[16] Besides the programs mentioned specifically, Janson designed costumes for such series as the *Performance*, or *Off Air*, (which offered home viewers studio reconstructions of theatrical productions), and dramatic series *Sidestreet*, *A Good Place to Come From*, and *Vanderberg*.

[17] In 1979 *Captain Brassbound's Conversion* from the Shaw Festival was taped for the *Off Air* series, and in 1981 a studio television production of the Stratford Festival's *H.M.S. Pinafore* featuring the entire theatre cast was broadcast as part of the *Super Shows* series. Janson was involved with the costumes for both of these productions.

[18] Janson designed costumes for many hour-long dramas for this series and other similar series, among them, *Brooke*, adapted from Betty Lambert's play *Visiting Hour*, and *A Population of One*, based on the novel of the same name by Constance Beresford-Howe.

[19] The program was nominated for an Emmy award in the Variety category and won the prestigious Anik Award in 1979 and the Rose d'or de Montreux Award in 1980.

[20] This work in dance for television was soon matched by designs for the National Ballet of Canada: *Playhouse* (1980), *Portrait of Love and Death* (1982), *Musings* (1991, 1992) and for the Royal Winnipeg Ballet *Firebird* (1982).

[21] *Home Fires* was broadcast on CBC for three seasons 1980–82.

[22] *The Rivals* was part of the CBC series *Off Air*.

[23] Janson won the Dora Mavor Moore awards for her costume and set designs for this production.

[24] Janson's costumes-cum-scenery were also a particularly effective way of coping with the lack of wing space in this former vaudeville house. The Elgin Theatre opened as

the vaudeville house Loew's Yonge Street Theatre in December 1913. (The companion to this theatre is the Winter Garden Theatre, which sits above it, and was opened three months later.) The Elgin had been part of a Cineplex during the seventies until the complex was bought and renovated by the Ontario Heritage Foundation during the eighties.

25 This design elicited one of the most vociferous and most venomous reactions from the critics, who responded primarily to the departure from the film and to a design which occasioned a totally distinct playing style. American movie icons were still sacrosanct, it appeared, for Canadian critics of experiments in musical theatre.

26 Designing this production was also significant because it marked the beginning of collaboration between three female theatre artists. Martha Henry, a long-time actor at Stratford made her directing debut with this production. She later went on to become artistic director at the Grand Theatre in London, Ontario, from 1989 to 1995 where Astrid Janson designed eight productions. Playing the role of Mrs. Temptwell was Diana Leblanc, a bilingual actor who would later make her directing debut at Stratford with Martha Henry as Mary Tyrone and with Astrid Janson as the designer in the very highly-acclaimed production of *Long Day's Journey into Night* during the 1994 season which was revived the subsequent season. During the 1995 Stratford season the three came together for the production of *The Stillborn Lover* and in the spring of 1996 for the production of *Three Tall Women* at the Citadel Theatre in Edmonton.

27 While designing costumes for *Home Fires* Janson became convinced that period costumes must be designed from the underwear to the outerwear in order to seem authentic. This conviction seems to have been expressed with great wit in these late-eighteenth-century costumes for the theatre.

28 Janson had previously experimented with exaggerated silhouettes in the 1975 production at TWP of *The Captain of Kopenick.* The scenery for the production, which unfortunately was not chosen for the actual production, because it made too much noise, was to be a series of oversize (8–12 foot) cardboard forms lined in copper mylar and set on casters. See Mallet.

Works Cited

Carson, Neil. *Harlequin in Hogtown: George Luscombe and Toronto Workshop Productions.* Toronto: U of Toronto P, 1993.

Collins, Winston. "The Fervid Designer." *Today* (23 August, 1980): 16.

Janson, Astrid. Artist's Statement. *Theatre Design Explorations.* np.

———. Interview with the author. August 1995.

Langer, Susan. *Feeling and Form.* New York: Routledge, 1952.

Lotman, Yuri. "Painting and the Language of the Theater: Notes on the Problem of Iconic Rhetoric." *Tekstura, Russian Essays on Visual Culture.* Ed. and Trans. Alla Efimova and Lev Manovich. Chicago: University of Chicago Press, 1993. 44–55.

Mallet, Gina. "Designer Sculpts space to illuminate stages of Toronto Theatre." *Toronto Daily Star* (25 September 1976): H3.

Doherty, Tom. "Preface." *Theatre Design Explorations.* np.

Theatre Design Explorations: Exhibition Mounted for the Prague Quadrennial, 1979. Toronto: Associated Designers of Canada, 1979.

Editorial Note

For photos of *Reflections* (Expo 86), *Jacob Two Two*, and *The History of the Village of the Small Huts: The Great War*, see illustrations 9–11 (66–67).

The Cosmopolitan Classroom

by Ronald Fedoruk

For a few days in March, students at the University of British Columbia occupied the office of President David Strangway, their reason being dissatisfaction with the University's decision to raise tuition fees for foreign students. This decision could mean that some international graduate students could be paying up to triple last year's fees to go to school here.[1] In the face of continuing budget cuts to education, it is understandable that the university should cast about for alternative sources of income. Raising fees is to be part of the larger proposed solution to budgetary problems and may be justified on those terms alone. But the arguments surrounding this issue reveal our ambivalence toward students from abroad. There is more to this decision than mere economics, and in this context, it is worth examining the value of international students and what their presence means to the university.

Not All Mosaics are Cast in Stone

We Canadians are preoccupied with concerns about national unity and what we have come to call the cultural mosaic. There is a huge worry that multiculturalism just is not going to work. Granted, the way the whole concept is defined and implemented by Ottawa, there is room for skepticism, but the angst is somewhat misplaced. Multiculturalism is already a fact. As time goes on, there are many more varied and more easily recognizable cultural groups. Cultural identities are becoming stronger, and cross-cultural influences are a more important part of the Canadian experience. We have been living with the concept for quite some time. We are far beyond any discussion about whether it is a good idea or not. I suggest we stop worrying about how this is fragmenting our society and start recognizing how multiculturalism enriches us.

At UBC, the multicultural classroom is having an impact both on the curriculum and on the teaching methodology in the MFA degree. The program currently has students from Taiwan, Iran, Romania, Belgium, Mexico, and mainland China. Approximately 40% of the Design Program is made up of international students, and about 30% of the Directing Program. Our undergraduate BFA has students from Hong Kong, Taiwan, Poland, and the United States. UBC also seems to be a destination of choice for Australian exchange students. Internationality has become a major consideration and is changing the teaching of design at UBC. Foreign students bring a completely different set of skills with them compared to students educated in Canada. It is to the benefit of the program that we are developing an increasing emphasis on an international approach to design education and to finding ways of accommodating students of many diverse cultures.

Visual Dramaturgy is Something Worth Seeing

The entrance requirements for a Master's Degree in any discipline almost always stipulate an undergraduate degree, and naturally enough we find a good deal of merit in students having an undergraduate degree in theatre. In the case of the MFA in Design, some demonstrated design ability, of course, is required, but students coming from Canadian or American schools will often have completed a BA in Theatre, which is more likely to have placed an emphasis on dramatic literature. Even BFA and MFA programs in most places put a high premium on the written text. But these academic skills often come at the cost of manual artistic expertise. It is a rare student who excels in both manual ability and dramaturgical insight.

At this point we have to carefully examine the very basis of our curriculum and methodology. This is not as treacherous as it sounds, and there are models. A source of great insight and education for me over the past few years has been my association with OISTAT (Organisation International des Scenographes, Techniciens, et Architectes de Théâtre). Through that organization, I have been made aware of the many different ways there are to approach the subject of Scenography. Successful designers from different countries have often been trained in very different ways. Maybe we need to question our traditional teaching methods. They are certainly not the only option.

In China, Japan, Russia, and most of Europe designers typically go to art school before theatre school. Most of the international students we get at UBC are very capable drafters, painters and sculptors. A dramaturgical background has not been their foremost consideration. Some very exciting designers have come out of this tradition. *Theatre Design and Technology* has recently done a series of articles on international designers. The many different approaches to scenography can be seen in the renderings of Russian emigrés Boris Anisfeld (Brandesky 46–55), and Danila Korogodsky (Korogodsky 10–17), the sculptural models of Slovakia's Jan Zavarsky (Unruh 23–30), or England's Pamela Howard (Howard 5–7), the wonderfully architectural costumes of Chilean-born Amaya Clunes, or the painted fabric robes of Japan's Setsu Asakura. These are designers and teachers of design who are picture painters or sculptors first. Theatre history is full of examples of visual artists who have designed for the stage: Natalia Gontcharova, David Hockney, Maurice Sendak, Matisse, and even Picasso. The dramaturgy that all these people bring to the craft is visual rather than textual and is every bit as valid.

There are obviously alternative ways to learn design, and we should be able to appreciate an artist with a broader range of experience than just a knowledge of how to paint or how to act. According to this approach, it might be appropriate to consider students with degrees in disciplines completely unrelated to the theatre. Since MFA students will be expected to interpret the text in visual ways, perhaps it is more likely that we should require their entrance portfolios to show evidence of a visual dramaturgy that is equally as important as textual expertise.

Fodder for Multinational Canons

The textual familiarity required for graduate school is quite often very strictly prescribed. Most schools have established a canon of plays that students are expected to have read upon entrance and upon graduation. The canon is pretty predictable and usually emphasizes English, or at least Western, drama. This is natural given that most theatre schools have grown out of English departments. In many universities, the connection between Theatre and English is still extremely strong.[2]

Too much emphasis on Western or on English literature will be an increasing problem in a global education system. Students from other countries are naturally going to treat English a little differently than we do, and more importantly, students with other languages are going to bring with them a different dramaturgy. We have to acknowledge the value of that experience. We have to be able to give an international student credit for what s/he already knows, and we have to be able to recognize that alternative literature may be just as relevant to a Design Program.

It is often very difficult to apply or enforce a rigidly prescribed bibliography of required reading in the case of design candidates. At UBC, as I suspect is the case in most universities, the reading list was first devised for MA and PhD students, most of whom were studying theatre history. With the introduction of the MFA, the same list was adopted with minor modifications and has been used ever since. The reality is that many design students have neither the interest nor the time for that sort of research. There is already a temptation to reject some of the textual material in order to pursue more compelling design issues. If all of the textual material we demand is in the student's second language, this temptation is made even worse.

We must be able to encourage the well-educated artist, but at the same time make it possible to accept talented candidates who have training that deviates from the usual BA or BFA. One of the ways to accomplish this is to be more flexible about recognizing study in other languages. This has made us want to redefine what a designer is supposed to have read, and we are working towards a smaller core canon. Each student is then able to add titles and establish an individual bibliography suited to her/his own needs and previous experience. Consultation and advice are needed of course, and approval of this personalized canon must become part of the entrance requirement.

Father Knows Best

In some cultures, age is actually an advantage in getting respect. International students often bring with them a different set of expectations about the relationship between students and professors. Having to deal with such students may require different methods of teaching. I very much enjoy challenging other people's ideas, and I am equally prepared to defend my own. I believe that through this sort of challenge and defence a concept is more fully articulated. It can sometimes be useful to take a provocative or argumentative stand in order to initiate a debate. This is based on the assumption that our irreverent students will be only too happy to try to slaughter my opinions. Not so with most Asian students. After a lifetime of obedience to the teacher, this argumentative approach does not come easily. I have to be careful about any idea that I advance for discussion. Someone out there may actually believe it. After all, it is coming from a Professor. For some students, conditioned to respect their elders, it is unthinkable to question or argue with the teacher. Our presentation of material has to be sensitive to that fact.

I've learned not to expect that everyone will participate in a round-table discussion. At one time I thought that this was merely a result of linguistic skills. That is not it at all. In some cultures it is considered bad form to propose your ideas so brazenly. It is more polite to wait until someone asks for your opinion. This means that in order to include everyone in a discussion, the teacher has to be able to distinguish between those who are being quiet because they are waiting to be asked for their thoughts and those who are being quiet because they don't have any. This has had an impact beyond just international students. In all of our classes we are now more conscious of actively engaging all students, not just those who are naturally forthcoming.

Learning and the Work Ethic

Education in many countries is a privilege allowed only a fortunate few. Students coming to Canada with this mindset are likely to work very hard indeed at maintaining the highest possible grades. These are often students from families who have a very high regard for excellence. Many Canadian students can learn from this sort of example, and having international students in the classroom almost always raises the level of productivity.

There is a downside to this industriousness. In many cases, it is a disgrace for the whole family if a student does not do extremely well. On one hand this makes for some amazingly dedicated students, but on the other hand, we must be very aware of the consequences at home that poor performance might bring. There is a lot of pressure on most foreign students, and a good deal of tact is required if a student is not doing well. Teaching a class with a lot of international students can be an object lesson in diplomacy.

Immigration Policy in a Country of Immigrants

A number of students who come to Canada to study actually end up staying. There is a connection between international students and new Canadians. In many discussions of Canadian immigration policy, we hear the argument that newcomers will not be able to find work and will therefore become a drain on our social insurance system.

The parallel belief is that newcomers who will be able to find work will take jobs that could be occupied by people who are already here. These views contribute to a widely held belief that immigration is a liability. The problem is that neither of these preconceptions is correct.

Many people coming from other countries do not understand a welfare system. Most are accustomed to earning their own way. They will most often endeavour to find work in Canada in order not to starve. In addition to this, immigrants are often entrepreneurs at one level or another. Many of them actually create employment rather than take jobs away from established Canadians. Far from being a liability, immigrants have always been the people who have made Canada prosper. A large reason that British Columbia's economy is currently more buoyant than some in Canada is because of the influx of Asian entrepreneurs and Asian capital.[3]

Increasingly, there is a feeling that those who use the universities should be the ones to pay for them. There is a protectionist mood in the general population which gives support for higher fees from all students, and foreign students are perceived as being a greater burden on our resources. Even tax-paying Canadian students are being asked for increased tuition, so it is not much wonder that international students are an even more likely target.

UBC has traditionally had lower fees for international students than most other schools and, granted, some adjustment is probably necessary. My concern, however, is that I hear this being discussed in purely financial terms, with cost savings as the only motivation. I do hope that we are also prepared to examine the benefits that international students bring to the educational experience and the value that they are to the university. It is worth the expenditure of some of our precious resources to be able to have them contribute.

The Glass Menagerie is a Fragile Concept

During an OISTAT conference in Beijing in 1994 the delegates were treated to an exhibition of the works of Chinese designers. One of the most bizarre items was a student set design for *The Glass Menagerie.* It featured swagged fish netting liberally adorned with huge spherical glass floats. It makes no sense, of course, but the "glass" image was being rendered in a new and provocative manner impossible from a designer who is more familiar with Tennessee Williams's work. For years I have had trouble with the imagery of those silly little glass animals. They are just not big enough or visible enough on stage to have the kind of impact that is needed to support the text. The fish ball idea is unusable but it is big. It made me question whether maybe Williams got it wrong. I now have to pursue this investigation. I must do the play to see if I can find the answer. It took a Chinese student to show me where to start. I get at least one startling idea from every foreign student I meet. I consider myself privileged.

(1997)

Postscript:

In the eleven years since I wrote this article, I am pleased to see just how much of it still applies. In the Theatre Program, three of our seven current graduate design students are from outside Canada.

The observation I have these many years after the fact is that the article does not address the vast diversity of cultures already represented in the Canadian mosaic. Neither landed immigrants nor recently naturalized Canadian students are discussed simply because they don't appear in the international statistics. But they also bring a multicultural imperative to the classroom. We can also add to this cosmopolitan mix all those thousands of second generation Canadians. There is indeed a very diverse and eclectic cultural milieu at UBC. The dynamic in our classes can be extraordinary and I continue to be challenged by it.

(2008)

Notes

1 The UBC Board of Governors has approved new tuition fees for international students. The proposed fee of $7,087 is 3.1 times higher than the current level.

2 Frederic Wood taught English at UBC for many years before there was either a Theatre Department or a building to bear his name. Drama at McGill is still taught in the English Department.

3 According to Statistics Canada, the current census figures give Vancouver a population increase of 14.3% since 1991 (compared to the Canadian average of 5.7%). Most of that increase is due to immigration.

Works Cited

Brandesky, Joe. "Boris Anisfeld and the Theatre." *Theatre Design and Technology* 31.1 (1997): 46–55.

Howard, Pamela. "The Creative Imagination of a Stage Designer in Modern Theatre." *Theatre Design and Technology*. 24.2 (1988): 5–7.

Korogodsky, Danila. "Dinosaurs: Fragments of a Designer's Notebook." *Theatre Design and Technology* 32.2 (1996): 10–17.

Unruh, Delbert. "Speaking the Truth: the Stage Designs of Jan Zavarsky." *Theatre Design and Technology* 32.2 (1996): 23–30.

Editorial Note

For a photo of *The Rez Sisters* (UBC 2007), see illustration 12 (68).

Discipline Makes Better Art: Michael J. Whitfield Talks About Repertory and Opera Lighting

by Allan Watts

Michael J. Whitfield is a prominent international lighting designer who is currently Head of Lighting Design at the Stratford Festival of Canada. Michael is a member of Associated Designers of Canada. Allan Watts recently [in 2001–ed.] talked to him during a rehearsal break at the Stratford Festival.

Michael Whitfield: What we do as lighting designers should definitely be collaborative. I think sometimes that in this business the most flattering comment is no comment. If an audience member comes out of a show saying it was terrific, but they can't tell whether it was the lighting or the set or the performances that made it so good, then the whole company has done its job well. So lighting design is about creating a supportive atmosphere for what everybody else in the company is doing as opposed to grandstanding or running away and doing your own thing. I am a collaborator, not a stand-alone artist. Lighting is the most ethereal of all theatrical design elements. In the design stage, the lighting plot doesn't look like what the audience sees in the way that a costume sketch or a set model does. The lighting plot is symbolic rather than pictorial. With every other area of design, you can walk away from the show with something tangible like a prop or a costume as a partial record of what happened. When the show is over, the lighting is gone. Photographs taken of the lighting during the show are not really a representation of what the audience saw because the camera can't see the range of contrast.

Allan Watts: Cameras don't see the same way eyes see.

MW: Exactly. To see the lighting you have to see it in the context of the whole show. If somebody asks to see a record of my work, I tell them to see a show I've designed in performance because lighting is really something that needs to be experienced. If I show people my cues, they mean nothing until they're put together with all of the other elements. When we do cue testing on the stage here at Stratford it looks like nothing until you put it all together with the performers and the costumes. Then it comes to life and makes some sense. So it's kind of fun because, in a way, I pass through a production, but I don't leave any tracks. It is a strange thing to say, but when the production is over there is nothing left of the lighting but a bunch of paperwork. I have a garage full of the bloody stuff, but it's really of no use to anyone.

AW: Could you briefly outline how you came to be a lighting designer and just sketch in your professional path? I know this will be difficult because your career has been so extensive.

MW: The really funny part is that I started out in science at the University of Victoria. I had never even gone near the theatre in high school. My parents both worked at the university. My mother was a stenographer in the English Department, and my father was Head of the Buildings and Grounds Department. Through the English Department they both got involved with the beginnings of the theatre program at the University of Victoria. My mother suggested to me after my first year that I fill out my course schedule by taking one of the new theatre courses being offered. I took this one course and decided that theatre is a lot more fun than science. So I actually took an extra year to get through an undergraduate program because I switched into theatre. I landed in lighting because of my interest in the art and the science of lighting together. It was also because I was the one that seemed most available and adaptable to doing lighting. After the five years of undergraduate school, I went to Britain and saw lots of plays. I then had an offer from the University of Victoria who desperately needed someone who could light for them. They asked me to come as a graduate student in the MA program. I had a great time because it was a small and very diversified program made up of people who were not necessarily specializing in theatre but who were interested in it. I didn't act, but I built scenery and lit productions.

Then I taught for a year at the University of Windsor. I had met Sue [set and costume designer Susan Benson], my now wife, in Victoria, but we met up again in Windsor. She was offered a position as Head of Design for a brand new centre in the theatre program at the University of Illinois. The centre was a huge complex, bigger than anything we have in Canada. It had three theatres, plus a small theatre on the roof. I was interested in theatre history as well as lighting and thought this would be a great opportunity to get a PhD. I became a teaching assistant, teaching lighting and working on my PhD. At the point when I was done everything except the dissertation, I had an offer to come up here to Stratford. My wife and I had both decided that we had been there four years and it was time to move on. The offer was to work with Gil Wechsler, who was one of the foremost lighting designers in North America. I could not miss that opportunity, so I came up here, and it really turned me over from the world of research. I never finished the PhD. As well as working at Stratford, I also worked at the University of Toronto at Hart House Theatre and at the Glen Morris Studio Theatre.

Just about the time I was leaving that job and going to teach at York University, the Opera program at the University of Toronto got to know me and invited me to come in and light some of their operas.

AW: Was that at the McMillan Theatre?

MW: Yes. That got me into doing opera. I had always enjoyed music, so it seemed like a logical development. After three-and-a-half or four years of teaching at York, while running back and forth to Stratford and doing a lot of commercial work all over the country, I decided I needed to make a decision. I was getting enough commercial work that I felt I could strike out on my own and become a full-time freelance designer. In 1979, Lotfi Mansouri came to Stratford to do *Candide*. We worked together on that production and sort of clicked. He invited me to come and light for the Canadian Opera Company, which I did for the nine or ten years he was there. When he moved to the San Francisco Opera Company in 1989, he asked me to come there. Ever since then I have been lighting a couple of operas per season in San Francisco. From there it has developed into picking up offers to light other operas in other places. As well, for the past three years the University of Victoria has invited me back to do short guest spots, and I've enjoyed that a great deal. So with Stratford, the operas, a little teaching and commercial ventures, I've been very busy. I really enjoy my work because it's always different. I've done the same play five times, but it's never the same.

AW: What do you like about lighting opera?

MW: Opera I find particularly special because it's such a rich form. You take the score and build level on top of level of interpretations. Doing *Salomé* with Atom Egoyan was amazing. It was astounding what he got out of that material. I think a score has even more you can tap into than a playscript. And I love cuing to music. Another difference between opera and plays is that, with opera, the scale tends to be large. If you think of the designer as painting with light, then the opera designer paints with big brushes, bolder strokes and a bolder colour palette. I enjoy letting one kind of work influence another. I like to incorporate into opera some of the detail and precision from smaller plays and some of the broader strokes from opera into plays. Mixing styles helps keep you on your toes.

AW: Most of your work in the past twenty-five years has been with the well-established, more prosperous companies. Do you ever work in small spaces with very limited resources?

MW: I don't necessarily work much in the smaller theatres, but I do enjoy the challenge of resources. Sometimes we don't have the right instrument or the right equipment to do an effect, and I enjoy figuring out how to make do with something else and use it in an unconventional way. I drive the technicians crazy here at Stratford because I'm always coming up with crazy ideas using found objects—a little electric motor, a piece of plastic, an elastic band, et cetera. It's fun to cross that threshold and make something work by using your imagination.

AW: What area of the sciences were you into before you switched to theatre?

MW: I think I was going to specialize in physics.

AW: That explains why you like to engineer things.

MW: Yeah, I like building things… especially little gizmos. It's the other side of the big strokes, I guess. I like fiddling with something in my garage and bringing it into the theatre. I have this reputation. The crew sees me coming and starts to laugh. I cut a lot of my own gobos as well. You would think that out of a catalogue of 500 gobos there would be one for just about every application. But I often can't find one that is just right, so I cut my own out of aluminum oven liners. The Canadian Opera Company is filled with templates that I and others have made over the years.

AW: Are there significant differences between lighting opera and spoken theatre other than scale and the rhythm of cuing encouraged by music?

MW: The expense. Every minute of opera is so expensive. Because of scheduling and the size of the crews, you are often on a faster track. You have to work quickly and in a very concentrated fashion. It's probably good exercise to have to use that discipline. If you know your craft, you know just how far you can go with the time you've got, with the size of the crew and with the equipment available. I think any art is more successful when it is clearly defined in terms of its boundaries. There is nearly always a time constraint in opera. With the biggest companies in Europe, you have a little more time, but typically in North America time is an issue. Because you are working on a large scale, you really have to nail it the first time. You can't afford the time to do it again. Working so quickly you may not be able to do your most polished work, but sometimes your work is more exciting. So in opera you are constrained by time, which is money, whereas in smaller theatres you may be constrained by equipment. If you have only fifteen lamps and five dimmers, some people say there is nothing you can do. I don't agree. There is a principle in art that less is more. I think on both the larger and the smaller scales, good art is about refinement and clarity.

AW: Often in opera, and certainly at the Stratford Festival, you have to deal with repertory scheduling and its implications for lighting. As Head of Lighting Design for the Stratford Festival, is it your responsibility to design the basic repertory plot for the season?

MW: Much of the repertory plot that we are working with now goes right back to good old Gil Wechsler. My attitude is that if it works, don't fix it. Some repertory companies do what is called a saturation rig, which is where you put up every instrument you've got and go from there. But Gil's original plot works on general coverage in terms of illumination and colour control. At Stratford, the Festival Stage and the Tom Patterson Stage are thrusts and pretty fixed in terms of their maps from year to year. So we use pretty much the same basic plots from year to year. At the Avon, a proscenium stage, the use of the stage is more set-specific from one season to the next. As a result, we consider a new plot for each season and make more concessions to each individual show. The Shaw Festival will tend to work toward a composite plot by getting all of the lighting designers together in the same room and saying, "This is the equipment you've got, so you fight it out." What we do here at Stratford is closer to what most of the repertory opera companies do.

AW: It's a way of saving time and, of course, money.

MW: It is. If you had to start from scratch with each show, it would be an impossible situation. I think to work well in a repertory situation you have to have the discipline to be able to get the most flexibility you can out of the basic plot. The first thing you need to do is study the plot and learn as much as you can about what you can get out of it.

AW: At Stratford do you afford a certain number of instruments beyond the basic plot to each specific designer?

MW: Yes. This is fairly standard practice because the resources are not limitless. We try to apportion the instruments according to the size and the demands of the show. Ultimately there has to be some balance between real demand and the resources available. Ironically, some of my best moments in shows have been with an absolutely minimal rig.

AW: I tell students that limitations are not the enemy. They facilitate and prompt your doing things you wouldn't do otherwise.

MW: I always observe that a poor director will add things when they get in trouble and a good director will take things away. The same is true for lighting designers or any other type of artist. It's amazing what can be done with modest resources if you really apply yourself. Again, discipline makes better art.

AW: Do you allow colour changes between shows?

MW: The general rule here is that if you can reach it safely and without ladders you can make a change. In the Festival Theatre, virtually everything is accessible. Even then it is necessary to exercise restraint because if you changed everything you'd be there all night doing it. We have more and more colour scrollers all the time, and that certainly speeds up the process. I will usually poll the designers and come up with a colour string (thirty-six colours) that will do the season. We can't afford to do multiple colour strings for each instrument, so each designer needs to work within agreed-upon limits.

We also do what we call photo templates instead of doing time-consuming re-shuttering between shows. What we do is shutter the instrument for each particular show and photograph the shuttering. Then we translate those photos into gobos or templates for each instrument in each show. During the changeover, instead of re-shuttering, we simply change the gobo, and the look is always consistent with a minimum of labour. We don't allow physical refocusing. Now at the San Francisco Opera, there is a huge refocus between operas. I still find it amazing to watch a really slick crew with three people directing focus and a dozen people at various positions around the theatre re-pointing instruments. All of that happens at the same time. It's a wonder of orchestration.

AW: How do you work out the logistics of reaching consensus with lighting designers who are typically all over the country on very different schedules?

MW: What I try to do is disseminate information to them, making sure that everyone gets a copy of where I'm trying to go with the plot. Then I use all the communication means possible or necessary to talk to them. With the Avon Theatre, we actually try to get the lighting designers in the same place at the same time.

AW: Are you now using computer software when you prepare a lighting plot?

MW: I am trying to do some of it with computer, but I still find that in the process of drafting the plot by hand there is a mental link that helps me catch my mistakes before we get to the stage. I think the danger with the computer-generated plot is that it looks so slick that you are lulled into thinking that it must be right. Then the errors start to creep in. Good old hand drafting has an edge and a thoughtfulness to it that I miss when using a CAD program

AW: Do you have any particular directors you like to work with?

MW: That's difficult to answer because the circumstances are always so important. Sometimes a director will be just great to work with on one show, and you'll wonder what happened on the next one. What I will say is that I like directors who will honestly challenge you and will not fall into a routine. Directors who are visually sensitive are the most fun to collaborate with. I learned something really interesting once when I was working with a ballet director. He had worked his way up to director as a dancer. We were setting a cue, and suddenly he ran down to the stage and walked around, then came back and said, "That feels right." There isn't usually a lot of scenery in ballet, so the light is something the dancers really connect with. It becomes their world, and they are very sensitive to the feel of it. Now, whenever I light ballet, I talk to the dancers about how it feels.

AW: Do you like working with a director who really knows lighting and can read a plot?

MW: There can be a danger in that. I was in a barbershop one day, and I was watching the barber cut the hair of the customer ahead of me. The barber was having an awful time. It was obvious that this relationship had tension all around. When the customer left and I took my place in the chair, the barber said, "You know, what I want from a customer is for him to tell me what he wants his hair to look like, not to tell me how to cut it." I think that illustrates a very important point about collaboration. I will say to a director, "Let's talk our way through this. Let's find out what you want from this, and then trust me to call up the right channels." I want a director who is sympathetic to the process of collaboration. I don't for a minute think that I have all the answers. I try to avoid the whole ego thing. As long as I have the chance to try what I want to try, that is fine. There has to be an ongoing collaboration.

(2001)

Seeing the Light: Montreal's Axel Morgenthaler

by Ana Cappelluto and Edward Little

Before moving to Canada in 1991, Swiss-born Axel Morgenthaler worked as a lighting designer for Italian actor Massimo Rocchi, toured international festival circuits and worked as assistant painter for Sol LeWitt. Since his arrival in Montreal, Morgenthaler has established a reputation as one of Quebec's leading innovators in visual and lighting design. His work has been seen across Canada, the United States and Europe, in production with companies including LaLaLa Human Steps, the Alvin Ailey Dance Foundation, Montreal's O Vertigo Danse and with directors and choreographers such as Robert Lepage, Wajdi Mouawad, Alonso King, Jocelyne Montpetit, Marie Chouinard and Stephen Petronio. Work such as his design for the opera *Kopernikus* (produced by Autumn Leaf, Toronto, and the Banff Centre for the Arts in 2000) is resulting in growing recognition for him in the English-Canadian milieu.

Morgenthaler is a *concepteur visuel.* His work encompasses lighting installations and set and lighting designs for dance, opera, theatre, multimedia, film and television. He describes his preferred manner of working as a "global approach to all the visual aspects of a show." He prefers to design both set and lighting. In his latest show with O Vertigo, he designed set and lights, as well as video components, and spent three full weeks in the studio working alongside the dancers and choreographer. His total length of involvement with the piece spanned an entire year. The relatively high level of support for artistic residencies in Quebec makes this kind of working arrangement possible—a situation which Morgenthaler admits is seen as a "luxury" in English Canada but one which is a precondition for ongoing innovation.

Morgenthaler's use of moving lights is the very essence of much of his work. Often beginning with only two instruments, he spends hours programming, refining and working to make moving light function as an integral and integrated presence in the show itself. To realize his design for the *Lulu, le chant souterrain*, Morgenthaler attached tracking devices to two performers to enable the computer to respond to their exact positions and actions. The show's rig was less than 100 instruments—Morgenthaler spent over 200 hours programming the lighting board.[1]

Morgenthaler describes his approach as a kind of "organic research" akin to cooking; knowing the type of meal he is to prepare suggests the kind of pot and the essential ingredients, while much of the rest will stem from inspiration and improvisation. With energy, direction and ideas as the starting point, he develops what follows in collaboration with directors, choreographers and performers. Sound and music are major inspirations for his designs. Many of Morgenthaler's most striking effects combine moving lights, a "hazer" and computer guidance to create a sense of making visual the very essence of light as interpenetrating waveforms orchestrated with colour, rhythm, direction and speed.

Critic Linde Howe-Beck has described Morgenthaler's approach as

> equal to that of the choreographer-interpreter, providing intoxicating technological illusion through which (Jocelyne Monpetit) floats erotically. In both Icone and Transverbero, the dance and the light serve each other in a quest to reach a higher dimension...

For Manon Richard of Montreal's *La Presse*, in Morgenthaler's work light "uses space freely, crossing mirrors, drowning our senses, amplifying shadows, inching slowly, furtive and agile, like the rapid fluid of troubled thoughts that lead to the abyss...." Director Andree Martin has praised "the subtlety of the marriage between light and gesture" in Morgenthaler's work,[2] and Linda Boutin, writing about *Le Fou*, a 1997 dance piece choreographed by Ginette Prévost, describes an effect in which

> the shadow of a dancer joins its movement to those of Kathleen Dubé on stage. At first it looks as if it is her movements that are being projected, and then we realize it is actually her colleague Marianne De Grace hiding in the wings. Brilliant![3]

Morgenthaler had been experimenting with these kinds of effects as early as 1996 in productions such as *L'Amande et le diamant* at the National Arts Centre, Ottawa. The production used fifteen Martin MAC 600s and four Martin PAL 1200 moving lights, plus eighty conventional lighting instruments. One of the moving lights was used to slowly encircle the dancers in an organic way designed to match the sensuality of the dance. The effect depended on a combination of computer programming and manual control of the instrument using the track ball. For another effect, a single PAL 1200, in combination with a reflective mat, was used to project an image of a dancer's shadow onto an upstage scrim. The instrument's ability to frame a light beam in a manner similar to the shutters of a Leko was used to "cut" exactly on the edge of the mirrored mat in order to produce a cleanly defined shadow image. The dancer performed while lying on the mat, which was cushioned by rubber. This enabled the dancer to influence not only the shape but also the quality of her shadow—any shift in her weight distorted the mirror, the light's reflection, and thus the shadow.

Morgenthaler has taken these kinds of interactive effects even further in *La Traversée du temps*, a 16mm short film project directed by Andree Martin and shot in Montreal's L'Agora de la Danse in late 1999. The concept for the piece involved the lighting serving both as set design and as interactive partner of dancer/choreographer Heather Mah. To accomplish this, Morgenthaler created a performer-influenced lighting set-up using sixty Fresnels and Lekos, plus two Martin PAL 1200 moving lights rigged in the air and two others mounted on rolling structures. All four moving lights were linked by a three-dimensional ultrasonic tracking system.

This effect uses a large sheet of Mylar to catch and reflect waves of light in order to create a playful, kinetic and interactive lighting entity. Using similar techniques and effects, the lighting also creates the three-dimensional architectural space for the performance.

In addition to serving as set and dance partner, light is also, of course, called upon to provide visibility. Balancing these needs requires three distinctive approaches to lighting which must be integrated in such a way that each contributes to the whole without interfering with, or even destroying, the effect of another.

In a similar vein, O Vertigo's 1999 *La Vie qui bat* required an environment in which the excitement generated by the rare opportunity for ten highly kinetic dancers to perform with a live orchestra of thirteen musicians could be manifested on stage. With the decision to move the musicians out of the "pit" and onto the stage, a way had to be found to visually control when and how much the audience could see the orchestra in order for a precise balance between music and choreography to be maintained.

Morgenthaler's solution involved the creation of a large "cooler" constructed from the kind of PVC strips used in industrial refrigeration applications. This became a canvas for the lights that could be altered from transparent to opaque as desired.

In O Vertigo's latest piece, the choreographer's concept was to scrutinize some of the details in the movement of the dance that would not be visible in a normal stage presentation. The (relatively) limited budget required especially creative ideas, and to this end the final rig incorporated two MAC 500s, two MAC 600s, a video projector mounted on a computer-controlled Compulite yoke, three live videos cameras and nine custom-built magnifying lenses.

In order to optimize the use of video images, the projector was mounted onto the yoke of a moving light placed above and behind the proscenium arch. This position allowed the video beam to function as another moving light. Images could thus be projected onto the upstage painted scrim or used to shoot top-down onto the dancers.

This arrangement also made it possible to project a live image of a dancer in a round shape across the horizon. This created a stunning illusion of a person moving on the moon. During the scene, this "inhabited" image of the moon moved across the scrim to create a palpable sense of the passage of time.

Morgenthaler's work is characterized by an ongoing desire to define and refine the language of interaction between light, space and material. This was clearly represented in his "Phototonic Playground," an outdoor lighting sculpture/installation exhibited during Montreal's first annual Highlights Festival (Festival de la lumière) in February–March 2000.

Set in an empty urban space in downtown Montreal, the installation consisted of a powerful multilayered, modular beam emitting from ground level and focused upwards. The beam itself consisted of five separate moving light sources that could be combined to appear as one. Ten feet above the light sources, the beam was "captured" by a parachute-like reflective veil held in place by the upward air pressure created by four industrial fans. Reflecting off the veil, the light was then redirected to the ground in the surrounding area of the public space. The lights were programmed to change beam shape, colour and texture in thirty- to sixty-minute cycles. During its journey, the path of the light became mobile and visible as it interacted with a multitude of canvases: the varying amounts of haze introduced into the airflow supporting the veil by a MDG 5000 smoke machine; changes in the shape of the veil from modulations in speed and pressure exerted by the fans; the changing elements supplied by nature (snow, rain, ice crystals); and the naturally reflective surrounding surfaces of the icy and snowy space itself.

Among the next challenges which Morgenthaler has set for himself is the creation and refinement of software-based approaches which will reduce the optimal time required for "organic, in-studio research." This requires a next generation of computer simulation.

The purpose is not to minimize the importance of the collaborative in-studio process but rather to enable more in-depth modelling, experimentation and creation of desired effects before, between and during actual rehearsal times. Morgenthaler sees this as key to producing his kind of innovative work within the tighter time constraints imposed by American and English-Canadian models. This approach will also provide the kind of flexibility which should prove especially advantageous for applications in film and television.

The financial resources necessary to invest in these new technologies are significant, and Morgenthaler is embarking on another significant innovation that may well signal an inevitable trend in the way in which contemporary designers will compete for projects. Morgenthaler has recently teamed up with fellow Montreal designer Martin Gagnon to form PhotonicDreams, a company offering a complete range of visual design services, from lighting to set design, video elements and integration of multimedia for theatre, dance and opera, as well as film and video projects.

(2001)

Notes

1 This opera by Chants Libres opened 10 February 2000 at the Usine C in Montreal. The show was remounted in spring 2001 at Montreal's Centre Pierre-Peladeau and opened on 24 May.

[2] Andree Martin speaking on SRC Midi Culture. Martin's remarks were translated by Bob White of Language Lunch. [The date of this broadcast could not be retrieved—ed.]

[3] Translated by Bob White.

Works Cited

Boutin, Linda. Review of *Le Fou. Journal Voir* 22 May 1997: 48.

Howe-Beck, Linde. "Beyond Theatre and Dance." *Montreal Gazette* 9 October 1998: D9.

Morgenthaler, Axel. Telephone interview. 12 March 2001.

Richard, Manon. *La Presse* 17 May 1997. SRC Midi Culture, Radio Canada, Montreal. 15 May 1997.

Editorial Note

For photos of *La Vie qui bat, Lulu, le chant souterain*, and *Don Juan*, see illustrations 13–15 (69–70).

For photo and illustration acknowledgements, please see pages viii–x.

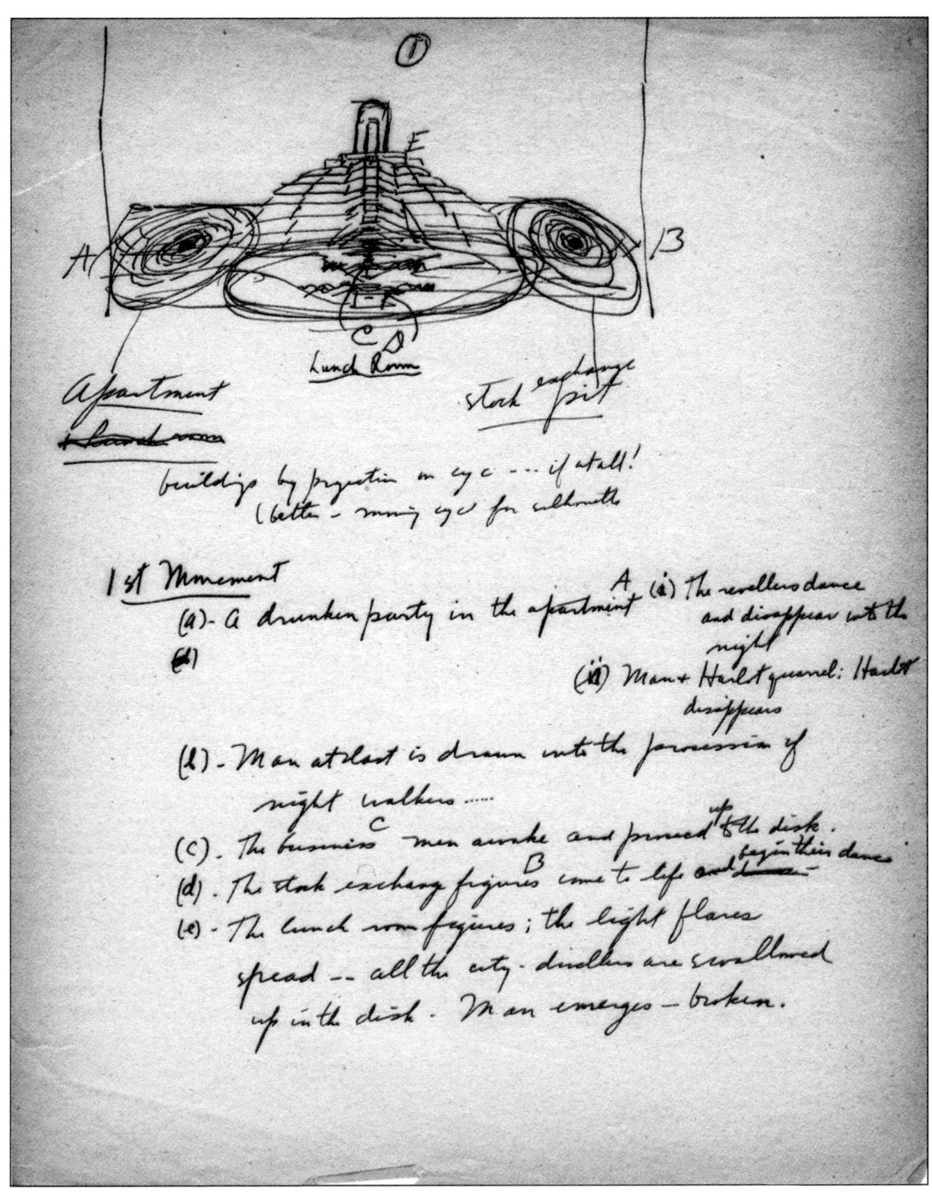

1. Sketch by Herman Voaden. Scenario for First Movement of *Symphony* (*c.* 1930). Seen here Voaden conceptualizing a stage space that could facilitate highly abstract and ritualistic choreography on a central staircase, in a dynamic tension with the more pragmatic range of locations along the downstage—an apartment, a lunch room and the unsettling third location of a pit for the "stock exchange."

2. Sketch by Lowrie Warrener, possibly for the Fifth Movement of *Symphony* (1930). Warrener fills the space with abstractions of natural form in an apparent reorganization of a logical order in favour of a volumetric effect achieved by emphasizing lighting as taking precedence over the physical space. The overwhelming relationship between Man on the ledge is seen here with the rising of the sun as an illumination from *within* the centre of the stage space.

3. Sketch by Lowrie Warrener on reverse side of first page of Second Movement of annotated draft of *Symphony* (1930). The sketch presents Man as a counter-rhythm to his environment, the shapes rising and encircling him, an approach that reaches out to an experiential impression of the environment rather than the more locational one shown being developed by Voaden.

4. *7 Stories* by Morris Panych, Arts Club, Seymour Street, Vancouver, 1989. With the apparent stage reduced to a narrow ledge and seven large windows, Ken MacDonald's set challenged spectators with a theatrical version of René Magritte's surrealist disruption of a sense of "here and now."

5. *7 Stories* by Morris Panych, Arts Club, Granville Island, Vancouver, 2004. Fifteen years later MacDonald's scenography is in tune with a postmodern emphasis in architectural detail that plays out the surrealism in the paradox of a reflection of the sky on a stonework building.

6. *7 Stories* by Morris Panych, Arts Club, Granville Island, Vancouver, 2004. Architectural details and painting (close up) show skewed perspective with the corbels receding into the building itself and attest to a postmodern fascination with quoins, seen here grafted onto the building.

7. Deanne Taylor in *The Patty Rehearst Story*. By Deanne Taylor. Hummer Sisters. 85 St. Nicholas Street (1976), Frank's Place (later Ydessa Gallery) 1976, The Kitchen Centre for Music and Video, New York (1978). Deanne Taylor in performance shows the juxtaposition of video and live performance in gallery settings emphasizing the simultaneity of mediatized and embodied narration.

8. Deanne Taylor as Sister DeeDee in *The History of the Village of the Small Huts, Part 1, New France*. By Michael Hollingsworth, Theatre Passe Muraille (1985). Iconic images created by costumes contribute to a sense of anachronistic photo opportunities derived from history and aimed for an audience raised on televised historical "re-enactments."

9. Janson created a series of eleven installations entitled *Reflections* organized as a spiral path of galleries through the Ontario Pavillion at Expo '86 (Vancouver). Seen here a selection from Modern Ontario celebrating culture and sports in which images of recognizeable figures from theatre, dance and sports were projected onto "canvases" enlivened by Plexiglas tubes that slowly rotated. Lighting of the images in sequence gently ushered the spectators through the exhibit.

10. *Jacob Two-Two*, adapted from Mordecai Richler's story, for stage at the Young People's Theatre (Lorraine Kimsa Theatre for Young People) in 1989 featured scenography by Astrid Janson. Projections replaced cumbersome physical scenery, allowing scale and narratival perceptions to be played out visually as the stage environment.

11. *The History of the Village of the Small Huts: The Great War.* VideoCabaret, 1993. Janson's oversize costumes pad out the actors and mimic period military uniforms. Constructed as they are from shiny laminate fabric and festooned with bottle-cap buttons and mock medals their details invite closer scrutiny from the spectators beyond the "portrait" of the past that they initially signal.

12. Ron Fedoruk inquires into the effect on design education in Canada when an international student cohort brings with it influences of visual traditions of stage design. This production of *The Rez Sisters* by Tomson Highway was mounted at University of British Columbia (2007) with a design team of Parjad Sharifi from Iran (set), Jay Haven from Canada (costumes), and Chris Littman (lighting).

13. *La Vie qui bat.* Choreography Ginette Laurin, musical direction Walter Baudreau. O Vertigo Danse/ Société de musique contemporaine du Québec. Salle Pierre Mercure, Montreal, 1999. Morgenthaler employed PVC strips—the kind used in industrial refrigeration—to create a canvas for the lights that could be transparent or opaque depending on the desired precise balance to be struck between isolating the ten kinetic dancers and including the thirteen live musicians on stage.

14. Axel Morgenthaler prefers to design both sets and lighting to engage the spectators in a highly integrated performance environment. For *Lulu, le chant souterain* Morgenthaler attached tracking devices to the performers to enable the computer to respond to exact positions. The lighting traced the perimeter of the built stage, highlighting the treads of the encircling staircases and defining the space volumetrically as an enormous light box. *Lulu, le Chant Souterain,* composed by Alain Thibault and libretto by Yan Muckle (Chants Libres, l'Usine C, Montreal, 2000).

15. Axel Morgethaler's *Don Juan*. By Felix Gray. Chants Libre, Théâtre St.-Denis, Montreal, 2004. Described as a *concepteur visuel* by Cappelluto and Little, the lighting designs by Axel Morgenthaler develop out of collaboration with directors, choreographers and performers "to make visual the very essence of light as interpenetrating waveforms orchestrated with colour, rhythm, direction and speed."

16. *Concerto grosso pour corps et surface métallique*. Choreography by Danièle Desnoyers. Carré des Lombes, 1999. Nancy Tobin's soundscapes occasion a distinct landscape in the theatre—a mic-ed metal floor and speakers suspended above the stage in plain view of the spectators. The dancers interact with the speakers and the feedback from them is made integral to the choreography.

17. "The Funeral Procession." *Ra* by R. Murray Schafer. Patria Music/Theatre Projects. Holland Festival, Leiden, 1985. Jerrard Smith's scenography incorporated the spectators into a chorus of priest and priestesses who were included in the ceremonies of the funeral for the Egyptian King. His scenography for the nine-hour performance created environments for ritualized events in the streets, parks, a church and a museum in Leiden.

18. *The Palace of the Cinnabar Phoenix* by R. Murray Schafer. Patria Music/Theatre Projects (2006). Jerrard Smith's wilderness scenography integrates the surroundings of the Haliburton Forest and Wildlife Reserve into the experience of a Theatre of Confluence. Schafer's opera is seen here from the vantage point of an on-shore amphitheatre that looks out to a floating puppet stage and orchestra "pit." Entrances from around the lake are negotiated by canoe or kayak, and the performance is timed to coincide with twilight.

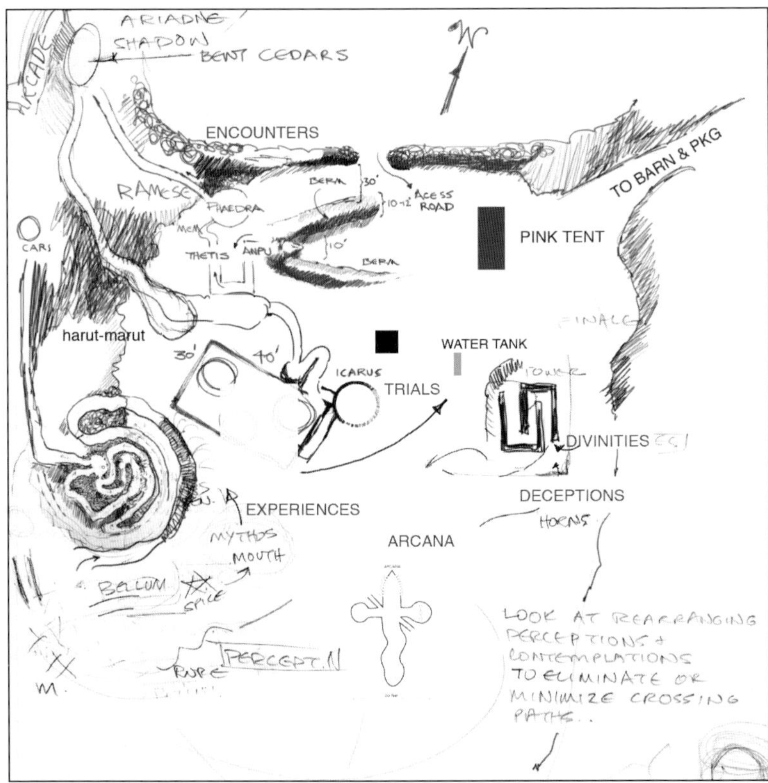

19. *Asterion* site map created by Jerrard Smith. In the *Patria* cycle the labyrinth stands as a metaphor for the search for personal and cultural identity. *Patria 7, Asterion* is intended as a journey to be experienced by one person at a time. Seen here a map that begins to space out the fifty events, each with its own environment, that constitute the transformative journey for the audience.

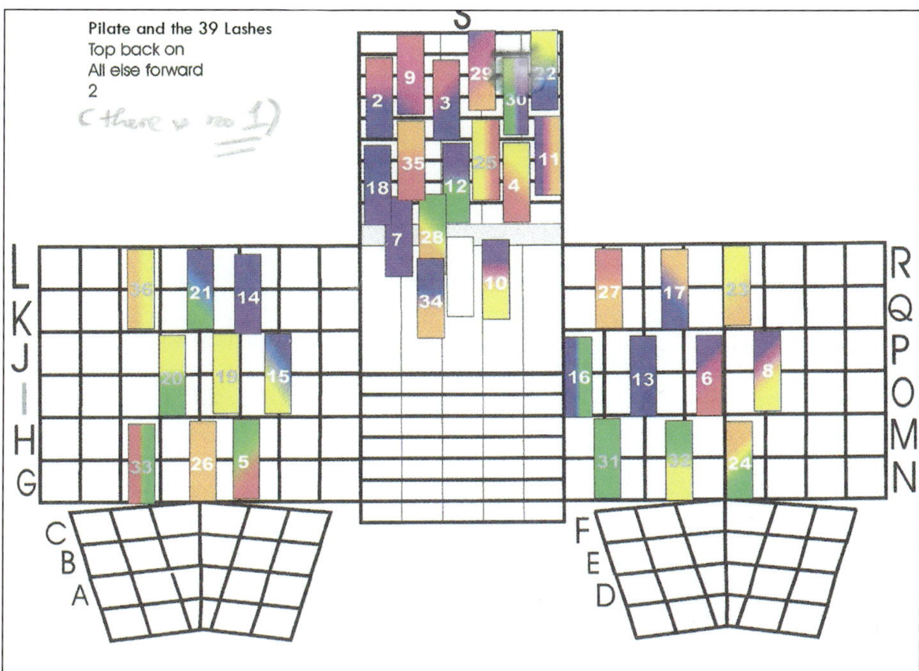

20. An example of the 2’x2’ grid employed for *Jesus Christ Superstar* directed by Jillian Keiley and musical direction by Petrina Bromley (Artistic Fraud, 1998). Using mathematically-based choreography, Keiley scores each performer’s presence on a grid; in the case of this production the kaleidography made use of the costumed figures to compose images on stage that approximate, by their effect, stained-glass windows.

21. Jillian Keiley’s kaleidography emphasizes choral movement as integral to the *mise en scène* drawing on musical scoring to achieve its rhythmic and spatial analogues in her scenographic dramaturgy. See here a scene from *Jesus Christ Superstar* (Artistic Fraud, 1998); note the visible grid on the stage floor.

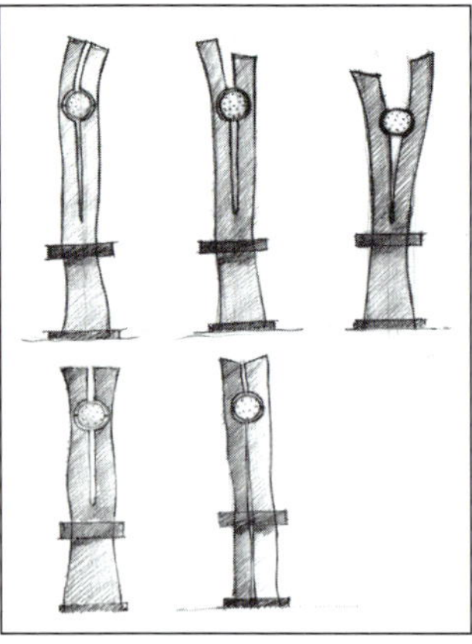

22–23. *The Bus Project.* The kiosk located in the Regina STC Bus Depot, designed and constructed by John Reichert, 2004. Another such kiosk was located in the Saskatoon station. Together, Irwin argues, they redefined the perception of the depots by allowing the idea of art to become part of the milieu.

24. *Candide.* By Leonard Bernstein. Directed by Robert Carsen. Théâtre du Châtelet, Paris, 2006. Considering the way in which we view cataclysmic events and to find contemporary resonances with Voltaire's satire, Carsen and Levine developed a dramaturgy for the production drawing on the imagery of a 1950s televsion with environments that receded upstage a little like a Las Vegas set.

25. *Candide.* Preliminary sketches by Michael Levine. Artist's sketchbook. A page from Levine's sketchbook shows how Levine was conceptualizing the television set as a frame for the stage space and considering its potential contribution to enable a re-orientation of perspective if it would simulate an overhead camera angle.

26. *Madame Butterfly.* By Giacomo Puccini. ENO (English National Opera), London, 2005. The scenographic design by Michael Levine, created in dialogue with director Anthony Minghella, provided a highly flexible environment to allow development of the *mise en scène* in rehearsal. Drawing on Bunraku theatre's energy of real scenery used with an awareness of the artifice of performance, this scenography employed manipulators to remake environments using mobile shoji screens, an overhead mirror and puppeteers.

Robert Lepage's *Zulu Time*: A Colonialist Fantasy

by Rahul Varma

Zulu Time, a lavish multimedia event created by Robert Lepage and star Peter Gabriel, was billed as the centrepiece of Quebec/New York 2001, a month-long festival celebrating Québécois culture that was scheduled to open in New York on 21 September 2001 but was postponed in the wake of 9/11. While ex-Premier Bernard Landry and his Minister Louise Beaudoin personally expressed their condolences to the victims, Lepage benefitted from the postponement when it was revealed that *Zulu Time* was set in airports and had terrorism as a central theme.

Now, as President Bush's "liberation" of Iraq has finished off the unfinished business of Bush's Senior's "Operation Desert Storm," Lepage's *Zulu Time* continues its world tour, supporting a particular world vision defined by US militarism.

Zulu Time consists of 26 scenes, each named after a letter of the international radio transmission code used by aviators: A for Alpha, B for Bravo,... I for India,... and finally Z for Zulu. Lepage's "Zulu Time" refers to the military's universal clock. Apparently, Lepage was "blown away" by the profundity of the idea of the whole world agreeing on a common concept of time. He told Don Shewey of the *New York Times* "When they bombed Belgrade, bombers leaving from San Diego were synchronized with bombers leaving from Italy, and they were on Zulu Time."

The action of *Zulu Time* unfolds on a giant metal catwalk that moves up and down and from side to side. A huge projection screen moves in and out of the scene while a soundscape—a mix of hip hop, (distorted) Indian classical, and other musical styles—pulsates in the background. The play chillingly depicts a terrorist-instigated plane crash, punctuated by breathtaking footage of warplanes and accompanied by deafening thunder, smoke, sparks and fire to convey a sense of urgency, panic, and destruction. *Zulu Time* employs a cavalcade of character-types: pilots, stewardesses, drug traffickers, a golfer, travellers, acrobats, contortionists, singers, DJs, robots, and more. *Zulu Time* is an air travel fantasy—bodies floating through an airplane cabin, divers searching for underwater remains, an upside-down tango, an energetic robot dance, and a golfer repeatedly swinging his golf club. It depicts a flight attendant's sexual fantasy in which a black robotic figure jumps on her from the ceiling and repeatedly lifts her in the air and slams her back on the bed before disappearing into the ceiling, only to reappear and repeat the same actions but with more intensity. Each repetition leaves her more exhausted and with fewer clothes on her body.

Lepage's fascination with technology represents a form of cultural colonization in which the technological means of his art form masks the hidden message. *Zulu Time* is an exemplary demonstration of how multimedia art that is developed and controlled by the West can misinform, misinterpret, and malign the reality of the East in order to exercise political, social, and economical control over it.

Beneath the mesmerizing glitter and technological excellence of *Zulu Time* lies a perverse and dehumanizing show. In scene after scene, peoples and cultures other than Lepage's own are consumed to feed Western colonial fantasies. We are presented with such images as a South Asian woman carrying a candle and shabbily dressed in sari, a Muslim woman in a burka who lets out a piercing scream, and a male terrorist who loosely resembles a Sikh, (even though by Lepage's own admission the show was triggered by Middle Eastern terrorists). In another scene, entitled "India," the face of an East Indian woman with a large bindi and luscious lips is projected on a giant film screen as a male percussionist effectively "plays" her: each time he strikes an electronic drum her mouth emits a classical Indian taal/alap. Between each beat, her face is electronically frozen in a contorted grimace, drawing chuckles from the audience.

Even more disturbing is the depiction of Africans as dumb savages: a Zulu warrior tries hopelessly to learn to use a microphone (finally shoving it in his mouth) and a woman dressed in a black monkey suit "apes" for a white man while a video shows Peter Gabriel teaching apes to play the keyboard. All of these images demonstrate a colonial mindset, one that hasn't yet freed the white man from a paternalistic desire to civilize others—the animal, the woman, and the natives.

White actors played all but one of the non-white "characters" and ethnic stereotypes. In this regard Lepage's instinct perchance turned out to be a good thing, as no actor of colour (except the "ape woman") was made to conspire against the dignity of their culture and history. If casting the actor as monkey woman wasn't degrading enough, however, Lepage decorated the lobby with a larger than life-sized photograph of the naked actor standing upside down in a balancing act.

Lepage, who sees the art of the twenty-first century as a convergence of the disciplines, told Shewey in the same *New York Times* article, "it's not a homogenous group of people doing the same craft [...] you have interesting artists finding a coherent balance in an elegant way of telling one story." I take Lepage to suggest stories about loneliness and travelling, or about misunderstanding different cultures, or about men and women.

Lepage's team adheres to the theory of rock musician-philosopher Brian Eno, who maintains that the postmodern artist is primarily a curator. In *Zulu Time*'s program Eno is quoted as saying, "There is no longer such a thing as art history, but there are multiple art stories."

If *Zulu Time* is to be seen as an example of Eno's theory, it raises the question, can Lepage's idea of postmodernist creation be considered a legitimate multiple art story when it utilizes a menu of myths, metaphors, and languages of the Other while sacrificing their dignity, culture and history?

Lepage argues that *Zulu Time* presents an example of "technology's new vocabulary connecting dramaturgical ideas and heartfelt emotions." But in reality it is a smokescreen masking the old colonial attitudes under the guise of a new technology. *Zulu Time* is nothing more than a sense-pleasing artistic product devoid of any serious dramaturgical ideas, revealing more about Lepage's expanded beliefs and fantasies than the actual cultures and people he depicts in the show. Lepage's *Zulu Time* sells itself as cross-cultural, but in reality it's nothing more than a collection of constructed images of the Other. The real Other is politically, historically, and artistically absent. The potential for contrasting ideas and ideologies or for sophistication of analysis is sacrificed for a few simulated images, which range from superficial to exotic. Cultural diversity is diminished to a simulated likeness, which reveals the colonial mindset of historical superiority. For example, *Zulu Time*'s white characters—doing drugs, living out their sexual fantasies, playing golf, and frequenting night clubs—are perceived as engaged in "civilized" pursuits, but only because his non-white characters display primitive idiocy (e.g. eating a microphone, acting like an ape, emitting a piercing scream, disrobing, or performing an erotic dance).

Zulu Time is a regressive show in so far as it claims to present a cross-cultural perspective but it fails to recognize the degree to which its own colonialist assumptions and arrogance are reified in its attempts to sympathetically depict the Other. It is regressive because while it is not pitched as a righteous artistic response to the events of September 11, in reality it reaps the benefits of the present climate by capitalizing on the grief, anger outrage and fear of terror that followed the terrorist attack of 9/11.

It is regressive because it keeps the public and its audiences distracted from questioning whether the US warmongering is any different from terror America claims to be fighting.

It is regressive because it conspires thoughtlessly with a US media caught up in a shameless game of one-upmanship to provide news entertainment: a game designed to demonize those very countries that had previously carried out US-backed terrorism but are now seen as a counter to the hegemonic purpose of the US.

It is regressive because of its superficial research. While Lepage acknowledges that Middle East terrorism played a prominent role in his conceptualization of the show, his "research" focused on terrorist training camps in Kashmir (Hays). Perhaps nobody told Lepage that Kashmir's "terrorist training camps" are the Kashmiri people's attempt to defend themselves in a disputed land occupied by the armed forces of both India and Pakistan, which vastly outnumber the defenseless men, women, and children.

It is regressive because of its racist world view. Lepage told Matthew Hays of *The Mirror* "we kept wondering if we had the right turban, if the guy would wear a beard. Then we sent all of this stuff to New York just five days before the attack." Not only does Lepage lack a clear understanding of the nature of the enemy—the "terrorist"—he sacrifices his objectivity for superficialities: rather than looking for cause and content he restricts himself to costumes, turbans, and beards. Much like a racist to whom all ethnics look alike, Lepage perceives that all "terrorists" look alike.

It is regressive because of its superficial look at airport security, which distracts attention from racial profiling that routinely targets Arabs, Moslems, and South Asians as terrorism suspects at our border posts. In one scene, a white man fails a metal detector test until one by one all the metallic objects are removed from his person, including "ornaments" from his nipples and genitals. He is gradually stripped naked, to the audible delight of the audience. By stripping a white passenger to the amusement of his audiences, Lepage desensitizes surveillance and control that non-white passengers are regularly subjected to at our border points.

We must question the show's patronage given the fact that Louise Beaudoin, then Quebec's Minister of Culture and International Relations, had been enthusiastically citing *Zulu Time* to elevate Lepage to an iconic status as representative of cross-cultural attitudes on Quebec. In promoting this vision of Quebec, Landry and Beaudoin failed to recognize that Quebec, like the rest of Canada, is a multi-ethnic and multi-racial society in which misrepresentation and non-recognition seriously diminish the other. Lepage's *Zulu Time* exhibits a colonial mentality in which the dignity of the other is sacrificed on the altar of an assimilationist cultural agenda.

(2003)

Works Cited

Hays, Matthew. "Theatrical Premonitions—Robert Lepage's Eerily Prophetic 9/11 Parable *Zulu Time* arrives in Montreal." *Mirror.* (13 June 2002): 67.

Shewey, Don. "Robert Lepage: A Bold Québécois Who Blends Art With Technology." *New York Times.* (16 September 2001): Section 2,1,6.

The Loudspeaker as Instrument: The Soundworks of Nancy Tobin

by Anna Friz

I first encountered Nancy Tobin's work through her Web site, RestArea, featured in Studio XX's Les HTMlles/Maid in Cyberspace festival in Montreal in 2001, and accessible on the Web at www.mmebutterfly.com/restarea/. The site is "an ambient Web site for relaxation," a soothing blue plane inhabited by coloured rectangles slowly drifting across the screen, intentionally reminiscent of a television test pattern or a Piet Mondrian painting. The accompanying soundtrack is of the microsound ilk—a clicking rhythm layered with other minimal tones. The overall aesthetic is like Nancy herself—unassuming and deceptively spare, with layers of complexity at work behind an uncluttered presentation.

RestArea won the First Prix du Public at Les HTMlles 2001 and was shown at the New Museum of Contemporary Art in New York; but Nancy Tobin is best known as a sound designer for stage. Her work has been part of the Festival de Théâtre des Amériques, the Festival International de la Nouvelle Danse, the World Stage Festival, the Festival d'Avignon, the Edinburgh International Festival and the Berliner Festwochen. In 2002, she was nominated for the "Masque de la contribution spéciale" by the Académie Québecoise du théâtre for her sound design of *Intérieur*, directed by Governor General's Award winner Denis Marleau. She works primarily with experimental theatre and dance directors such as Danièle Desnoyers, François Girard, and Denis Marleau, people who are, she affirms, "good ear people."[1] Tobin specializes in subtle systems of amplification, resulting in intimate atmospheres; innovative use of loudspeakers; and electroacoustic work inspired by microsound and glitch music forms. She works with the acousmatics of the presentation space, with the tonal qualities of amplified voices and the "voice" of pre-recorded sound sources amplified through various speakers.

Formation

Tobin entered the field of sound production very casually, almost accidentally. Like many children, she listened to pop music and had a little musical training, but her first real exposure to sound equipment and experimental soundmaking was at the radio station at Collège Limoilou in Quebec City. There she hosted a weekly program, and had the opportunity to fool around with Revox reel-to-reel recorders, splicing, and mixing. She later moved over to CKRL (campus and community radio) in Quebec, and continued her radiophonic explorations there. Tobin remembers "spending nights in the station, having a show the whole night, having four turntables and three Revoxes and an open mike and open telephone—that kind of fun." Her show was open format and often hours long (filling in the wee hours on campus and community radio is a special kind of madness); and here she truly played with the available equipment, "slicing tape, throwing it all on the floor and picking it up again, putting it back together to see what it does." Though the station provided basic training, what was most valuable for Tobin was having license to play, to try different techniques in a casual and non-serious way, but within the discipline of a weekly commitment to do a program. Tobin's inspirations at this time included Laurie Anderson, Brian Eno, Klaus Schultz, and Meredith Monk.

Tobin began studying dramatic arts at the Université du Québec à Montréal (UQAM) in 1986, where she began her technical training in earnest. Initially she was interested in theatre direction, but felt insecure about her ability to make a living in theatre, so opted instead to become a technician, which she viewed as a "more concrete" profession. Because of her volunteer radio experiences, Tobin gravitated toward sound, and so studied sound engineering. Digital editing was still very new and expensive, while MIDI was state of the art. She gathered a solid basis in studio operation, theories of sound, and technical concerns specifically for stage. Tobin notes that she has consistently improved her technical knowledge, partly to maintain professional excellence and partly out of a desire for job security. "For the last ten years what was important to me was to get some serious training in theatre… to have a really solid thing that I could rely on to make a living." Tobin has worked professionally in theatre and dance since graduation.

The Intimate Voice Onstage

Upon graduation in 1989, Tobin worked for several years for smaller theatre and dance companies in Montreal. "But what I do now, I certainly didn't learn in school," Tobin attests. "I feel sometimes that in Quebec I'm a pioneer in the development of a unique approach that is specific to Québécois theatre." The successful adaptation of multimedia for stage is a hallmark of Québécois theatre. Tobin's work with Denis Marleau and Danièle Desnoyers is particularly rich, in part because the directors themselves assign a significant role to the sound design of the production. They integrate amplified and composed sound, not as embellishments, musical interludes, or background, but as central elements of the presented works. Sound is the medium in which the performers exist and move, their voices seamlessly amplified, their bodies causing audible change, the soundscape challenging and leading the choreography as much as integrating with it. Tobin is called on early to participate in a production, so that sonic elements are created simultaneously with choreography and character development, in many cases enabling actors and dancers to become amplified sound sources themselves, through the use of wireless microphones and controlled feedback systems. Tobin is particularly known for her trademark natural-sounding vocal amplification and manipulation of sound with various types of loudspeakers. These skills were developed through experience in the field, especially working with directors who provided time and equipment to experiment during the production phase of a show.

With the help of a professional development grant, Tobin went to Broadway and to London's West End in 1997 to observe sound designers at work on huge musicals like *Oliver*. In particular, Tobin was interested in the technique used for amplifying voices so they could be heard in the back rows of large concert venues while remaining synchronized with the acoustic voice onstage. These halls are so large that it takes a noticeable period of time for the sound from the stage to reach the back rows. This results in a lack of clarity in the sound. Very little was written about ways of dealing with the situation, so Tobin engineered a kind of apprenticeship for herself, where she learned "through observation, and by listening to experienced people discuss their techniques." Tobin spent a month in New York observing a production during its creation by sound designer Tony Miola, and Miola put her in touch with Andrew Bruce in London, where she spent another month's internship. Upon her return to Montreal, Tobin worked with the techniques that she had learned, adapting them to smaller venues and budgets, and began to establish her distinctive style.

In order to create the illusion that actors are not amplified, invisible mikes are used, and loudspeakers must be synchronized to the acoustic voice on stage. This involves delaying the amplified voice in the speakers to match the time it takes the acoustic sound to travel from the stage to the spectators' ears. Tobin says that while she interned in London, calibrating the speaker delays was a fun group activity. The technicians would people the balconies farthest from the stage, while a single speaker onstage emitted a regular pulse, and the speaker delays were set by consensus among the group. Nancy still invites friends to come in when she sets delays in Montreal, so I joined her one afternoon on the set of Théâtre UBU's *Quelqu'un va venir* at Usine C to see how the process works.

Usine C is a renovated factory used for theatre, dance, and multimedia presentations, and as such does not possess the flawless acoustics of a concert hall. However, by the time Tobin has finished setting up the sound system, the most intimate sounds of an actor's voice and breathing can be projected to the audience without any separation between the acoustic and amplified voice. For this production, there are five speakers hanging from the ceiling, and four on the floor in front of the stage. Tobin works with another technician to first angle the speakers to cover all the seats in the house—a finicky and tedious task. The uneven contours of the room alternately reflect and diffuse the sound, depending on where one sits in the audience, causing hot spots and dead spots. Checking the angles involves slowly creeping up and down each row, hunched over to the same height as a seated person's head, while the same song plays over and over again though the sound system. Speakers are minutely angled, adjusted, and readjusted. Once Tobin and her assistant are satisfied with speaker placement, we convene near the front row to calibrate the delays, beginning with the two middle speakers on the floor. An additional speaker is set on stage to emit a high frequency click track. First we just listen to the clicking speaker, concentrating on the attack of each click; then the two front speakers are faded in to the maximum possible volume until we are aware of a separation. Tobin methodically calls out each delay value in seconds, and we listen and hear the acoustic and amplified sounds draw closer together. By the end, the difference between an audible and an inaudible delay is a matter of milliseconds. Consensus with this group is astonishingly easy—we all hear it the moment the speaker synchronizes with the acoustic sound. We move further back in the seating, and the same procedure follows for the suspended speakers.

Tobin first adapted this method of imperceptible vocal amplification to more intimate venues under the direction of Denis Marleau of Théâtre UBU, in 1997, for a production entitled *Les Trois derniers jours de Fernando Pessoa.* Tobin also notes that this was the first time that she was really asked to do sound design as opposed to sound production. "My challenge was to create an audio space where the acoustic voice of the actor and the amplified voice of the playback would both seem to be in the same space—as if they were talking to each other in a realistic manner. There was a clear function that the sound should achieve, specified by the director. Usually in a stage production, if there is voice amplification, the idea is just to make the actor's voice louder, and there is no specific role for the sound." Thus Tobin's job was to craft the mediated voices of the characters through amplification techniques and speaker choice. Only a single physical actor was on stage, and he played all the characters in the piece, video images of the other characters projected onto his face as he played each of them. For the recorded voices to seem as real as the actor's voice, the live actor was also amplified by a small invisible microphone and played back through a speaker with the right tonal quality, thereby allowing him to share the same acoustic space as the recorded voices. Through Tobin's design, the live quality of theatre encounters the intimacy of cinema, as the actor can whisper or make small expressive sounds instead of using the exaggerated effects of stage projection; thus her techniques transform the methods of both actor and director and enable poetic, abstract, and minimalist theatre experiments.

Les Aveugles

Denis Marleau's staged video-art installation *Les Aveugles, fantasmagorie technologique* (2002), is an adaptation of Maurice Maeterlinck's static drama from 1890.The staging is extremely minimalist, consisting of a dark room containing twelve masks on which are projected the faces of two actors, each playing six characters. Each projected character also has his or her own speaker. The premise is simple: twelve blind people go out with a guide for a walk in the forest; at a certain point, the guide announces that he will leave for a moment, but in fact dies suddenly and silently among them. The play takes place with the blind characters stranded in the forest awaiting their guide's return, with the projected actors made truly blind to the audience by being physically absent. The aural aspects of the piece are central to the success of the production—from the amplification of the actors' recorded voices through natural-sounding speakers, to the soundscape of the forest.

Maeterlinck's text describes the sounds the blind hear—breathing, wind, oceans, birds, leaves, steps on leaves, and the sound of stars—and Tobin wanted to integrate these sounds without relying simply on foley effects. After listening intently to recordings of oceans, winds, leaves, etc., Tobin noticed that all these sounds met in the very high and very low registers. "I realized that all the sounds Maeterlinck wanted included in his play could somehow come from a single instrument. All these sounds are quite similar at the extremes of the human audio spectrum." She began by emphasizing each sound's texture in its extremely low or extremely high frequencies. For instance, the sound of waves against a gravelly beach becomes a fragile rustle when the high frequencies are foregrounded, or can sound like the land itself breathing when mostly lower frequencies are heard. The final soundscape conjures an abstract yet recognizable environment, as ghostlike and subtly evocative as the actors' faces suspended against black, drawing the audience into the dark wood that can only be apprehended by listening.

Concerto grosso pour corps et surface métallique

Nancy Tobin has worked with choreographer Danièle Desnoyers and her company Carré des Lombes through a series of productions, each one an exploration of the body as sound subject and as object moving through a sonorous environment. *Concerto grosso pour corps et surface métallique* (1999) featured six dancers moving, predictably, on a metal floor. Some dancers wear tap shoes—not for a tippy-tapping percussive effect but for scraping the metal surface like skates applied to ice. The ice rink metaphor continues with fluorescent lighting overhead and a rack of battered eighteen-inch hockey-arena loudspeakers. Two dancers have wired into the bottom of their tap shoes small microphones, whose signal Tobin transforms in the latter part of the piece by considerably lowering the pitch, broadcasting the altered sound through subwoofers stationed at the edges of the metal floor. Additionally, when a dancer with miked shoes comes into proximity with the speakers, a controlled feedback rumble arises, creating deep eddies of bass harmonics offset by the earlier harsh scour of metal shoes on the metal surface. Only some of the dancers wear tap shoes, and only two at a time are amplified, rendering different members of the company audible while others become mute, and in some cases are characterized by their choreography as deaf. These elements in turn are heard in relation to recordings of piano music by Morton Feldman and Alfred Schnittke, which are sometimes played through the tinny rink loudspeakers rather than the PA.

The overall effect is one of intense contrasts: Desnoyers has set the organic body in motion between these cold unforgiving elements of metal and fluorescent lighting, which Tobin supports with sounding tools for the dancers that create a sonic landscape, alternately murky and dark or sharp and thin. The piano score played through the rink loudspeakers takes on a nostalgic, distant tone, due to the compression of the sound and emphasis on high frequencies, evoking the feeling of a song half-remembered from a dark dream of a family skating outing.

Bataille

Desnoyers and Tobin continue a study in contrasts in Desnoyers' *Bataille* (2002), which also shares similar staging elements with *Concerto grosso*—the cold fluorescent lighting and the white square floor functioning more as a plane of inquiry than as a stage. For this production the dancers do not themselves create sound, but there are two dialogic sound sources: Violinist Malcolm Goldstein's live improvisations as he moves around the perimeter of the stage, and electroacoustic pieces by Tobin, created from baroque recordings on vinyl. Desnoyers arrived at Tobin's house with a bag of baroque records one day and asked Nancy to DJ at a rehearsal with these recordings with "the basic aim [being] for it to become something else." After listening to the records and trying some mixes at home, Tobin preferred to keep working at home, as she felt "quite negative" about the material and the possibility of transforming the baroque music into something else through turntablism: "I would pick any album from the pile and try mixing it to the record already playing. This method was very haphazard." She recorded those mixes to DAT, and began experimenting with the raw material on the computer, which began to yield interesting results. Her compositional method was "inspired by the microsound musical genre; every small crackle or noise that revealed the vinyl format was taken as an opportunity to create a rhythm or a melody. Small vocal excerpts were integrated in an attempt to emphasize the emotional quality already present in the baroque style."

The results are sometimes crackling loops and undertones of dub, layered with haunting choral samples, sometimes lurching and looping rhythms of records winding up and down—arpeggiated horn solos engaging with full orchestral samples, and ending with a tiny spectral echo like a transistor radio playing in the apartment next door. The emotions reflected from the baroque pieces into Tobin's compositions are grand—voices swell in requiem, a single horn renders a noble but melancholy tribute—yet the crackles and the pitch-shift of a record suddenly slowing remind us that this is all artifice. Tobin's processing of the vinyl reflects Desnoyers' process for the choreography: "[Desnoyers] explained to me that her piece, *Bataille*, is not really about a battle, as in a fight, but more about oppositions being confronted.... What is left? What is created?" Two very different worlds collide in this composition by Tobin, the sound creating a counterpoint between the ornate grandeur of baroque music, and the "aesthetics of failure" inherent in glitch and microsound genres that enhance the smallest sounds and create rhythms from tiny fragments.

Though Tobin learned her DJ skills not with any intention of playing live, but to improve her sense of beat, DJ techniques in this case helped her shape the raw material into something she could work with. "From that experience," Tobin notes, "I realized that you can compose an emotional musical piece without knowing the traditional musical language of chords and melodies. I never read music. I speak in tone, I speak in hertz, I speak in noise I don't speak in notes. But somehow the result is the same. It's just a different path to go toward it." Considering that Tobin came to sound through cut-up tape and mixing experiments on campus and community radio, it is no surprise that her entry into musical composition evolved from the role of technician.

Desnoyers' initial goal with Bataille had been to create a piece with the sensibility of a museum installation, and that formal aesthetic led Tobin to an interesting aural augmentation: six piezo speakers were placed in a row along the back of the performance area. "The frequency range of the piezo speaker is very high and the result is a very thin piercing sound. Sometimes the soundscapes would be amplified by these special-effects speakers, as well as by the main sound system, as if suddenly another instrument was playing the same parts but in a much higher range." Tobin often employs specialized speakers for their diverse tonal qualities, much like minimal dub producers enhancing high or low frequencies: "I consider the loudspeaker as my instrument. I play and interpret sounds through it, as a musician plays an instrument."

Playing the same track through different kinds of speakers greatly affects not only the equalization of the piece but the texture of the sound as well. Tobin often augments the main PA with other speakers to exaggerate high or low frequencies, thus enhancing or quickly shifting the intensity of the soundscape at a critical moment in a choreography. Choosing specific speakers has also led Tobin to experiments with controlled feedback, as with Concerto grosso. *Duo pour corps et instruments* (2003), Tobin's most recent collaboration with Desnoyers, is a further exploration of controlled feedback, this time placing speakers prominently onstage and teaching the dancers to improvise with sound creation.

Duo pour corps et instruments

Inspired by Patti Smith, Desnoyers wanted to work with rock music for *Duo pour corps et instruments*, particularly sampling and building soundscapes from guitar solos. Tobin employed some of the same techniques of sampling and mixing from vinyl as she used for *Bataille* to create raw, loud, highly charged pieces out of fragments of guitar-god onanism. The dancers, three women, all dress in late '70s, early '80s high heels and black and taupe dresses, their movements enacting a kind of desperate distracted beauty, suggesting an era both decadent and hollow. The piece, however, centres around units of one dancer and two speakers (the body and instruments of the title—because the speaker truly is Tobin's instrument). Each dancer works with a guitar amplifier (commonly used by bands in the '70s and '80s as a personal stage monitor) and a small wearable speaker that functions as a high impedance microphone. Depending on where the dancers position their small speaker-mike in relation to the guitar amp, varying tones of feedback result, and in some instances, two dancers form another kind of duo when creating feedback tones at the same time. Thanks to an octave pedal and other effects pedals rigged up between speaker-mike and guitar amp, the sound is piercing but syrupy, sometimes a morse code of dashes when just at the edge of effect. The dancers learned the sensitivity, range, and tonal quality of the equipment in rehearsal, and developed a vocabulary of movements with which they improvise to make sound for the performances. Meanwhile, the speakers themselves are far from static: the dancers sit like nervous party girls on their guitar amps, fall off them, haul them across the stage and back again, unplug and replug them. "The guitar amp," says Tobin, "was integrated in our sound system as part of the set, but also as a way to give to the audience another aural perspective that is more direct, as opposed to the main sound system, which is more surround." In this way, the three amps do not merely amplify, but take on a role parallel to the three women; though they are controlled by the dancers, the amps move, they sound, and they have distinctive voices. There is a compelling subtext at work in the tension between dancer and speakers: proximity creates sound and can be very beautiful, but bringing the wearable speaker microphone and the amp too close together results in shrieks of angry feedback. Playing the speaker is an exercise in managing intimacy.

Collaboration

Tobin emphasizes the importance of becoming involved in a production early in the creative process, establishing communication with the director or choreographer, allowing time for development, experimentation, and for coming up with new methods—"kind of like inventing a tradition… I don't work alone, trying to invent a precise and developed idea and then delivering it, saying 'Here is the finished product.'" For *Bataille*, it was a "teeny" loop that led to a whole structure of loops. Desnoyers would ask for fifteen minutes of one loop, and then work on it with the dancers. "Somehow the root of the work was the same for me and for her," says Tobin.

Work in a theatre is undoubtedly teamwork, an aspect of her profession that Tobin relishes. "I like it when you create work that becomes something outside of you, that exists without you, something that has nothing to do with you anymore, but that you're part of, that you've helped to happen." Tobin also stresses that it is important to relinquish proprietary feelings when working collaboratively: "You have to be sort of free, you have to be generous, but not like you're giving something of yourself, it's just this thing that exists, that happened to occur in an afternoon in front of the computer." Tobin considers herself lucky never to have had to produce theatre clichés, like creating a storm, or cuing a train whistle while the curtain drops. "Somehow I've always been in contact with people that wanted more."

Prendre sa place

One of my aims in interviewing Nancy Tobin was to determine what she had experienced in her field with regard to gender. When I asked her about gender distribution and her experience as a woman in her field, she confidently asserted that she has not experienced gender discrimination while working within the Montreal experimental theatre and dance scene. And during her technical training at UQAM, while she may have been among a minority of women, she "certainly didn't feel like I was invaded or was invading an environment." She did add, however, that if she were to move into bigger mainstream productions, she would need to expend some energy maintaining the level of respect that she currently enjoys. When observing Broadway and the East End, Tobin found the situation very unbalanced in terms of gender, and bigger productions also have intensive organizational hierarchies that often reflect mainstream social stereotypes—for instance, the captain-like sound engineer at the mixing console is most often male. Tobin comments that if she were to move to bigger productions, she would need to elbow her way in.

On the other hand, there are so few people employed to do experimental sound design for theatre that gender is not an issue for Tobin in her professional life at the moment. She notes that there are only three or four people in Montreal who work in this way, and two of them are women. "It's as if I'm setting a standard," she says; and so this new tradition includes women from the beginning. For Tobin, the more immediate challenge is for sound designers as a body to garner respect in theatre and dance. Though lighting design is receiving more recognition, the sound designer is still brought in last for most productions, and is allotted the smallest budget, the least amount of time to work, and the lowest fees. Tobin and her peers are developing new ways of working and new expectations of a theatre experience, but are also showing the way for future sound designers in terms of fees and work conditions. Importantly, Tobin is also learning to value her own work as being professional. For instance, she demands to be billed on the show poster and in the press when significant original creative and technical work is done.

In a Simple, Slow Way

Meanwhile, I am starting to believe that Nancy Tobin needs a break at her own RestArea for a while. She works at a relentless pace, going from production to production, causing me to wonder what energy she has left for her solo artistic practice. She describes each production as its own all-consuming world, dictated by deadlines—"so you have to find solutions, the ones you think are most authentic, and you have to find them fast." The time pressure is not always a problem, however. *Duo pour corps et instruments* and *Les Aveugles* were both developed during residencies at the Musée des Arts Contemporain in Montreal. "Working at the MAC is always a great situation," notes Tobin. "I think in any creative project the most important thing is to have as much time as possible in the actual context where the final result will occur."

Though Tobin could surf on her contacts and technical abilities for years, she would like to set aside time to contemplate and to play solo: "I feel I have this vocabulary now in sound that I can make little planets or places to experiment on one sound idea." RestArea is a perfect example of such a place. It is a little pause created in response to an increasingly mediated world where, particularly on the World Wide Web, flashing text and images compete for our attention at high speed. RestArea unfolds slowly and simply, beginning with two small bars of blue and white moving across the screen, and eventually evolving into a more densely choreographed landscape of striped and coloured bars floating across a blue background. The viewer has not stepped off the so-called information superhighway, and is still staring at the computer screen, a screen also reminiscent of television and animated advertising hoardings. Yet there is no text, nothing to be bought or sold, and no story told. There is, rather, a moment unfolding, over five minutes, again and again, as long as our attention holds. We are made aware of our expectations and impatience with regard to media, and of ourselves staring at the screen, at the same time enjoying the minimalist sound and abstract shapes. We find ourselves caught in a little paradox—that the screen is providing a rest from the screen.

Tobin wants to highlight listening in a socially relevant context, unlike much new media work that she sees as superficially beautiful but often unemotional and empty. Her work with Desnoyers and Marleau has set a high standard of challenging audio that seems to lead naturally to her current aspirations. "What I really want to work on is something that's a merging of visual art, new media and theatre, in a simple, slow way: something relatively simple that really talks." Nancy Tobin's latest solo undertaking is aptly titled *Risk*, which features a rare instance in which she herself will be onstage at the Société des Arts Technologiques (SAT) in Montreal, manipulating sound through some of the feedback tools created for *Duo pour corps et instruments.*

Whether designing the overall sound environment or specific tools for sound play, Tobin's work brings listening to the forefront of experimental theatre and dance.

(2004)

Notes

[1] Quotations from Nancy Tobin are from an interview with the author, the date and place of which are not recoverable—ed.

Editorial Note

For a photo of *Concerto grosso pour corps et surface métallique*, see illustration 16 (70).

Collaboration and Confluence: A Multidisciplinary Approach to Environmental Scenography

by Jerrard Smith

February 14, 2005

The sun sets.... An audience is gathered near a canal; a barge carrying the sarcophagus of the dead Egyptian King and a chorus of priests and mourners slowly arrives, stops and disgorges the ceremonial funeral party. They form a solemn procession through the streets. The audience follows, beginning a journey in which they will participate in the birth of the sun god RA as he is transformed from the hawk-headed god of the daytime skies into the ram-headed manifestation who must endure the many perils of the underworld before being reborn as the sun the following morning. The audience must also endure a series of challenges in the form of preparation rites, culminating in the ceremony known in ancient Egypt as the opening of the eyes and mouth, whereby the dead King is brought back to life so that he may follow RA on his journey through the underworld. The spectators, now robed and hooded, are themselves transformed into initiate priests and priestesses who will follow the King and by morning all will be reborn as divine.

This nine-hour event of ritual, theatre, opera, dance and spectacle took place in the streets, parks, a church and a museum in Leiden in 1985 as part of the Holland Festival. *RA* is a work by Canadian composer R. Murray Schafer and is just one of the series of environmental music dramas he has devised and called the *Patria* cycle, for which I have been a designer of sets, masks and puppets since 1980.

My current interests in scenography grow out of my work with Schafer and in this paper I will examine a number of works created for presentation in unusual spaces, with an eye to seeing how the space itself brings a sense of theatricality to a work of theatre art. With particular reference to a current project, I will examine also the methods by which the research process might incorporate a number of students, volunteers, artists who by sharing in the exploration may help to realize a new work of theatre.

I will begin by describing a few more of the *Patria* works, as the venues and performances have varied wildly. My introduction to Schafer and the *Patria* cycle was *The Princess of the Stars*, the prologue to the *Patria* series. Here, the audience is led to the shore of a remote lake before dawn and as the day breaks, musicians and singers who have been stationed around the shore of the lake create a haunting soundscape as a story unfolds, told by costumed creatures in canoes on the water.

Patria 3, The Greatest Show requires a venue suitable for recreating a small fair or carnival such as might have been found in a previous and less technologically intensive era. In 1987 and 1988 the *Patria* team took over a park in a small city in Ontario and we created a fairground in which 120 performers presented a spectacle of wonder and confusion. On the surface, *The Greatest Show* seems like any small fair, but as the audience becomes more involved, they realize there are threads of themes running through the work. The Grand Finale collapses in chaos and the performers literally herd the spectators out to the streets in simulated panic as the fairground erupts in smoke and flame while a shadowy monster prowls through the ruins.

There are twelve parts to the *Patria* cycle of music dramas, and while they differ from one another in form, they are connected by common characters and common themes.

The chaos and disassembling of *The Greatest Show* are necessary parts of the cycle of death and rebirth and can be likened to the symbolic destruction of the elements in the alchemist's furnace in preparation for the marriage of the Sun and Moon and the eventual birth of the Divine Child. In fact, this is the theme and subject of the next work in the series, *Patria 4, The Alchemical Theatre of Hermes Trismegistos*, in which a chorus of alchemists orchestrates a transmutation of the elements and creates the gold of the alchemists' quest.

These works are difficult.

They are difficult to create and they are often difficult for the audience to experience, and intentionally so. Schafer wants his audiences to work, to get up in the middle of the night to travel to the shores of a remote lake or, as in the case of *Patria 10, The Spirit Garden*, to join a group of actors, dancers, musicians, singers and gardeners in a ritual in which an actual garden is planted and later harvested.

There is a work being prepared for presentation this August in a remote wilderness area of Northern Ontario where the audience will follow a group of children on a journey of a few kilometres through the forest at night, where strange characters will come out of the darkness to tell the story. The hardships endured are rewarded by a unique theatrical spectacle accompanied by beautiful music ringing across the water and through the woods.

Difficult enough for the audience, these works are also very difficult to create. We all know that presenting a work in a well-equipped theatre is at times difficult enough. Creating works in the wilderness adds a whole new set of challenges. First, our production team must establish an on-site infrastructure. This involves a shelter and workspace—usually for us a large tent. Tools and materials have to be brought to the site and electricity or generator hooked up. Communications must be established. Transportation around the site may require off road vehicles and paths must be established for the "backstage" crew. Our crew often camps on site for days or weeks at a time and so care and feeding becomes a production concern. Careful planning is essential as the nearest hardware store may be an hour or more away. Facilities for the performers including shelter and change areas must be set up. Then the audience must be accommodated. Signage, seating, first aid, toilets and transportation must all be considered. This kind of undertaking, much like film location work, obviously requires significant financial support.

Canada is not known as the best place in which to raise money for unusual projects. Sponsors are not exactly clamoring to put their money into work that will be presented in the most remote venue imaginable and whose limited audience might have to give up some creature comforts.

Patria has a fairly traditional administrative structure. We have a board of supportive people who gamely struggle to raise funds and promote our events. As is the case with anything that is worth doing, we all put in extra effort to realize a production beyond the immediate means available. Like many organizations, we often rely on the involvement of a number of volunteers—mainly interested amateurs who are attracted to the work out of interest or possibly through association with someone else involved.

A lot of what we are trying to do can be done and in fact is done by amateur and community theatre all over the world. There is virtue in the rough edges and honesty of many community productions. There can be a sense of charm and wonder in the simple theatrics and swirl of colour and movement in many of the pageants and festivals that use parks and fields and farms as their stage. I have participated in many such events and have come away from them enthused and enriched by the innovative solutions to the problems posed by the limitations of space, facilities and funds. Schafer's work, however, is sufficiently demanding, complex and intricate that we cannot rely on charm entirely. In the realization of the visuals the designers seek the same standards of excellence as is expected from the actors and musicians.

How can this kind of work be realized in a way that is rewarding artistically for those who will experience it and satisfying for all involved in its creation? The solution must go beyond simply raising enough money to hire the best craftspeople. I think the key lies in developing a community of committed people who have the talent and training along with that particular sensibility that attracts them to this kind of performance. It is not enough to have the skill; this kind of work demands people with the ability and willingness to apply that skill in difficult remote circumstances.

How can we attract these people? Certainly the unusual nature of the performances and the unique venues can capture the imagination. Once involved, most find the work to be exciting and interesting. It is certainly exciting to design and in spite of the difficulties, satisfying to realize. While not entirely unique, the work of R. Murray Schafer is often groundbreaking in many ways and must still be considered experimental (at least from where I sit: after 25 years we are not getting any closer to what would be considered mainstream).

We are firmly planted in the realm of research and development—fantasy division.

But given a climate where funding for the arts is on the decline, how can we continue to do this kind of work successfully?

Let me first outline some theories of Schafer's about the nature of theatre.

To begin with, Schafer is a harsh critic of the current state of the arts and the way civilization in general and commerce in particular have destroyed what is intrinsically valuable in art.

> This must be the first purpose of art. To effect a change in our existential condition. This is the first purpose. To change us. It is a noble aim, a divine aim. And it existed long before the stale word "art" was coined to describe the last tremor of transformative power accessible to civilized man. Once it was drumming, prolonged drumming until its beats fused into a spellbinding hysteria. Once it was dancing, eternal dancing, until the dancer's feet left the ground and danced in the sky. Once it was singing, singing the turnings of the melody until they became the trail of life, following it back open-mouthed and breathless until the spirit became as light as a swan's feather and ascended out of this world. Once it was looking, intense looking and neither to the right nor to the left but directly at spectacles in which beating hearts were plucked from victims, in which dead men were brought back to life, in which gods boxed with thunderbolts, or the dead sun was kindled to life again and restored to the sky, or ghostly spirits were released from their wanderings—a world of miracles—that is what we were made to see. (Schafer 83)

He decries the commodification of art whereby the centres of production send their product to the margins to displace that which is locally produced, that which is unique. His aim is to reinvent, to put art back to being a medium of wondrous transformation.

He would like to circumvent the hierarchy inherent in performance. Most forms of theatre place one discipline in the forefront, with others playing a supportive role. Opera puts the music forward, drama the text. Dance celebrates movement and so on. Design too takes centre stage in visual spectacles, parades and pageants. But like Wagner and others, Schafer envisions a form of performance where these disciplines flow together as more or less equal partners, each supporting the others in an attempt to bring each art to the highest possible level. He calls his theatre the Theatre of Confluence.

> Ideally what I want is a kind of theatre in which all the arts may meet, court and make love. Love implies a sharing of experience; it should never mean the negation of personalities. This is the first task: to fashion a theatre in which all the arts are fused together, but without negating the strong and healthy character of each. (Schafer 26)

Schafer feels we have lost much through the process of becoming civilized. We have for example lost the ability to celebrate the important events in our lives. Death and dying have been institutionalized. Love is measured by others' values that we cannot attain ourselves. Conversations are based on repeating phrases from popular media. We have no rituals.

In order to encourage the audiences to be receptive to an art that is not based on revisiting known or familiar territory, Schafer strives to find ways of presenting his work that are appropriate to the sense of ritual and of celebration with which they are suffused. To hear a song from across a lake at dawn will provide a richer experience than listening to the same work on CD.

As a composer, Schafer is especially particular about the music. The music is often difficult to perform and requires a particular musicianship to play it well and there is no question that we are striving for excellence in every aspect of the production. Musicians of this calibre are in demand and don't have to risk precious instruments and vocal chords by traipsing out into the forest to pursue their art. There are, however, many excellent players and singers who are attracted to the experience that Schafer's work presents to them, and we try to work with these people again and again when possible. In fact participating in Schafer's works has created a kind of community of players who might be considered specialists in the field of bringing wonderful talent to unusual situations. So the community that I referred to earlier does in fact exist, and it includes actors, singers, dancers, puppeteers and the theatre craftspeople required to realize these unique events of a Theatre of Confluence.

The Auxiliary

In addition to the highly skilled and trained professionals who make up the team of people working on *Patria* events, there are a number of ancillary workers whose contributions are essential to the success of the work. At times, there has been frustration in situations where we have been obliged to rely too much on unskilled help to realize our dreams. I have often complained that I could have realized a task in half the time it took the helpers, done a better job and I wouldn't have had to stay late and wash all the brushes they left behind. But rather than deny their support, they must be encouraged because there is always something of value brought to a process by people who are there because they are genuinely interested.

Over the years, the involvement in our projects of volunteers or people who have not been trained in theatre arts has had some surprising results. A case in point is the experience we had in Holland mounting the production of *RA*. Part of the team that was found for us by the local production manager was a group of students from a museum and display program. They were enthusiastic and intrigued and excited by the unusual nature of this production and I encouraged them to bring the expertise they were developing in their field to the project. They turned out to be very resourceful in bridging the gap between their world and ours and their contribution to the production was a factor in its success.

Let me go back to another unusual theatre situation that had positive effects from the involvement of a group of non-theatre people. *Patria 10, The Spirit Garden* celebrates the cycle of planting and harvesting—birth, maturation, death and rebirth. The work consists of two parts, Spring and Harvest. Spring takes the form of the ritual planting of a real garden with the help of the audience and is a daytime celebration with orchestra, choirs, actors and dancers and takes place in late May. Throughout the summer the Gardeners tend the garden and harvest it in the fall. The Harvest section of *The Spirit Garden* takes place on or near Hallowe'en and consists of a ritual burning of the remains of the garden before passing it over to Winter, who arrives with his Four Winds to take possession until next spring. The audience then proceeds indoors and the Spirit Garden closes with a ritual banquet at which the produce of the garden is consumed.

The Spirit Garden is probably the *Patria* work that most closely resembles community theatre. Gardeners are recruited from the local community and it is this team of perhaps 24 or 32 people who actively prepare the garden for the event. But they are also the interface between audience and cast. When the audience members arrive for the performance, they are met by the gardeners who try to convince each of them to join one of the eight "vegetable clans." Once sorted into cabbages or tomatoes, they are told stories, given tokens, learn songs or chants and are quickly initiated into the group. It is the enthusiasm of the gardeners that brings the audience into the spirit of the event, allowing the barrier between audience and performer to be lowered.

Theatre should be a transformative experience for the audience and the performer.

In the case of *The Spirit Garden*, the gardeners begin their involvement by signing on to do what they like to do… tend a garden. But before long, as the realization that they are to be "performers" as well starts to set in, they realize that this ride is much more than they bargained for. But with guidance from Schafer, the *Patria* team and the professional actors, they are gently encouraged and helped to take on their roles of guides and mentors for the audience. By the time the show is on, they have become "actor-gardeners" but still amateurs, which allows them to successfully bring the audience into the work by being on their level. They talk to the audience as equals and provide a context for the activities. It proves to be a comfortable level of involvement for most audience members. They feel a part of the performance, yet are still able to maintain the appropriate distancing from the singers, actors, instrumentalists and dancers who exist on another plane, representing archetypes (the King, the Sun, the Mistress of the Planting, the Corn Mothers). Thus the spectators are at the same time integrated as active participants in the theatrical ritual and still audience for a spectacle that (seemingly) would be played out whether they were present or not.

The natural outcome of working with Schafer and of engagement in work of this nature is thinking about new paradigms. His work has redefined many of the relationships between performer and audience, and use of space. It allows us to question the nature of theatrical experience within a broad set of parameters. So... what if we eliminate the audience?

...and Wolf Shall Inherit the Moon.

Every August for the past twelve years, approximately 60 people gather their tents, sleeping bags and other camping equipment. They pack the food and clothing, tarps, canoes and other gear needed to camp for a week. They also include costumes, masks and musical instruments. They then drive to a remote private forest in North Central Ontario and take a logging road to its end. There they load the canoes with their supplies and canoe for 45 minutes through a spectacular landscape to four different sites where they set up camp and embark on a week of ritual theatre and music, culminating in a day-long performance of a scripted and scored work performed for its own sake and not for an outside audience. The same work is done every year and mainly the same people return to participate. It is not funded beyond the extremely nominal fees the participants contribute to cover the costs. It has been self-sufficient to the point where surplus funds have been used to subsidize travel for participants from Europe, Brazil and Western Canada.

The week-long event, which is the epilogue to the *Patria* cycle, is titled, "*...and Wolf Shall Inherit the Moon*," although the participants simply refer to it as "The Wolf Project." It is an attempt to reaffirm our need for ritual and is a celebration and reaffirmation of our relationship with nature. Every year the people involved come away refreshed and energized by the experience, and looking forward to the next year. As many as are able meet two or three times throughout the year to discuss the logistics and other practicalities, to refresh the themes and share good food. There is in fact a community of people which has developed out of their involvement with this project and whose talents and energies are sometimes called on when we are preparing other *Patria* works. Group members often get together for presentations of their own.

Although there are many very talented singers, instrumentalists, actors—artists of all kinds, the Wolf community also includes many people who simply enjoy wilderness camping and who contribute to the overall theatrical presentation in other ways.

Having eliminated the audience, let us also, at least temporarily, eliminate most of the performers.

Theatrical space

We are left with only the space and the questions of the innate theatricality of the space. Putting aside for the moment those defining elements of theatre: the performer, the audience and in many cases the text, I wish to look at just the space, to try to determine what it is that makes it theatrical, that makes it a "seeing place."

I think it is safe to assert that some physical spaces are more innately theatrical than others. It might be the quality of the light, the balance of architectural elements, or a particular aspect of the natural environment that speaks to us in a way that implies a story, because I think that the notion of storytelling is an essential element in the transformative experience that is theatre. I do not mean the particular text or story but rather the idea of storytelling or perhaps simply the possibility that a story is attached to a place.

This search for theatricality of space takes the researcher into the realms inhabited by installation artists, museum display designers, sculptors, architects, landscape architects and others.

When I enter a space, I am sometimes aware that someone has made an effort to influence the direction of my gaze or to elicit an emotional response. If I feel the tendency to look up in a place of worship, I know that the intent of the architect is to change my sense of awareness, to cause me to look away from the realm of the mundane and up to the realm of the divine. A carefully contrived interior setting can evoke appropriate responses or establish a mood. But it must be carefully contrived to be effective. In fact the most effective design is often the one that seems spontaneous and uncontrived. In these examples, I am responding to an attempt at theatricality. I am even more impressed if the theatricality has been achieved without my being aware of the hand of the designer.

But even without that conscious effort on the part of a designer, there is something about space that can be evocative and make the visitor want to start filling in the details of the story. A space, much like a smell, can call up associative responses and memories. This is certainly the case if you have ever entered someone's private space without his or her knowledge. There is theatricality in the way someone may arrange a room for visitors but there is also theatricality in the randomness of a room that simply reflects the way in which it has been inhabited. Our natural curiosity starts to fill in the blanks, to look for a story, to create theatre. This is particularly true of old spaces—spaces that have survived from a previous time. The very nature of antiquity implies that the interactions of the space and those who have come in contact with it over time have somehow clung to the walls and can perhaps even be read by a discerning eye. This is particularly true with spaces that have been abandoned.

There are spaces that are designed for ritual activities such as churches, banks and schools, which can by the nature or simply the fact of that activity, have theatricality. The way a space can reflect a sense of power relationships is an intentional theatricalization of the space. A space can be theatrical if there is a known history; if there is evidence of conflict, if there is choice… or if there is ambiguity (our first impulse upon entering an unknown space is to try to satisfy ourselves that we have a rationale for everything we see, as unanswered questions set up a tension within a space). We are encouraged to be engaged. We can't be passive when we come to a fork in the road. We must think when we encounter a broken window or door. A maze presents us with twists and turns, choices and tension and may be the most theatrical of spaces.

But it is not just buildings and rooms that I wish to examine. Landscape too can evoke emotional responses, whether a grand vista or a dark region that may beckon and repel at the same time. Harmony of forms, lines, colours, textures arouses in us a response that we can't necessarily define but has the potential of setting us up to be transformed.

I'm not ready to bring in performers yet. In describing spaces with theatrical potential I do not mean that I am thinking about an appropriate place to bring in actors and audience and put on a show. I am still trying to think of the space as the theatricality, not simply a venue for a theatrical event. This is not such a stretch; most of us are so used to being in some proximity to other people most of the time that an empty space can easily be populated by our imaginations and I think it is that tendency that helps to make an empty space potentially theatrical.

The search for a suitable framework for this examination of space for its theatrical potential leads me again to R. Murray Schafer and an outline of a work based on the myths of ancient Crete.

Asterion—A journey through the Labyrinth

In *Asterion*, Schafer has created the blueprints for a particularly unusual and challenging work. Part of the *Patria* cycle, *Patria 7, Asterion* fits with *RA* and *The Enchanted Forest* as works that embody a journey of self-discovery. Based on the Cretan myth of Theseus, Ariadne and the Minotaur (a myth which resonates through all of the *Patria* works) the text of *Asterion* outlines a series of approximately fifty events each with its own unique environment. Both the form and content are that of the labyrinth and the work is intended as a transformative journey through a series of intertwining passages and rooms to be experienced by one person at a time. In the *Patria* cycle, the labyrinth stands as a metaphor for the search for personal and cultural identity and *Asterion* is intended to make that search manifest. As I begin to explore the possibilities inherent in the work, I realize that the project lies at the intersection of a diversity of artistic disciplines including theatre, architecture, music, and installation art.

This diversity appeals to me very much and I am using the multidisciplinary potential of *Asterion* to inform the methodology of my research.

I have outlined a number of questions to use as guidelines for the exploration, all based on the primary question: "What is it about a given space that is innately theatrical?"

Environment

What elements or aspects of a geography inform the decisions for placement of events? What parts of the environment draw my attention and why? What can I use the way it is, and what would I reconfigure? With a variety of terrains, which are most appropriate for a given section described in the text of *Asterion*?

Structure

How can the shape of the 3-dimensional space help to tell the story? What surfaces and textures are most evocative and appropriate? What is the appropriate form for each of the spaces described? When a structure is built, the form can be more or less apparent. When the underlying structure is apparent—as a tent or a glass wall, or if there is either obvious mass or fragility, how do these affect the response of the person passing through? The nature of the transitions from one space to the next is extremely important to the impact of the spaces on the observer and will be a significant factor in the design of the labyrinth. Each corner that is turned has the potential of enhancing the experience. Each door becomes an important event (consider the difference between opening a door and walking through a curtain). What might be the reaction if the entrance door locks behind you and there is no perceivable exit? Perhaps some task must be performed in order to escape.

Space and time

I think the perceptions of time in the labyrinth will be interesting to observe. For example, imagine two identical spaces. One is filled with a wide range of objects—lots of information and clutter, like a second-hand store or a storage attic. The other has two objects, simply placed. The same amount of time in each space would be perceived very differently and the state of the person experiencing the spaces will vary accordingly.

There are forty-nine events described in the text. They are grouped in descending order. The participant first faces 9 encounters, then 8 trials, followed by 7 experiences, 6 perceptions, 5 contemplations, 4 arcana, 3 deceptions, a duet of divinities and a finale.

This structure will also disrupt the perception of time as a constant. There will be some events where it is desirable to proceed quickly. At other times in the journey, the participant may remain in an area that encourages contemplation.

Some events imply an interior setting while others could very well be placed outdoors. Some are dark, some light. Some are frightening; some are peaceful and beautiful. In order for the spaces to be theatrical, there must be tension or at least a sense of expectation. This tension may come from the anticipation of surprise (Will something move? What is around that corner?) or simply be evident in the balance (or imbalance) of a particular space.

Exposition

When it is not enough for the space alone to tell the story, how do I incorporate text, images, and symbols? Parts of *Asterion* will probably be somewhat like a museum. Some will require installations, which allows for the involvement of sculptors, painters, designers, craftspeople... each with the possibility of taking on the task of embellishing one of the described spaces within the labyrinth. Some are described in detail while others leave more room for interpretation.

A few of the spaces require the presence of one or more live performers.

The actors

We had to bring the performer back sooner or later. But only one or two performers will be encountered at a time and those events are not numerous. The performer usually engages directly with the person undertaking the journey. This also suggests interesting possibilities. In a given space, how does the location of the single performer affect the experience? The audience-performer proxemics will vary depending on the size and shape of the space, what the spectator has experienced, and finally the actions or words of the actor. What about a recorded voice?

Installations

Combining architecture, sculpture, simple mechanics, effective lighting—all will contribute to the creation of a scene. For example, creating a space where a creature has been, and may return, might be enough to represent the creature. Each description suggests a range of interpretations and is the raw material for much exploration and experimentation. The use of sound will certainly help transform the space to fit the experience. What would be the difference between a sound such as Aeolian harp (that requires no performer) and a flute or drum in defining the theatricality of a space?

Interactivity, whether electronic or mechanical, will be interesting in terms of the way the participant interacts with the space although I feel that the less obtrusive or contrived the better. I also think it best to keep it low-tech wherever possible. Perhaps the physical act of opening a door or turnstile might trigger an animation. This suggests the possibility of incorporating puppets. The use of moving figures or events will be an inevitable part of the design discussions.

All these questions and possibilities provide a framework for the development of *Asterion* and hopefully will be of interest to people who might want to participate with me in the exploration. The question of what? must then be followed by the question of how?

Developing a community

Encouraged by the success of the community that has developed around the Wolf Project, I can see that as a model for realizing *Asterion.* Let me explain how the *Asterion* team began and how I hope it will develop. Having agreed to pursue *Asterion,* Schafer and I met to look at the resources we had with the aim of putting together a team to at least talk about possibilities. Between us, we knew of a few interested people. These included a structural engineer, an architect, my partner Diana Smith (who is the costume designer for the *Patria* works), an installation artist who works in willow and other natural materials, a fine arts student and three graduate students in architecture, landscape architecture and drama. Starting with this core group, we had a series of informal meetings to generate some ideas of the direction and shape that the project (if not the ultimate structure) might take. The objective is to create a community of participants to develop the physical structure and to refine the dramatic component through a series of workshops. We have agreed on a number of basic elements:

- there are advantages to be gained by creating a full size model of some of the areas that are described in the text and to try the texts with an actor and a participant within those spaces.
- the particular attributes of any given section of the terrain will be allowed to influence the design decisions.
- the work will be allowed to grow as an organic process without imposing restrictions until a certain level of complexity has developed. That level will be defined as part of the process.

Schafer lives on a farm property east of Peterborough, Ontario and it is there that we plan to build the labyrinth. He arranged with the local municipality for necessary permits and permissions, and with a small grant from my University, I was able to plan a short on-site exploration. Three of the students, Diana, Murray and I and a friend who agreed to come and help made up the group of people who camped on-site for a week. Our plan was to explore the possibilities of the location and then have a public weekend workshop in which visitors would be introduced to the project, work with us and provide some feedback. We were fortunate in gaining the use of a large water truck, and a 4-wheel drive vehicle with a trailer. We had a large tent, which we set up as tools and materials storage as well as a kitchen. I was able to obtain a donated front-end loader and a supply of sand and gravel.

Our week was a great success. We explored the proposed site and created a series of paths and trails through various parts of the property. We allowed the varied terrain to inform the geometry of our labyrinth to a large extent. For example, we cut passages through a dense cedar forest partly by allowing the trees and spaces to suggest the route and partly following the design of a traditional labyrinth. We wove our paths in and out of the forest, looking for a balance between dark and light. We also levelled an area and started a simple straw bale construction, this time following a more formal design. In a short time we had developed over a kilometre of pathways.

Some were directly related to the text, others were simply interesting and I think both approaches are valid and in fact necessary. Schafer is willing to modify his text as our explorations open up new possibilities.

After our week of survey and experiment, we held our weekend workshop. Advertised through word of mouth and the *Patria* web site, the workshop attracted seven people, some of whom we knew (two were members of the Wolf Project), and some newcomers. They agreed to come and camp for the weekend, paying a nominal fee to help defray costs. We spent one day as the facilitators of the labyrinth experience by providing an introduction and tour, then taking on roles as described in the text and reading some of the lines. We also swam and prepared a great feast and talked about the experience. The second day, the new "initiates" took on the roles and we were the participants. Both experiences gave the team insight and fresh ideas.

I am now prepared for the second session to be held in early July, 2005. I anticipate that most of the same people will return, and I know there are a number of people who will be joining us for the first time and I invite you to be among them.

Information about the *Patria* cycle of music/theatre works and *Asterion—The Labyrinth Project* may be found on line at www.patria.org.

(2005)

Work Cited

Schafer, R. Murray. *Patria: The Complete Cycle.* Toronto: Coach House, 2002.

Editorial Note

For photos of *Ra* (Leiden) and *The Palace of the Cinnabar Pheonix*, and a drawing of the *Asterion* project, see illustrations 17–19 (71–72).

Keileidography: The Symphonic Theatre of Jillian Keiley

by Michael Devine

I first encountered the name of Jillian Keiley in 1997, when the general manager of Theatre Newfoundland Labrador, where I was artistic director, returned from a PACT meeting singing the praises of a talented young artist from St. John's. As no one ever says "No" to Gaylene Buckle for long I soon agreed to give Jillan her first opportunity to direct on Newfoundland's west coast. My friend John Mighton had written a challenging play called *Possible Worlds*, which I'd wanted to direct for years. Hearing of the intelligence and verve of this young, home-grown director, however, changed my plans, and I assigned her the project. Soon after, I saw her production of *UnderWraps* in St. John's, a production so mesmerizing that it remains, with Robert Lepage's *Polygraphe* and Carbone 14's *Le Dortoir*, on my list of the most significant Canadian theatre productions of the past fifteen years.

The significance of Keiley's work, which has developed since *UnderWraps* as a staging process called kaleidography, doesn't lie simply in her willingness to depart from the conventional forms of Canadian production. It has also to do with the positioning of the work and of the artist herself. For, although she now tours her work throughout the country, and opportunities for international work have come her way, Jillian Keiley is a Newfoundlander who has chosen to live and work in Newfoundland, to buck the "goin' on down the road" trend of out-migration. As it does for Andy Jones, who also chooses to make his home in his native city, St. John's provides Keiley with a creative context, a place where artists such as herself and Jones fit.

In one sense, coming home was the easy part. For when Keiley returned from Toronto in 1995, apart from the Resource Centre for the Arts Theatre Company (RCA), where Keiley worked as an associate artist from 1994–99, which produces a truncated season, there were no full-time theatrical employers in the city. She was forced, like the members of CodCo before her, to create her own opportunities, which she did by establishing Artistic Fraud of Newfoundland with collaborator Robert Chafe, now in its twelfth year.

Since then, Keiley's success has accelerated. She has received national honours such as the Canada Council John Hirsch Prize in 1998 and the Elinore & Lou Simonovitch Prize in Theatre in 2004. The increasingly national profile of Artistic Fraud, viewed by many as the most exciting and fertile theatre enterprise to come out of the Atlantic region in a generation, is due to a resurgence of theatrical activity in Newfoundland. The establishment of a professional theatre training program at [Sir

Wilfred] Grenfell College—and the employment offered to local actors by the string of summer theatres led by the Summer in the Bight and Gros Morne Theatre Festivals—has created a creative pool of artists from which Keiley can draw.

But the development of a truly independent world-theatre approach in the roiling waters of the St. John's theatre scene has not been without risk. Tightly knit, marked by generational divisions with respect to training and theatrical structure and forever brimming with passionate debate and colourful invective, the St. John's theatre community teems with talent and yet demonstrates a manifest insecurity. Keiley directs differently than any Newfoundlander has ever directed before, and the path to acceptance of her style has not always been smooth. In the following excerpt from a chat that I had with Keiley in December of 2005, she talks about how her work was received after she returned to St. John's:

Michael Devine: How do you feel your work fits into Newfoundland theatre… the culture as a whole?

Jillian Keiley: I think it's one of those anomalies that grew out of the fact that it was not allowed… in fact, it was the opposite to what was happening here when I came back [in 1995]. It grew out of… when I first came back to work here they didn't have stage managers… they had directors who were not directors…. It was a very strange time and there was a high degree of paranoia. There was a lot of infighting. The money was pretty scarce.

MD: This is when you were working as artistic associate at RCA.

JK: And even before that. I learned later… because I was tied up with Gordon Jones [at Memorial University's Drama program]…. There was a big divide between the university and the downtown… the [LSPU (Longshoremen's Protective Union)] Hall… a tremendous divide between the two. The university disregarded us and the people in the downtown thought the university was stifling or killing [independent work] and creating expectations of mainland or British or American art to be forced into Newfoundland.

MD: They were setting up that kind of expectation that the Arts and Culture Centre had become known for in the 1960s?

JK: Right… with John Perlin… who would bring in—like wouldn't ever allow a Newfoundland play—but would bring in a forty-person production because that was what theatre was…. Our artists downtown rejected that model and were doing collectives.

MD: But the era of the collectives had largely finished by the time you were starting to train. So what did you feel was the environment that you came back to?

JK: Well that was the tumultuous time… a very tumultuous time. There hadn't been an audition at the RCA [Resource Centre for the Arts] for seven years.

MD: An audition?

JK: And so I held auditions. I was crucified for doing so. Crucified. How dare I come in there and… when I first showed up I was pretty innocent. I didn't realize; I didn't know the history and I didn't realize… I know I had sympathy for both sides but I was so raised by both sides… and so pulled apart by both sides.

MD: It was really a very difficult time. But… they'd done so much work on their own, without help from the university, without support from the government… I was telling Ann (Brophy, general manager of Artistic Fraud) the other day that I remember sitting in the Duke with you, listening to Rick Boland rag on you for the better part of an hour… mostly about the fact that you had gone away to train at York University.

JK: I was given a lot of grief about that. People have come round… it just doesn't happen anymore (grumbling from Ann Brophy); that's been dying out. I don't see it happening with the new generation.

At York University, Keiley was exposed to the work of Peter Brook, Robert Lepage and early twentieth-century director/scenographer Gordon Craig. She developed an interest in *commedia dell'arte* but was stymied by the demands of the genre until she discovered what she regards as its secret, which has come to define her directing style: timing. Timing, however, cannot create a unified work in and of itself. Thematic unity needs to be created first. In working with Bach's *Fugue in G minor* as an initial template for kaleidography (in Keiley's later work Chafe's scriptwriting came to fill the role that Bach's *Fugue* played here), Keiley developed a beat-by-beat transformation of a precise musical equation (the *Fugue*) into a precise theatrical equation (*The Cheat*). *The Cheat* involved eighty-one people working on a nine-by-nine grid. The recapitulation and contrapuntal variations for which Bach's music is famous served as touchstones for which Keiley sought to find "harmonizing actions… instead of the notes having a tonal value they have an action value" (Artistic Fraud).

These actions may seem sufficiently specific to create paroxysms in that demon sub-species of Canadian theatre, the indulgent, pause-taking, wildly inconsistent, pseudo-Stanislavskian actor. An example from *The Cheat*: Beat 4 of bar 42 instructs an actor to extend his left hand and drop the pen he is holding. The actor standing stage left of "actor 1" (as marked on the grid) is instructed on beat 3 to hold out his hand and on beat 4 to grab the incoming pen. The pens were not insignificant; at points the actors used them to underscore action and text through a soft percussive rendering of the fugue (Artistic Fraud). The beats form a set of interlocking musical units, accompanied by music in various forms such as percussion or vocalized sound produced by cast members. Actors have the freedom to interpret the movement; the key to the process is that they have precise parameters within which to complete it. The intent is to create a context within which actors can use their skills to invest themselves in the creation of the piece with a sense of clear artistic direction and support.

But surely wrong choices are the path to correct choices, just as the idea of sin enables the definition of virtue? Aren't actors the artists and directors the traffic cops? Of the eight countries in which I have worked as a director, Canada remains the only country where, at least in the major regional theatres, a director is often implicitly instructed to work without a concept and simply to "stage the play," performing the role of what in opera is called the "stage director"—making sure the scenography is collaborative rather than evocative and adhering to a playwright-centred notion of text interpretation. Canadian theatre has only recently begun to question its fealty to text-based realistic theatre and this marginalization of the director. Keiley's staging vocabulary explicitly valorizes gestural and sonic expression over pure spoken text. In one respect, this explains her insistence on working with a small number of artistic collaborators in whom have been inculcated her working methods and physical vocabulary and on grounding her most creative work in the supportive framework of her own theatre company.

Kaleidography owes at least part of its process to musical scoring, but the connection runs much deeper, to the idea that every gesture, every choice within a performance, has both a discrete meaning and an inextricable link to a greater totality and that this totality can be composed. It is the director's responsibility to create a score the actors interpret, rather than to coax out the direction of that interpretation in rehearsal, a situation where experienced actors often may seem to be more in control of the production than the director. The idea of a unified set of rhythms to a production is not new, but in the New-World eagerness to define realism in psychological terms, this approach has been largely confined to the major works of artists such as Robert Wilson.

In the early years of the twentieth century, Vsevolod Meyerhold, adapting industrial movement theory to the stage, systematized stage movement through his bio-mechanics; and there is perhaps a more direct link to past avant-garde theories of rhythm and movement in the work of Rudolf Laban, whose movement system still bears his name, and of Émile Jaques-Dalcroze, eurhythmics. "Scoring," too, derives from Stanislavski, although the meaning of the term has been reduced to the simple tracings of character and event arcs throughout a text. Keiley's scoring is at once more ambitious and more methodical. Frame by frame, movement by movement, it transcends the dogged realism of mainstream Canadian productions.

Kaleidography itself describes a "mathematically-based choreography and directing system in order to produce very specific movement and sound instances on stage, like symphonic music but created with an actor's speaking voice, natural movement, technical elements, and blocking" (Artistic Fraud). The performance floor is charted prior to rehearsal to produce a grid, using various forms, including musical notation, a vestigial benefit of Keiley's background in choral music. The execution of the system changes for every new-production, while retaining the system's core principles. My own characterization of these principles would be *precision*, an executed unity of form and content; manipulation of *tempo* through the integration and layering of physical and vocal expression; and *thematic harmony*, comprised of actions and sounds that break apart and re-integrate (harmony and dissonance), recapitulate and continually underscore each other, often in counterpoint. Kaleidography cannot be described without the use of such appropriated musical terms. The complex layering of rhythms and the shifting nexus of action creates the visceral impression in the spectator of a living animal in constant and unpredictable motion.

Kaleidography encompasses much more than formal patterns of movement, though. With *Under Wraps*, Keiley, Bromley and Chafe began to work out the methodology of "fuguing" text; that is, synchronizing it with the musical score while keeping it comprehensible (for actors and audience). Months before rehearsals even began for the production, actors were given a "click track" so that they could become comfortable with delivering their lines within set metres, and the technical demands would not impede artistic instinct. Other Keiley co-creations have involved the incorporation of new casts in a touring show (*Icycle*), characters matched with specific musical instruments (*The Chekhov Variations*) and actors interacting in real time with shadow characters and props (*Empty Girl*) or with audience members (*Signals*) or with mirror-image film (*Belly-Up*). In almost every instance, the effect is harmonic, if not symphonic, and the visual result is arresting. The sensation in watching a Keiley/Artistic Fraud production is one of almost Mozartian lightness, the depth of talent, intuition and preparation neatly concealed beneath a shimmering surface. It's a different ride for a spectator, one that matches the expectations of an audience willing to believe kaleidography owes at least part of its process to musical scoring. But the connection runs much deeper, to the idea that every gesture, every choice within a performance, has both a discrete meaning and an inextricable link to a greater totality and that this totality can be composed.

For those who want a cup of theatrical java, dark and bitter, rather than the deceptive latte froth of a Fraud production (the company name indicates a certain degree of irreverence), the results may sometimes be frustrating. While the idea that the kaleidography process is a dictatorial one that allows actors little or no scope for interpretation has been proven false in a stream of kinetic and engaging productions, Keiley's work remains, at times, unable to plumb darker emotions and reach the deepest depths of psychological complexity or emotion. It needs to be said, however, that this could only be considered a deficiency within the conventional mindset of North American psychological realism. There is a function for a theatre of wonder, too. While Keiley does not demonstrate much interest in psychologically-driven narratives, and it must be said that the work of her co-creator, Chafe, tends far more to the wistful and elegiac than to *stürm und drang*, their work is not devoid of emotion. Unlike the clinical Gordon Craig, the mechanical Meyerhold or the worst technocrats of the 1980s Québécois theatre scene, Keiley has a soul. She likes to fly, in a metaphorical sense, rather than dig deep in the ground.

Groundhogs in the audience, accustomed to bathetic fare, may grumble but what Jillian Keiley achieves in her work is hard to achieve. In this her work has a close affinity to that of Robert Lepage and Robert Wilson and other directors of the International School. Like Lepage and Peter Brook, she has a personal humility and directness that have enabled her to reach audiences and sponsors who might normally find such work abstract, such as those in her home community.

In the ten years since the success of *UnderWraps*, Keiley, working both independently and with Artistic Fraud, has created a body of work, in various forms, that features Newfoundland writers, established and new. She has helped develop adaptations (an environmental production of poet Michael Crummey's *Salvage*), brought new verve to the work of established writers (Rhonda Payne's *Stars in the Sky Morning*, Berni Stapleton's *The Pope and Princess Di*), created new work with musical collaborator Petrina Bromley (*Icycle*, *SIGNALS*, *UnderWraps*) and championed emerging playwrights (Torquil Golho's *Beyond Zebra* and *Ragarnok*). Above all, she has matched her directing approach with the luminous, lyrical writing of playwright/actor Robert Chafe (*Empty Girl, UnderWraps, Belly Up, Burial Practices, Nightingale*).

Jillian Keiley's work has won awards and prizes because it has been successfully promoted as innovative or ground-breaking. What is truly remarkable about her work, however, is its old-fashioned theatricality. Large casts, swirling images and the use of music and direct address engage audiences. The theatre is never free of its storied and tumultuous past, and those of us who devote our lives to it pay tribute to our ancestors through the integrity of the work we do. In recreating a sense of wonder, in giving her audience wings, Jillian Keiley's work harks back to the best traditions of the theatre while living resolutely in the present. The fact of her residence in Newfoundland, her insistence on working with and training a new generation of Newfoundland-based theatre practitioners and, increasingly, in productions like Chafe's *Tempting Providence* and *Nightingale*, mining the rich vein of Newfoundland's history provide some demonstration of an artist firmly grounded in her own culture, determined to integrate that culture with outside influences and, in the ceaseless touring of Artistic Fraud, to carry the resonance of her culture far and wide. Keiley, at present, is only in her early thirties. It is more than plausible to observe that she is really at the beginning of her career as a director and that the integrative power of her theatre will only grow in execution and scope.

(2006)

Works Cited

Artistic Fraud. "Artistic Fraud." Powerpoint presentation. Presented at Shifting Tides: Atlantic Canadian Theatre, Yesterday, Today and Tomorrow. (Conference) University of Toronto. 31 March–3 April 2004.

Keiley, Jillian. Interview with the author. 9 December 2005.

UnderWraps. LPSU Hall, St. John's, Newfoundland. April 1997.

Editorial Note

For photos showing the grid for *Jesus Christ Superstar* and the effect achieved in performance, see illustrations 20–21 (73).

Acceptance Speech at the 2006 Siminovitch Prize in Theatre Honouring Designers

by Dany Lyne

The following acceptance speech was made by Dany Lyne at the 2006 Siminovitch Prize in theatre honouring designers on October 24, 2006. The Elinore & Lou Siminovitch Prize in Theatre honours professional directors, playwrights and designers by acknowledging excellence and encouraging further exploration in Canadian theatre. The Siminovitch Prize was created in 2001 and is dedicated to distinguished scientist Lou Siminovitch and his late wife Elinore, a playwright. A jury awards the $100,000 prize annually. Direction, playwriting and design are recognized in three-year cycles. As a condition of the prize, one quarter of the prize amount ($25,000) is be awarded to a protegé designated by the recipient or to the recipient's choice of institution (theatre or educational facility) that contributes to Canadian theatre. At the discretion of the primary prize recipient, the secondary prize may be split between no more than two protegés and/or institutions. The protegé must be involved in professional direction, playwriting, or design in Canadian theatre.

Merci infiniment aux fondateurs du Prix Siminovitch de théâtre. Merci à vous, Lou, ainsi qu'à votre regrettée épouse Elinore. Merci à Tony et Elisabeth Comper et à BMO pour cette magnifique soirée qui célèbre la scénographie canadienne. Et finalement, merci à vous Peter Hinton, pour avoir proposé ma candidature et pour votre collaboration remarquable et passionnée à nos projets.

I must also give a big thank-you to my chosen family—to my parents-in-law, Helga and Gerhard Rudolph, who have been unfailingly enthusiastic about and interested in my work, and to my partner, Katja Rudolph, whose unflagging support has helped to get me to this podium. She has never once questioned the sacrifices required to do art, and I am inspired by her own artistic journey as a writer. Hers is the best novel I've read this year—still in manuscript form, but hopefully to be picked up soon by an agent or publisher!

Theatre has saved my life… and it has also almost killed me! As melodramatic as this may sound, I mean it quite literally.

I have wanted to be an artist ever since I was very young. Growing up in a family ravaged by violence and abuse, the *mythos* of the artist was like a beacon to me. It was an identity that I could aspire to, one that promised more from existence than the pitiful prospect around me. I even dressed up as an artist for Halloween—it was a clichéd caricature that I created, including black beret, suspenders, round glasses, grey mustache like my beloved Monsieur Bertillon, my Grade 4 art teacher. But even at that age I knew the artist to be a potent force in society, to be a poetic investigator and a political agitator. I saw the artist as a creator of beauty, as a challenger of beauty, as a consummate observer and reporter, as a committed iconoclast and visionary. Somehow, even as a young child, I knew that it is the artist who takes on the role of relentless storyteller in our culture and society. It is the artist who takes up the narratives in circulation there—dominant narratives, lost narratives, narratives of desolation and despair, narratives of hope and redemption—and transforms them into a poetic, stylized form that an audience can encounter like a mirror. It is the artist whose sole purpose is to experiment, expose, propose, engage, uplift and challenge us to confront ourselves. Challenge us to confront our own humanity and inhumanity and thereby perhaps support a united attempt to reach for a peaceful, spiritually vibrant future for us all. For someone suffocated by a deathly familial silence within a worldview that had no meaning for me, this vision of a life of conscious, purpose-driven storytelling kept me going. It kept me literally, too many times to count, from plunging off the Jacques Cartier Bridge into the St. Lawrence River. As melodramatic as that sounds.

During my tumultuous twenties, I was a Fine Arts student at the Ontario College of Art and Design. It is there that I met Dr. Paul Baker, the professor of an introduction to theatre course. I instantly fell in love with theatre. I also fell in love with Paul as a teacher. I was 26, and had already worked in interior decoration, graphic design, font design and was attempting to become a painter. It clearly took me a while to find my medium!

There had been no theatre in my childhood. So, when I found it, I was stunned and amazed. The sheer multi-dimensionality of theatre filled me with incredible awe: not only is it three-dimensional visually, it is space-specific, unfolds in real time, includes spoken or sung word, explores the truths and lies of existence through narrative, and engages the soul of the musician and the expressiveness of the human body. Further, it miraculously weaves together the passion and vision of many collaborators—and I emphasize the word "miracle" here—from the psychological, spiritual, and political insights of the writer to the musical vision of the composer to the interpretive will of the creative team—director, conductor, designers, stage manager—to the generosity of actors and singers and musicians to the technical and artistic skill and dedication of the production teams. Finally, and equally miraculously, it demands the commitment and openness of an audience. The artist in me saw in theatre and opera the most exciting, complex and ambitious of mediums. I succumbed fully to the rich world of words, music and images and through this began to understand my own personal world, to finally see it reflected back at me. Translating the texts into images empowered me to engage in my own act of transformation.

Set and costume design allows me to turn a physical space into a psychological and symbolic setting. In close collaboration with the director, I strive to create a visual poetic-arc that best supports the unfolding story and best represents the emotional landscape of the characters. Focusing on the scene-sequence and the metamorphosis of the protagonists, I search for a central visual metaphor that emphasizes underlying themes and resonates with the author's symbolism. Whether the text is about the politics of war or the most modest of personal events, one striking image can, in my view, encapsulate the drama. Within this one cohesive poetic visual field, my goal is to articulate the story in such a way that the impact of each scene is accentuated. Subtle and transformative set and costumes convey what is at stake in the unfolding story.

Process plays a critical role in the creation of this represented world. I invite directors to work with me in my studio for days at a time at several stages of the design. We sit at my desk and go over the text line by painstaking line. We discuss everything under the sun in relation to this text—our political views, our aesthetic longings, our own biographies. And we order a lot of Thai food! Eventually, we develop a shared understanding of the story and its mythic relevance to us and to our time and place. The electricity that is generated from such a design process can, if all goes well, carry through to the rehearsals and technical rehearsals. The actors, singers and lighting-designer participate in this creative act and the accumulation of their insights refines our dramatic world further.

It is hard to convey the euphoria of a perfect opening night. One experiences that only a handful of times in a career. I felt it once in particular at the Cincinnati Opera House with a production of Strauss's *Elektra* directed by Nicolas Muni. At the end, there were several seconds of absolute silence, then an enormous rushing sound as a conservative Midwestern audience rose as one to their feet and began clapping and shouting, applauding a crazed, atonal, out-of-control, exquisite operatic rant. They clapped for ten minutes. In that brief time, everything expended in the creation process and more was given back to me. As empty as I'd just been feeling—I was exhausted and already mourning a finished project—I was filled instantly, and knew in that moment that I had my creative fuel for the next few years.

So what about theatre is almost killing me? As I said, very early on I clutched onto the arts and later specifically theatre as a lifeline. For me, it became part of my daily life-and-death struggle for a better existence. Everything was invested in the creative process and the journey required to put something substantive, beautiful, and poetic on the stage. The sheer effort of doing this is indescribable. I myself can never fully grasp how it can take so much time and energy. I fear that sometimes the intensity—the very life-and-deathness—that I bring to theatre makes me less than relaxing to work with at times!

But in addition to my own life-story and personality, there are very real obstacles to great theatre and opera design in Canada. Theatre really does kill you a little bit every day while it is saving you from yourself, lifting you up. It's just so damn hard. Firstly, in Germany, a designer makes an excellent living designing two shows a year.

Here it is impossible to make a living designing two shows a year. One has to book oneself absolutely solid and overlap projects to make a moderately decent living. This is exhausting and unsustainable. The PACT minimums set by ADC, which are the current industry standards, do not in any way recognize the expense of maintaining a studio and the incredibly time-intensive occupation that design is. If broken down into payment per hour, designers probably make amongst the least in theatre in Canada. I once actually calculated that I'd done a design for $6.35 an hour. Quite a big design, too, for a big company. Where others in theatres have contracts that last a few weeks, designers often have contracts that last many months over a period of years and their lump-sum payment does not reflect this. Secondly, designers cannot experiment, cannot push their art, test their materials, without having a theatre support the essential research and development required to grow and develop. Theatres are often reluctant to pay for this risk and the designer finds her or himself fighting for resources. Therefore, the designer is always in the end, unlike other theatre artists, inextricably linked to money, to the pesky, unpredictable financial figures of set, prop and costume production and can rarely simply be an artist attempting to push themselves to greater artistic heights. Thirdly, the financial burden of the ever-growing administrative side of theatre shifts the focus away from the stage to the office and to other programs theatres now offer. The corporatization of theatre is a real concern of mine. I hope we don't go too far down that road, where theatre is run like a value-added business. Businesses sell products, but theatre isn't selling a product: theatre is a participant in the life of the people. Theatre is the heart of a nation, a place where we can face ourselves, we can tell our stories, break our silences, save a few lives, literally and spiritually speaking. Or so it should be. Governments need to realize this, and it will take inventiveness for theatres to balance the books while at the same time building creative, artist-friendly, democratic administrations. We have to remember that without the stage, and the artists who fill that stage, theatres could not run their other programs and arts administrators would also be out of luck.

The above struggles push designers perilously close to burn-out. Burn-out is death to an artist, and for me, this means also a kind of death of myself. The struggle to get my vision on stage really has been kind of killing me in the last little while, with notable exceptions. Young designers are not lasting long enough in the business to become the great designers they could be. If the artist is to continue to be a beacon to generations coming up, if these generations are to continue to aspire to that mythic persona, we need to make sure that artists don't all drop out and take jobs in banks. We need people to work in banks, but we also, as a society, need artists. A prize such as this tonight is a huge symbolic boost, as well as, to a few of us, an incredible material boost when it counts the most, mid-career when energy is flagging, and all artists here tonight are very grateful for it—Let's have more of them!—but we also need systemic change.

I never cease to be in awe of the theatrical endeavour. It is my hope that this miraculous collaborative act can itself be a kind of exemplary metaphor for life outside of theatre. It is a source of hope to me to see what people can accomplish together in the spirit of a shared creative vision. Let's bring what is vital and transformative in theatre to the outside world, rather than let the norms of the outside world run our theatres. We need to decide that we are a nation that values the art that enriches the life of the nation, the art that sometimes even saves individual lives, literally and spiritually speaking.

This is the really fun part. It's an unbelievable pleasure to be able to honour two designers whose work and commitment I admire very much: April Anne Viczko, a discerning, architectural and poetic artist. I have worked with April a great deal in the last two years. Her passion, skill and unsurpassed sense of humour go a very long way to making a project fly high. And Camellia Koo: a meticulous, sculptural and symbolic interpreter. She brings precision, patience and great theatrical vision to her work. It's been my pleasure to work with her over the last four years.

We also wish to encourage a recent theatre design graduate: Jung-Hye Kim, whose talent and determination to become a designer are remarkable. I've been really impressed by her hard-working ethic and initiative.

(2006)

Editorial Note

The author would like to thank Katja Rudolph for her editing of the original text.

The Box: What Happens When You Place the Audience and/or a Performer Inside an 8' x 8' Box?

by Camellia Koo (with Guillermo Verdecchia and Christine Brubaker)

"Nightswimming" (www.nightswimmingtheatre.com) is an award-winning dramaturgical theatre company devoted, since 1995, to developing new plays, performance works and dance. The company explores new forms by commissioning Canada's leading artists in the fields of theatre, music and dance. Nightswimming commissions, develops and workshops these projects and seeks out established performing arts companies as partners in an extended developmental process leading to premiere productions by our partner companies. Nightswimming is devoted, through the creation of these new works, to advancing the field of dramaturgy and play development in Canada. Nightswimmming's "Pure Research" program—in association with the University of Toronto's Graduate Centre for the Study of Drama—challenges artists from across Canada to investigate new ideas in dramaturgy. The company provides space, money and resources for studio-based research into provocative theatrical questions of form and performance. "Pure Research" is designed to foster theatrical experiments which are not linked to a particular project. In the spirit of inquiry, the company assists artists to discover what they need to explore in order to further their work. What follows is a report on one "Pure Research" project.

Introduction

Going into Pure Research, I was very interested in experimenting with putting a barrier between a performer and the audience. We chose to use an 8' x 8' box in order to do this and contain our research as well as our audience and/or performer.

Fundamentally, what I was interested in exploring was the blurring of roles of performer and audience member, who is leading whom, who is driving the piece, and who is watching whom.

Some questions that initiated the research:

- How can a performer communicate to or with an audience through the box?
- How can an audience interact back?
- Who is the viewer and who is being viewed? And does this perspective have to remain static, or can it be fluid and keep interchanging?
- What types of barriers can we place between the performer and the audience?

- How can an audience learn through the performance what the rules are and what they are allowed or required to do in order to experience the piece as a whole.
- How can we implicate the audience into experiencing what they are watching so that they do not remain a passive "watching" audience?

Participants in the experiment were: Camellia Koo, Guillermo Verdecchia, Christine Brubaker, Brian Quirt, Jessica Glanfield.

DAY 1

The Frame

Day one started with us assembling the pre-built, 8' x 8' box frame. Once assembled, our progress quickly came to a stand-still. Guillermo, Christine and I stood around it, then eventually went inside it and still had no idea what to do with it.

The box frame provided an interesting "stage" in which performers could perform to an audience on the outside, and vice versa, but it did not provide many opportunities for interaction because there was no barrier between the two; no mystery.

The Skin-Ply Box

We then moved on to covering the sides of the box frame with 8' x 8' sheets of skin-ply wood, leaving only a narrow doorway into and out of the box. The ceiling remained open and we had two lx instruments focused directly down into the box.

First, we started placing as many chairs inside the box as we could for a potential audience, making them face the same direction to start, then making two sides face each other next, then making them all face the walls etc. This did not get us very far as we quickly ran out of variations.

Second, we removed all but one chair. We aimlessly walked around the box, walked into the box, brainstormed as a group inside the box, using it as our sort of think tank of things we could do. But it did not go much beyond just talking about what we could do with just the three of us. One idea was to close the audience up in the box, box them in, and then do things to them or to the box to provoke them to interact with us on the outside.

Then, Brian and Jessica joined us. We did more of the same aimless walking around and into the box until only Brian and Jessica were in the box by themselves.

Experiment #1 – Spontaneous Entrapment

Guillermo, Christine and I spontaneously and silently mobilized and decided to trap Brian and Jessica in the box. They did not know of any of the ideas that we had come up with earlier. Quietly sliding the door piece into place then very quickly using screws to drill the door piece permanently into place before they could escape, we had finally tested our first idea. (This idea would later go on to greater experimentation even beyond Pure Research, but more about this later.)

Then, we did nothing. We waited to see what they would do first. We found impromptu peepholes looking into the box (old screw holes), which allowed us to watch what they were up to. After awhile, we started provoking them. Guillermo, Christine and I did very little talking to each other and just ran around provoking the people in the box through silent agreements with each other and spontaneously improvising with the tools and objects we had in the room: hitting the box, kicking the box, hammering the box, throwing things at the box, tapping the box, writing on the outside of the box, running around the box, whispering around the box, and turning the house lights around the box down so that only inside the box was lit.

Discussion

From the *audience member's* perspective, this experiment became about experiencing an ordeal. The experience of actually being drilled into the box was unexpected and jarring at first. Then it became about what was going to happen next? What are they going to do next?

We, the *performers* manipulated the box or provoked the people on the inside of the box in order to try and make them react or engage with us. It became about us watching the audience, which blurred the lines between who the performers were and who the audience were.

Experiment #2 – Not So Spontaneous Entrapment

Brian then walked into the box by himself and before he could barely pull his leg in, instead of quietly sliding the door piece into place, we slammed the door into place and once again drilled the box closed. This time, we tried to be more selective about what we were doing on the outside of the box. Guillermo, Christine and I did a lot more planning and talking to each other.

We did more of the same as Experiment #1, this time with the introduction of tangerines which were originally brought in as snacks, but quickly became alarming noise makers when thrown directly at the box from the outside. We also started drilling new peepholes while Brian was inside the box.

Discussion

This time, for the lone audience member, the experience of being drilled into the box was still alarming as before. The person on the inside of the box was more aware of and more interested in what was happening on the outside of the box, about what we were doing, even if we were not directly manipulating the box, i.e. talking and planning our next move which could apparently be heard slightly from the inside.

As in #1, this experiment was also about ordeal, about putting an audience inside the box, subjecting them to things to try and raise a reaction from them. During the post experiment discussion of this, we all spontaneously gathered inside the box, pulling chairs inside and discussing what just happened from inside our makeshift think tank.

Experiment #3 – The Box Man

Then, at some point in the discussion, Brian slipped outside of the box, before drilling the rest of us into the box (Guillermo, Christine, Jessica and myself). Next, he slipped a handwritten note under one of the walls, which read, "Sit quietly and await instructions." We read the note, but kept on talking and wondering what he was doing outside of the box. Brian then slipped another note under the wall, which read, "I said quietly."

This time, we tried to listen for him on the outside but couldn't hear anything.

Suddenly, Brian began reading aloud some passages from a book that I brought in called *The Box Man*, by Kobu Abe. (A friend had lent it to me thinking it might be appropriate research for our experimenting.)

At first, we listened to the passage being read, about this man's experience of living his entire life inside a cardboard box. Then Brian stopped reading as suddenly as he had started and we spent the next couple of minutes trying to listen for his movements on the outside. Nothing.

Next, he began to manipulate the lights by turning them off in a snap blackout, dimming them up and down, and flashing them.

Then he read more passages from the book, and while doing so, we heard him walk out of the studio, still reading, and letting the outside door apparently close behind him. Then we heard nothing.

Discussion

This experiment was more theatrical in many ways. As audience members inside the box, we were asked to wait. Unlike the previous experiments, we were given instructions on how to participate. As a result, we remained audience members in that we were waiting to see what Brian, as the "performer" would do next. His choices of activities were decidedly not in direct contact with the box, such as the hitting and hammering etc. of the box, but instead atmospheric around the box, i.e. using his voice to read to us, manipulating the lights inside and outside of the box, and leaving the space entirely. Also unlike the previous experiments, the audience was not required to interact or react to what was happening.

For Brian, the trapper/reader, was still less of a conventional performer, and from his perspective, the event was more about taking care of the audience, giving them instructions, reading to them, trying to keep them entertained.

Experiment #4 – The Box Girl in the Box

The chairs were removed, and somehow I ended up in the box all by myself.

Somebody drilled the door closed and the game continued. This time, Christine, Brian and Jessica continued the activities of the first two experiments, this time throwing in a sweater at some point, throwing more tangerines, and also introducing the idea of moving the box. Since there was no floor to the box, it was easily movable. They pushed the box, with me inside it, out of the circle of light.

Since by now, I was very familiar with this line of experimenting, I began to repeat some of the same activities that they were doing, only from the inside; i.e. I listened to find out where they were on the outside, tried using the peepholes to look out, smacked the box from the inside when I heard Christine directly on the other side, and also managed to move the box a little by pushing from the inside.

Discussion

This experiment became a game between inside and outside.

Despite having been the driller of the door twice before and even having experienced it from the inside once before, it was definitely still surprising when it happened. I found out later that Guillermo sat on the side and just watched the interactions from the sidelines.

End of Day Discussion

Several questions came up repeatedly over the course of the day and during the end of day discussion about rules:

- How do you get the audience into the box?
- Do we blatantly direct them into the box?
- Are there signs that tell them where to go?
- Do we trick them to go into the box?
- Once they are inside the box, how do we keep them in there before the box is closed up?
- What if they escape before or while we are closing them in?
- What if they do not react/interact to what we subject them to?
- What if we put things on the walls on the inside to make the audience look at something to entice them inside the box?
- Why did no one just try to scream or yell out from inside the box?
- Why did both inside and outside participants always choose to whisper?
- Do we make them wait in line and take tickets before letting them into the box?
- What if we only put one chair inside the box?
- What if there were 12 people trapped inside the box instead of only 1 or 3 people?

DAY 2

Part 1 – White Transparent Tarp

Day 2 started with us removing the skin-ply sheets and recovering the box frame with white translucent plastic tarp (the kind you can buy in hardware stores to cover boats, cars etc). The tarps were stapled in place and covered all 4 walls of the box and also, this time, the ceiling of the box. Leaving one edge of tarp unstapled to create an openable/closable flap created a door. It resembled a greenhouse.

Experiment #1 – Light Box

The house lights were at zero, leaving the theatre completely dark. A floor float lighting instrument was put on the floor inside the box, and Christine went inside to play.

She created shadows using her hands and entire body, repositioned the light around the space, lay down on the floor so that she appeared to have disappeared from inside the box, then slowly raised herself up, and manipulated her own shadows and silhouette by moving closer or farther away from the light source.

Discussion

Christine was clearly putting on a performance for us on the outside. We all sat around the box and watched it and waited to see what Christine could come up with next.

A beautifully clean white translucent light box is inherently theatrical, in that it is attractive to look at and, once a performer is inside, incites shadow play, which is hypnotic to watch.

Experiment #2 – Flashlight Box

We removed the lx floor float and gave Christine a mini-flashlight only.

She began to reflect the light off herself, and off the material. Since the material was translucent, the closer she stood to the walls, the more colour and specific details we could see. She also began to turn the flashlight off, move to somewhere else in the box, and turn the light back on, requiring us to guess where she might appear next. She began chasing herself with the light around the box, leaving the flashlight on but somewhere stationary so that she could be hands free, and then she began to chase us around the space when she could see us moving around on the outside.

She then began to taunt us with the flashlight, using it to get our attention, using it to make us do something, and trying to get us to react to it.

Experiment #3 – We Play Back

We began to play back with Christine from the outside. Using another flashlight, we created a copycat game, then a game of light tag, then a sort of light dialogue between the two flashlights.

At some point, both Christine and Guillermo pulled out Sharpie markers and began writing on the material. Someone wrote KEEP OUT, someone else tried writing backwards to directly talk to the person on the other side.

Also, to replace the tangerines, Christine brought in soft rubber balls to throw at the box from the outside. Eventually some of them got stuck on the roof of the box and they became a performance onto themselves, especially when Brian began to poke them and manipulate and move them around the roof with his hands from inside the box.

Discussion

Even though there were chairs present in the studio, none of us felt compelled to stay sitting in them while watching Christine. We were free to walk around the box, which in turn gave Christine the opportunity to engage us and teach us how we could interact with her using only her flashlight, and then later with a Sharpie.

The rubber balls were amusing. It became a game to move them around and make them jump up by hitting the tarp roof from below, and from both the inside and the outside, it was compelling to watch.

Interaction began and remained fluid between the inside and the outside, between performer and audience because anyone can pass off the roles of who is leading whom, who is chasing whom and who is watching whom etc.

End of Experiment Discussion.

The clear plastic tarp material was inherently theatrical. It was attractive to look at even as a sculptural installation, and also as a device for shadow play.

The material also automatically invited play. There was still a very visible barrier to create both enough mystery and enough access to watch, to play, to interact and engage a person standing on the other side.

Some questions arose out of the experimenting:

- How do you engage the audience?
- How do you make them participate?
- And finally, what if the material were more transparent, would the audience play more?

PART 2 – CLEAR PLASTIC PAINTERS DROP

This time we covered the box frame with completely transparent plastic sheeting (hardware store clear plastic painters drops).

Discussion

It took ten minutes to put up, but only lasted another ten minutes of us standing around it staring at it before we took it down again. No one wanted to interact with it, or play with it or go near it. Christine attempted to go inside it and play around, but came up with very little.

We realized that there was no surprise, no mystery; therefore, no incentive to interact with it. It was too transparent. We discovered that we needed a barrier between the audience and the performer in order to give an audience a reason to get closer to the box to investigate it further and be drawn into it's mystery or reason for being there, and eventually make an audience want to interact with it.

PART 3 – WHITE PAPER

This time, we decided to explore what would happen if the material was more opaque than the white plastic tarps but not as solid as the skin-ply. We covered the box with white paper off a roll.

This time we lit the box from above and just let Christine play inside. Christine began simply with walking around inside the box, sometimes allowing us to see her shadow and singing.

Because the paper had seams where the reams of paper overlapped, Christine and then later Guillermo began interacting with their hands and shadows of their hands, through the paper.

Eventually, the inherent attractiveness of the paper light box and Christine's singing became hypnotic and we all just sat and watched her. This lasted for about half an hour of us just silently watching.

Next we gave her a bucket of water and a paintbrush and she began writing on the paper with the water, and letting the water melt holes in the paper.

Eventually, Christine started creating new peepholes for herself and then larger holes and rips in the paper by tearing at with her fingers. She re-found the flashlight and began using it to create shadows that she could control. Then hands and limbs started to poke through the paper, then eventually her entire head at which point she started to aggressively engage the audience by shouting at us and interrogating us, using the flashlight to indicate which of us she was talking to.

She began to rip the paper further so that we could see more of her inside it.

Discussion

Similar to the white plastic tarps, the paper light box was beautiful to look at as a sculptural installation. With the addition of Christine's beautiful singing, none of the audience members felt compelled to disturb her. The seams in the paper provided opportunities for immediate interaction between the inside and outside; hands, objects, etc could be passed from one side to the other, in addition to shadow play. The water writing was interesting, but also still just a performance, or something for us as audience members on the outside to look at.

With the exception of some shadow interaction between Guillermo on the outside and Christine on the inside at the very beginning, we all just wanted to watch from the outside. A pretty box, a pretty voice; you could watch it forever. It was inherently compelling to watch.

A number of questions arose from this experiment, though they started to ask questions that were about what the box meant as a metaphor:

– What if she were in an orange jumpsuit?
– What is the water?
– How did it get there?

DAY 3 – AN EXPECTING AUDIENCE

We invited a few people to come for Day 3 so that we could revisit some of the past day's work with unsuspecting audience members. They were all people who worked in the theatre community so they were not exactly "unsuspecting."

We began with the White Plastic Tarp box.

We left the flap open, and put a few soft rubber balls both on the inside of the box as well on the roof, and also left both a broom handle (to poke the roof with), a flashlight, and a few Sharpie markers inside the box. We hoped it would look inviting to an audience to want to go in and play inside.

We made the mistake of leaving chairs out in the space around the box.

When the 4 audience members entered the space, the box was beautifully lit, flap open and appearing to be inviting, but no one entered the box. They walked around it a bit, poked their heads in, then they saw the chairs or the edge of the stage and they all sat down and just stared at it. Christine eventually went inside it and tried to get them to interact with her, using the flashlight to get their attention and to try and teach them how to interact with her... but no one moved from where they were sitting. We decided to end it, then ushered the audience back out.

We did a quick changeover to the Skin-Ply box.

We left the doorway to the box open. But this time we placed a few chairs inside the box and arranged them around the box to be inviting, and let the audience back into the studio. Once again, the audience members followed the chairs and this time went into the box.

We slammed the door closed and drilled them in. Then we did nothing for a bit. We looked at them through peepholes, drilled new ones while they were inside, hit the box, dangled a c-wrench from the ceiling above them, threw rubber balls at the box, etc. and then the audience came to life.

Either boredom or survival instincts kicked in or the audience began to get ahead of us. We had planned to move the box across the floor while they were inside, but before we got that far, they began to push the box themselves from the inside. Then they started whispering and planning their next move and then to our surprise, lifted up the box and escaped from underneath.

Game over.

Discussion

Since our audience was invited, they were not completely unsuspecting. They entered the space expecting some sort of performance or demonstration, and not to be the instigator of the work. Since we were blurring the roles of performer and audience, the box as an installation requires that the audience drive the piece, and not a performer. Since the audience were either not given instructions on how to participate, and/or our signals were unclear, and/or because we have all been brainwashed to play the role of audience in a specific way, they did not participate so the demonstration was over before it began.

With the skin-ply box, the audience was put into a situation that invited interaction between the inside and the outside, but instead of being absolutely passive like they were with the Tarp box, this time they were absolutely aggressive and they completely took over the event. They created the event, which immediately relegated us, the demonstrators, suddenly to audience members since we could not longer do anything else but watch to see what they were going to do next.

This was a fascinating and unexpected turn of events.

FINAL DISCUSSIONS

One of the most difficult tasks to keep on top of during the day was keeping context out of the experimenting; for instance not making the box a metaphor for something else; i.e. a jail, a prison, a shipping container etc. As storytellers, it was extremely difficult to keep context and narrative out of our playing.

The day also became about "Rules," or theatrical conventions; how we have been brainwashed to watch theatre, how we are supposed to behave as an audience member, how we are supposed to behave as a performer, and how we use signs, signals or instructions to teach or condition the audience. When there are chairs present, the audience immediately knows to sit in them and expect a performance soon after. Also, who is the viewer and who is being viewed?

One point that was brought up in our final discussion was the idea that theatre touts its liveness, but we as theatremakers constantly strive to recreate the perfect show the same way each time every night usually (but not always) to a passive audience who have come to the theatre expecting to sit and watch a performance.

In reality, audiences love the uniqueness of those moments when something goes wrong, or is unexpected, or they are surprised; e.g., when watching a show in a park, unsuspecting dogwalkers always walk through the playing area during a performance.

Brian mentioned his dislike for cell phone announcements at the top of shows since they ruin the sound cues at the top of the show because it starts with an admonition directed at the audience. Discussion arose around the following: what if you left the houselights up during a show, then take them down or away, or what if they suddenly go up, and the audience suddenly becomes more aware of where they are.

The experimenting of the last three days became about social experiments and perceived preconceptions or "rules" of how to be an audience member.

- What are audience members allowed to do?
- How do they know what they are allowed or not allowed to do?
- How do we engage them directly?
- How do we make the audience drive the piece instead of a performer?
- How can we blur the roles or subvert the roles of audience and performer?
- How do we implicate the audience in what they are watching or experiencing?

GUILLERMO VERDECCHIA

"What happens," Camie asked, "when you put a barrier between the audience and the performance?"

People can't see? They get frustrated? They resolve not to go the theatre again? It seemed pretty obvious to me. So I figured there had to be more to it.

One

One of the most interesting things I learned was that the barrier to visibility presented by certain materials acted not as an impediment but as a stimulus. The completely transparent box was utterly uninteresting; it had no secrets. Everything was revealed at a glance. When the box was covered in a translucent material it became much more intriguing, inviting. Limits were created: an INSIDE, an OUTSIDE. The translucency of the material allowed for communication between the inside and outside. Games emerged, positions, dialogue of different kinds.

When the box was boarded up, everyone wanted to look inside. Though unappealing aesthetically, the box was interesting. What was INSIDE? Everybody eventually peeked in.

A dramaturgical analogy occurred to me. Delaying information is a good way to "hook" an audience. Tell an audience too much too soon and you risk boring them or overwhelming them. Don't give them enough "information" and they will eventually get frustrated and tune out. Give them a few key pieces of narrative information and they will sit forward, listen and watch actively, attentively. (Here the transparent material is the equivalent of telling an audience too much too soon.)

The box invites narrative. Who will make that narrative? What happens after I've looked inside the box? If something doesn't happen soon I'm going to get bored, resentful, leave. It's just like a regular, normal play. Or maybe I can't stop thinking like a "regular" normal play.

Two

We also wondered how an audience might be encouraged to participate, to engage.

It also became very clear to me that with a little bit of thought it was easy to control our audience. (Not all audiences—some will be less tractable, biddable than others.)

Questions of cultural "competence," as well as relationship to various kinds of authority—fields which are probably interestingly related—will enter into the equation at some point). Shine a light here, leave an opening there, arrange a few chairs to look like seating for a performance, and folks will march into the box.

The group of spectators who did not want to play in the lovely translucent box became surprisingly (to us, at the time) animated in the wooden box. But again there is a dramaturgical analogy. If you provide the right conditions, context, you can get your characters to do almost anything. If you lock a "passive" audience in a box, they quickly become active. Conditions impel them to act, to break through their reserve, shyness, to disregard the rules of theatre propriety. After all, by trapping them in the box, we showed a fairly blatant disregard for the rules so they were quite right to feel no longer bound by them.

Bourriaud (on relational aesthetics) says the aura of a work of art has shifted from the work to the viewer.

Three

And finally I was reminded how everything doesn't necessarily signify but everything does inform. We are constantly making judgments, discriminating at the minutest levels, piecing things together. Quickly. Often below the level of consciousness. The quality and level of light, the texture of materials, the arrangement of events and objects these things determine whether we step in to the box, if we stay long, if we feel comfortable, if we feel secure or vulnerable, what we are disposed to do once inside or outside. We immediately begin making associations, inventing, telling a (kind of) story based on the smallest stimulus.

Looking at the paper box after it had been ripped, my imagination worked to imagine what had once been there, what had happened. I'm tempted to say that narrative is everywhere. Unavoidable. That our minds are always making narratives as a way of making sense. Faced with a wooden box covered in ripped paper, the mind imagines multiple scenario that led to this state. But that's not true. I spend lots of my time not making sense of things, not making narratives, simply accepting things, figures, people at limited face value, not associating, not connecting.

• • •

It seems like an extremely simple project. You build a box, you cover it in wood or different kinds of plastic, you try to get people to go inside it, you try to get people to engage, to participate rather than simply watch passively.

But it's not simple at all.

Why a box? Why not a parachute or scaffolding? Why not metres of felt and bathtubs on wheels? Why not a floor covered with spikes or flowers or spoons?

Why not a swimming pool? The box is making all kinds of meaning all the time, suggesting possibilities.

And why do this in a theatre building? A theatre, empty and unloved as it may be, still comes with some very strong, if tacit, rules or if not rules, expectations. The box would "mean" something very different (or not at all) in a parking lot, a park, an art gallery, a shipyard, a slum.

And why should an audience participate, engage? What is wrong with watching? Is watching necessarily passive? Is engaging "better" than watching?

Sure, there's value in the sheer dumb fun of goofing in a box with others; it can be a way of re-figuring all kinds of relations—for a moment at least. But then what? What happens next? Sometimes some kinds of installation strike me as very slight, deeply unambitious, suspicious of the possibility of engagement with larger, more difficult, important questions. Long-term, larger scale.

Further, what is an audience? How is an audience constituted? How shall we know an audience? Are the people waiting in a foyer an audience, or are they something else? Are they in the process of becoming an audience? Are they an audience when seated? Are they an audience if they are scattered around the space? And wouldn't it be more accurate to speak of spectators rather than an audience? (Audience comes from *audire*—which is about hearing; whereas spectator comes from *spectare*, which is about watching). Or participants perhaps? People?

Anyway…

—Guillermo Verdecchia

CHRISTINE BRUBAKER

The Box, The Audience and a Space

Being the "hired actor" for this research project was interesting as there was actually no real performance, or actor technique ultimately required (that being said, there were moments of more conventional performance, but all of us agreed that that was not as interesting given what we were exploring). The project became more about a desire to explore the possibilities of space and audience relationship and I was more of a fellow researcher that a subject.

A few observations:

- Games involving unwitting audience members were fun.
- Real obstacles were fantastic (ie: REALLY being trapped inside a box—screwed in). It demanded a response, created energy where there was none before.
- Real obstacles activated our audience instantly—they became active participants in the event.

- Obscured sound is threatening—everything from whispers to loud thuds on the walls. Not being able to see where sound is coming from but knowing it's acting upon you can be disturbing, disorienting.
- Barriers of various materials really do evoke different emotional responses: the opaque plastic felt permeable, breathable and ultimately not nearly as threatening. The wood was solid, ultimately breakable, but not without a great deal of effort or tools. There somehow seemed a need to meet it with an equal amount of force or effort.
- It's very difficult for our "audience" to really step outside their conventional prescribed role of passive observer without really doing something drastic.
- Audiences will look for a place to sit.
- When asked to take a seat, audiences will choose a chair over the floor.
- Audiences will gravitate towards chairs in a space.

Acknowledgements:

This research was conducted at the Glenn Morris Studio, University of Toronto, December 14, 15, and 18th, 2006.

EPILOGUE – The Crate Installation

Back to the question of "how do we implicate an audience"? We were invited to bring the box out of storage after Pure Research was complete. We decided to use the Skin-Ply box and test it with unsuspecting audience members in a festival called Audience Re/Location TURN LEFT HERE FESTIVAL at Buddies in Bad Times on March 1st and 2nd, 2007.

On the inside of the box, we covered the walls with dates and statistics of people found in containers, in backs of trucks, body parts on lawns (having fallen from airplane wheels), bodies found in abandoned boats etc. We left the door of the box open, using the door piece as a pathway leading into the box. It was nicely lit, there were two nice big signs that warned people who were claustrophobic not to go inside, and we, the "workers" in black coveralls, just sat around, or nearby chatting. When the time was right, or when we felt like it, we snapped the room into blackout and slammed the door closed and then we pretended to drill them in. (We were not allowed to actually screw the door closed because of safety and health concerns.) Although, from audience feedback after they were let out, the slamming and the drilling sounds were scary enough for people.

Large groups never went in. The whole festival was sort of "walk around on your own time," so it was hard to usher people into the box. Instead we let them wander in. Sometimes we closed them in, sometimes we just let the box be its own mini museum of statistics. The only other sign on the outside of the box read "CAUTION—SMUGGLING AND ILLEGAL IMMIGRATION MAY BE ENCOUNTERED IN THIS

AREA." You only saw this once the box was closed as it was on the outside side of the door.

After closing the box, the lights slowly faded up along with a soundscape of wind and water and low rumbling music (provided by Thomas Ryder Payne). Also a live feed video camera and the TV's were turned on so that everyone on the outside could watch.

We found that we didn't need to do very much. Occasionally we would bang on the box if we saw (by looking into the peep holes) that people were too close to one side of the box; a few people we pushed into the box. But otherwise we let them be. And just watched them. During Pure Research we felt compelled to keep doing things to the audience on the inside of the box. After the initial shock of being drilled in, at first they laughed, one couple started slow dancing, some continued on with their conversations. But the longer we kept them in, the more dates and statistics they read and the more they became overwhelmed by them, it started to resonate—where they were, what they were reading, etc. The longer we kept them in, the more uncomfortable they became, but they kept reading. Only one person didn't fall for the illusion of being drilled into the box and subsequently bodychecked Jovanni Sy, who was holding the door in place from the outside.

Discussion

Unlike during Pure Research, we didn't do very much to the people on the inside. The people on the outside looked into the peepholes and watched the box people on the TVs, some joined in with the occasional banging on the box.

Also unlike Pure Research, this experiment had a very, very clear context and, with the help of lights and sound and our actions, we had a sort of beginning and ending to the "experience" for the people on the inside.

(2007)

The Bus Project: Technologies, Spectators and Locational Practices

by Kathleen Irwin

In Canada's foremost national English language newspaper we find the following description of Cirque du Soleil's production *KÀ* at the MGM Grand Hotel in Las Vegas: "Imagine a Broadway stage that can rise, fall, float, become completely vertical, or tilt, often at alarming, gravity-defying angles, and you'll have some idea of what [director, Robert] Lepage has conceived" (Posner). Commenting on this marriage of super-technology and the performing body, Lepage states, "the 19th century conception of the proscenium stage was based on a vertical world—with God above, man in the middle and the devils below the trap doors. [...] But the new world is horizontal, as much as vertical. [...] So it should be possible to have a theatre where everything is possible, where there is no floor, no ceiling, no gravity" (qtd. in Posner).

Certainly in Cirque du Soleil's mega-million dollar production, technology is foregrounded; "all the theatre's innards lie exposed—[w]inches, cables, conduits" (Posner). However, with all the technological trappings that purport to redefine audience perception in entirely new ways, the emphasis on spectacle and its conventions remain unaltered. What this explosion in entertainment technology, exemplified by *KÀ*, fails to address is its relationship to the spectating body and how techno-interactivity poses questions that address the specificities of the spectator in the twenty-first century.

In relative magnitude, *The Bus Project* described in this article falls at the opposite end of the scale of technologically-enhanced entertainments (see "Bus Project"). Nonetheless, *The Bus Project* departs from *KÀ* in illustrating how interactive technologies may be used to integrate performance into our everyday lives, how new audiences may be reached, and how preconceived notions of spectatorship, identity, and gender may be productively troubled through locational and intermedia practices. In provocative ways, both projects stake out a postcolonial, postmodern perspective and experiment with an aesthetic of multiplicity and heterogeneity, which make comparisons not entirely spurious.

As a secondary corollary, the paper addresses how creative interdisciplinary collaboration blurs the lines between art practice and research and problematizes critical evaluation of these processes. While these are "meat and potatoes" issues in a university environment where peer reviewed assessment is linked to advancement, they are equally relevant in professional arts practice where funding depends on juried proposals and measurable standards of excellence. While a key variable in assessment is inevitably the space between intention and results, *The Bus Project* illustrates the impossibility of foreseeing all possible outcomes in research driven by multiple agendas and cultural perspectives. Results rarely reflect the initial designs of its authors, and this can be advantageous for the creative process.

Organized under the rubric of Interdisciplinary Research, *The Bus Project* was a collaborative, media-based public art installation undertaken by theatre and intermedia artists, computer scientists, and graduate students and funded through the University of Regina in June 2004. The project offered an opportunity for academics to work across disciplines and with communities that are not usually linked.[1] Collaboration was central to the project as a means to connect scholarly research with local issues and to encourage joint approaches in an environment where single authorship is the norm.

While the research aims were multiple, the central focus of the project was to open up the idea of multiculturalism and the anxieties that have grown up around the multiple coding of this term[2] by investigating issues of immigration in the local communities of Regina and Saskatoon. In particular, the focus was on the diverse experiences of women from racial and cultural minorities and on how individuals cope with and articulate displacement in relationship to their adopted home. By focusing on the so-called "immigrant," we were also pointing to the two-facedness of Canada's multicultural policy in relationship to Aboriginal women, many of whom experience similar problems, not as a result of global economic shifts but as a result of abuse, isolation and lower self-esteem. The Canadian myth of a benevolent multicultural society imbedded in Canada's Multiculturalism Act is debunked by the fact that, historically, Native peoples were excluded from it. Karpinski writes that throughout the Act "multiculturalism emerges as a site of ideological power struggle and contestation of meanings, often polarized between traditional assimilationist, liberal pluralist, or anti-racist rhetoric" (172).

As the project moved from planning to implementation, questions around the nature of interdisciplinarity, community collaboration, and assessment also became central to the investigation. These ideas forced us to look beyond the initial research parameters and continually renegotiate our terms of reference. To provide some background, *The Bus Project* was part of a public art festival called SPASM II: The Couture of Contemporaneity, organized and curated by PAVED New Media Gallery in Saskatoon. The event was a significant one that brought together regional and national intermedia, installation, and performance artists. Invited to participate, Rachel Viader Knowles and I proposed an installation that spanned Regina and Saskatoon, two cities considered adjacent by prairie standards (275 kilometres). The venues chosen were two bus terminals, operated by the Saskatchewan Transit Company (STC), and an intercity bus. Funding was realized through the Saskatchewan Arts Board and the University of Regina, and other researchers, artists and students were brought on board as needed to assist in conceptualization, design and installation. Reflecting the disciplines of the participants, the project was simultaneously conceived of as a kind of site-specific performance/installation and as technological fieldwork.

Central themes of *The Bus Project* were displacement, leave-taking, and arrival. Conceptually, we aligned bus travel with virtual travel by enlisting the device of a video game into the public transportation network. Here the provincial bus system worked as a metaphor and a means of disseminating people and their "baggage" along the Regina-Saskatoon corridor. To highlight the actual mode of transportation and to connect the two primary locations through a third element, we installed a pair of upholstered seat covers in an intercity bus. Designed by fabric artist, Wendy Allard, using appliqué, dye, and resist, the surfaces were marked with playful and culturally significant images illustrating what migrant women might bring or leave behind. The appliqué was vibrantly coloured and textured suggesting the cultural and aesthetic value of such material objects. These seats took up the coveted front-row positions. Hence, watching the view and viewing the art (at least sitting on it) were concomitant.

Game stations, loaded with *The Bus Project* video game, were placed in the waiting areas of the Saskatoon and Regina bus terminals. Designed and built by sculptor John Reichert, they represent an abstract, non-gendered human shape and were built for durability using brushed steel. Displaying them along side rows of fast food and commodity dispensers encouraged interaction and with their tactile exterior and familiar computer screens; they attracted a steady flow of curious travellers. Our hope to install video monitors on the bus was abandoned at an earlier stage when the plan was deemed too invasive by the STC management from who we sought permission.

Upon entering the game, a player encountered a stylized road map of Saskatchewan, the main routes superimposed with exit signs representing bus stops within the province: Moose Jaw, North Battleford, Swift Current, etc. By touching the screen, the local destination dissolved into a point of origin: South Korea, New Delhi, Afghanistan, Ukraine, South Africa, Wales etc. Another touch triggered the image of a woman who recounted her arrival or departure story alternately in English and in her mother tongue. A player could choose the arrival narrative by playing the game in the Regina terminal. To hear the departure segment, the player had to become a traveller, in his or her own right, by completing the bus trip to Saskatoon and continuing the game there. Extracted from interviews with eight women affiliated with the provincial organization, Immigrant Women of Saskatchewan, their stories of choice, chance, and transformation illustrate the strength and resilience needed to confront another culture and fit in. Taken as a whole, the stories reflect and trouble the unifying rhetoric used to describe the Canadian mosaic. In opposition to this, our game plan aimed to infuse the undifferentiated idea of multicultural assimilation, Canada's unifying narrative of cultural multiplicity, with local specificities.

The placement of the game stations in the arrival and departure areas of the depots underscored the paradox of public space where private and emotional moments are frequently played out in full view of other travellers and where watching others is sometimes synonymous with the tedium of waiting. When, out of curiosity or boredom, a player approached the game station, he or she become complicit in an act of eavesdropping or witnessing highly charged, highly personal anecdotes. These, we hoped, might encourage players to empathize, compare local circumstances and consider the meaning of located identity from other perspectives.

When we initially approached the STC to discuss the project, they brushed us off by deferring our requests to higher authorities. We responded by repeatedly insisting that the STC was, in fact, a crown corporation (thus publicly owned and publicly accessible). After numerous meetings, we were finally allowed to set up the game stations and install the upholstery. While bus travellers readily accepted the presence of these devices, management representatives continued to be suspicious of our reasons for wanting to use STC property. Their primary consideration was for customer well-being and they were insistent that the game kiosks be unobtrusive and that playing the game be completely voluntary. Behind their concern, we speculated, was a fear that the central idea of the game might threaten, disturb, or subvert the "proper" activity of the bus depot. Central to this institutional anxiety were issues of race, education, and underemployment, currently front and centre in Saskatchewan, where demographics indicate a growing Aboriginal population. Here, the public transit system represents an affordable means of transport for a frequently itinerant population. The idea that a video game, addressing issues of global migration, might at best confuse or rankle, or at worst inflame was their central unspoken anxiety. Paradoxically, this was precisely the political imperative that underlined our desire to locate the game stations where we did.

Our own positions of privileged academics from the dominant culture placed us, however, in a vexed relationship in regards to our mediating role between the cultural groups. The intellectual ground that we were attempting to cultivate was a place of oppositions and paradoxes, asking questions about inclusion and exclusion. As Karpinski writes, "The principles of selection and compilation of 'representative' voices parallel the politics of multiculturalism as a site of power struggle over the definition of what constitutes Canada's commonality as a nation, a struggle often fuelled by assimilation, benign pluralist or racist tendencies" (113). The points of intersection among the women we profiled in the game and in our spectator community acknowledged a shared experience of cultural, racial and gender differences. All of these stories emphasized the women's relatively smooth transition into Canada (especially Regina) and the strong government support offered to them, underscoring how the quality of their lives had been improved by migration. Quotes from the women's narratives include, "We were very happy"; "I am here with my family; everyone is so good to me, everything is established and beautiful"; and "Happy things were coming to me."[3] These stood in stark contrast to statistics reflecting high rates of Aboriginal single mothers and children who live off-reserve and well below the poverty line.[4] Thus, we presented a multi-ethnic mix of women (Ukrainian, Russian, Korean, Indian/Hindu) not to support the notion of the Canadian mosaic but to foreground those—specifically First Nations—women who remain largely absent from the discourse of multiculturalism. While projects such as ours leave themselves open to critique around issues of misappropriation, misrepresentation and oversimplification, they also help to invigorate discussion around local situations that are frequently neglected or ignored and assist in developing models of cross-cultural encounter that are more complex and productive.

Another way of addressing the marginalization of culturally displaced women was through the location itself. The installation fit within the utilitarian aesthetic of the bus depot, a space already rich with symbolism regarding these issues. As a place of leave-taking and arriving, it is full of potential; as a border crossing marking "home and away," it is a place where identities are questioned. In this environment, seats are hard and do not invite relaxation, a video camera surveys the area, and fluorescent lights are harsh. The television is tuned to all-news or all-sports channels.

The bus depot is, superficially, a male space, wholly characterized by an absence of female indicators. Thus, the insistence of a women's perspective, inserted through digitalized narratives and the reworking of the serviceable bus seats with handcrafted seat covers, was incongruous, ambiguous and compelling. As Elizabeth Wilson writes in *The Sphinx and the City*, what women's presence represents in a controlled, rational male environment is feeling, sexuality, and chaos (87). Within the schedule-bound atmosphere of the bus depot, the women's voices were also dislocating and threatening. Their stories illustrated that identity formation is not fixed or static, illustrating Stuart Hall's description of identity: "identities are never completed, never finished; [...] they are always, as subjectivity itself, in process" (47). Within the context of the bus depot, the narratives suggested alternative perspectives, inviting a reconsideration of spatiality that blurred the binaries of private/public, personal/political, male/female. The depot became an "identity space" where notions of "selfhood" and "worldhood" might be addressed, where issues of race and gender might be considered the norm (Friedman 76). In the process, the space shifted from performing one function to performing multiple functions: as news spread, people called in to inquire about the arrival time of the upholstered bus. In other words, the stations could be seen as provisional galleries or theatres—spaces of reciprocity and interactivity.

What role did technology play in this project? In the rampant drive towards a totally tech-supported lifestyle in which BlackBerries proliferate and cell phones provide fingertip access to the internet, the use of the bus signalled a relatively "low tech" option of communication. The role of technology here was to interrupt the routine of bus travel and create an interface for the traveller that offered a more random and ludic trip around the province than the one on which he or she would normally embark. In the video mapping game, each mundane destination became a portal to an alternative world. The strategy was, to a degree, inspired by current experiments in algorithmic psychogeography in which the notion of the random stroll or drift is elaborated into a systematic practice codified into set patterns. The arbitrariness of the experience, the desire to satisfy one's curiosity about what is around the next corner, is key to the psychogeographic experience, and we wanted the same gentle pleasure of discovery to be part of the video game.[5]

While the game was used to provide a menu of playful possibilities for defining personal routes/roots, it also engaged with the traditional content of the video game. Typically in game environments, one encounters only virtual presences, ciphers or cyborgs engaged in often violent or aggressive activity. Embedding "real" people in the game posed questions not only about the conventional representation of virtual space but about the veracity of the stories told there. Does this game represent a world where such stories are verifiable or are they merely staged? Do I, as the player, empathize with these women or do I merely play the game? These questions are indeed critical for trying to understand the nature of spectator response to the immigrant narratives imbedded in the game stations. While the project cast "immigrant women" as participants, they were, of course, not simply defined by this designation. One of the women was an actress, two were intermedia artists, one was raising children and one seeking employment; all were aware of the mediating camera and their own ability to manipulate it to optimal effect. Each was asked to tell a story, not necessarily adhering to the facts; embroidering was allowed, even encouraged. Each was videoed against carefully chosen backgrounds, the lighting was controlled, several takes were done, and the stories written and edited by the women themselves. In post-production, certain words and phrases ("coming home," "I was lonely," "lost") were extracted and superimposed graphically across the screen, in comic book style. In other words, a performance was created that recalled other performative forms such as storytelling, documentary, and reality television. The level of veracity that first-person narratives assume shifts according to the nature of the media that frames the event. While news broadcast and documentaries strive for a level of authenticity, video games by no means attempt to make such claims; and the apparent incongruity might, I suggest, destabilize the experience of the viewer in productive ways and encourage a questioning of the language frequently employed to describe multicultural policy in Canada.

In the relative scale of technology-supported entertainment, *The Bus Project* was not a grand event. Part theatre performance, part installation, part research, it attempted to address local issues of race, gender, and immigration in a compelling and ambiguous way to a non-conventional audience. In doing so, it reassigned meaning in a place of prescribed activity and encouraged spectators to situate their immediate surroundings in a local/global context of interlocking networks and immigration patterns, where migrancy is the result not of choice, but of economic and political contingencies.

Too frequently, the spaces where we live and work are overly commercialized and controlled. Within these spaces debate and dissent are neutralized. Perhaps, the overarching achievement of *The Bus Project* was recognizing that public art can engage people in innovative ways and can challenge, in the process, conventional notions of appropriate time and place. It recognized that we live in a highly mobile society that engages in both low-tech and high-tech systems of communication and that these can be harnessed as metaphors to stimulate contemplation, conversation, and debate about the communities we inhabit. As well, it underlined the essential role that such performative events play in building and sustaining an urban community by foregrounding diversity and showing how single stories may overshadow multiple powerful narratives.

In dramaturgical terms, there are, of course, many differences between *The Bus Project* and *KÀ*, and the way each structures form and content is subject to discrete rules and traditions. I use the example of *KÀ* to illustrate how technology, however much it pushes the envelope, often merely supports performance as spectacle, appealing to a viewer who has learned over generations how to decode the work its form. Technologically enhanced entertainments such as *The Bus Project*'s game environment illustrate how the two-way communication of the conventional theatre is now joined by the operation of new interactive processes. The latter is defined by operating instructions and user rules that must be learned on the basis of new metaphors. Heide Hageblling writes,

> [...] the network among user groups that online media creates opens additional dimensions of exchange and competition on an extremely abstract level. In addition to the development of contents and characters or avatars, these programs are chiefly concerned with the development of a conception of dramaturgic rules that, in an open multi-user system independent of time and location, provides a binding operational context for an unknown user community and also wins their acceptance. Communication in these systems is defined by a high degree of anonymity and abstraction that practically presupposes the formation of interculturally acceptable metaphors and codes. (2–3)

This kind of interactivity anticipates an active participant whose ability to read the event is based on choices, interruptions, and jumps that distinguish individual communication from a more linear reception that takes place in groups. *KÀ* does little to redefine audience perceptions or shake up existing and sedimented attitudes and ideologies. This is illustrated by its conformity to a liberal pluralist discourse of global multiculturalism characterized by a levelling of difference and an aesthetic of homogenization. The cast of *KÀ*, representing a diversity of races and cultures, suggests a unified global community; its narrative based on a legend of "the conflict and love, of imperial twins who are separated at the prime of their youth and have to undergo the rite of passage of self discovery" (Lepage) might spring from any number of traditions. The show is marketed as a perception-changing experience that has the potential, through the extraordinary technology used to package it, to transform social perceptions—a faulty claim, indeed.

If the technology in Cirque du Soleil's *KÀ* does not redefine audience perception and cognitively engage the spectator in provocative ways, does *The Bus Project* come any closer to realizing this lofty goal? In considering community-based art practices, Lucy Lippard claims "[t]o affect perception itself, we need to apply ideas as well as forms to the ways in which people see and act within and on their surroundings" (286). She argues that the challenge of redefining perception is best addressed by reaching out to participant communities and marginalized audiences by whatever means possible and "allowing the art idea to become, finally, part of the social multicentre rather than an elite enclave." Reaching out in this way will inevitably result in crossing perceived boundaries and exploring new territories. Here the notion of "actual place" is fundamental. She suggests that shifts in perception are achieved when a work engages spectators on the level of their own lived experience; is collaborative to the extent that information, advice and feedback is sought from the community in which the work is realized; is generous and open-ended enough to be accessible to a variety of people from different classes and cultures; is appealing enough to engage the imagination; is simple and familiar enough on the surface not to confuse or repel; is complex enough to offer layers of experience to those who participate on different levels; is evocative enough to jog memory and emotions; and is provocative and critical enough to make people consider issues beyond the scope of the work. Most importantly, the event that successfully redefines audience perception is unobtrusive; it differs least from the space in which it is situated (Lippard 286). In the example of *The Bus Project*, it was, effectively, the technology that enabled us to locate the installation in the inhospitable environment of the bus depot and, in so doing, embrace a new spectator constituency.[6]

In the end, having overcome their initial distrust, the Saskatchewan Transportation Company wholeheartedly endorsed the project and opened the door to further collaborations with the arts community. In the process, they redefined the bus depot not merely as a place of arrivals and departures but as "art space" and "identity space." This was in itself a positive research outcome. For those of us involved in the project, our final assessment of the work was more ambivalent. Initially the project aimed to investigate representational strategies in non-traditional spaces, engage diverse spectatorships, and consider how technology might support the universal aims of conjoined research. Inevitably, in assessing the project, there arose other issues that merited consideration. While collaboration broadens a work's intertextual scope, the nature of this work is chaotic and inconclusive. The process of intersecting with multiple partners and constituent communities is, in many ways, as important as are the quantifiable and visible results. Where people and ideas meet and chafe are the defining sites of research, the "excess" that is never intentional and can never be planned for nor repeated. This tumultuous process is not easy to negotiate: the big picture is never available to everyone at the same time. For this reason, end results are difficult to evaluate by traditional yardsticks and are often disregarded as lacking merit. While intentions alone are not an accurate or definitive indicator of merit, they do suggest contexts and criteria useful for evaluation. They are important indicators of the values and meanings the artists/researchers attach to their work. Results-based evaluation does not take into account the multiple, sometimes unconscious, levels on which much art and community-based projects operate.

Within the academy, stringent criteria are placed on the evaluation process, yet this process is discipline-specific. While a project of this nature ideally exhibits the richness and depth that results from diverse input, at the same time its very hybridity makes it difficult to assess by such standards. In scientific or academic terms, the question begging to be asked is, "Are the goals of interdisciplinarity best served when individuals retreat to their own disciplines to assess and measure results or should a new model be considered?" In artistic terms, the question begging to be asked is, "Is it art and, if so, in what category should it be classified, critiqued and funded?" Any assessment must ultimately ask the question, "Is the work a substantial and meaningful addition to the cultural, social or scientific sphere?" In the case of multidisciplinary projects, a way of considering these questions may eventually be found in assessing, to the degree possible, the range of experiences and outcomes available to the wide spectrum of individuals who participated in or viewed the work. If intentionality is used as one yardstick for attributing merit, then it must also be understood that, in such events, there is an excess of meaning well beyond that intended or imagined by the authors at the outset, and this may itself exemplify a successful outcome.

In order to discuss the changing platform of performance and entertainment practices, I have attempted to weave several disparate threads: new performative technologies, community-oriented practices, and interdisciplinary methodology. For artists and researchers who deal with visual representation and audience perception and who look to technology for future directions, these considerations and the hurdles they present constitute ongoing sites of inquiry. This juncture marks, Richard Loveless writes,

> a most significant moment in time for performing arts and technology. [...] [O]ur challenge is to imagine a future for the arts that extends well beyond the human imagination that has shaped them in our lifetime. No matter what the time or place of our birth during the first half of this century, we all arrived as analogue babies, enriched and yet encumbered by traditions in the arts that were formed by a myriad of cultures. These traditions gave way to new trends, and in time were embraced by the immigration patterns that formed our nations. The last half of the century is another story; the new arrivals are digital babies. (283)

The challenge is to understand and use technologies to support innovation that breaks down boundaries between disciplines and communities and makes art and performance available to new audiences in untested places. Technology is pervasive, ubiquitous and can facilitate and support a range of creative and provocative activities in places normally considered purely functional, single-use and too "local" for broader consideration. Such approaches to place and space concern the conceptualization of the spatial in terms of social relations. Doreen Massey writes that

> [t]he spatial spread of social relations can be intimately local or expansively global or anything in between. [...] [T]here is no getting away from the fact that social is inexorably spatial. [...] "Space" is created out of the vast intricacies, the incredible complexities, of the interlocking and non-interlocking, and the networks of scale from local to global. (265)

An example of how this technology is being explored is seen in international networks like PLAN (Pervasive and Locative Arts Network) that consider the broader question that technology opens up: "what kinds of creative, social, economic and political expression become possible when every device we carry, the fabric of the urban environment and even the contours of the Earth become a digital canvas? (PLAN). A new generation of pervasive technologies is enabling artists in every discipline to break away from traditional desktop computers and games consoles and experience interactive media that are directly embedded into the world around them. For example, students at the School of Art in Utrecht studying Game Design and Development are trained to work in a multidisciplinary game team in such a way that the playability of a game reaches a high level, on both virtual and real-life platforms, and the game finds ways to include actual audiences. Such events are a hybrid of traditional performance and the gaming environment and are, by no means, unique experiences.

Looking to the future, new fields of interdisciplinary research foregrounding the use of pervasive technology and locative media will support experiences and social interaction that respond to a participant's physical location and context. Together these convergent fields raise possibilities for new cultural experiences in areas as diverse as performance, installations, games, tourism, heritage, marketing, and education. Many of these projects combine practicing artists and technology developers whose early research has frequently been delivered as public artworks or performances that have yielded new insights into the ways in which audiences experience technology. These are strategies that interrogate the very terms and conditions of the conventional audience and may, indeed, reshape the perception of digital babies.

(2008)

Notes

1 Kathleen Irwin, site-based scenographer; Rachelle Viader Knowles, inter-media artist; Daryl Hepting, computer scientist, and students form each area were involved in the project. These included Maki Nagisa (Theatre), Isabel da Silva (Intermedia), and Melissa Buhler (Computer Science). The women who shared their stories were Teressa Oliinik, Palwaha Humayun, Slava Gottselig, Neelhu Sachdev, Isabel da Silva, and Maki Nagisa.

2 In her essay "Multi-cultural 'Gift(s)'" Eva C. Karpinski writes that multiculturalism in Canada, since its introduction into public discourse by Pierre Trudeau in 1971, "has been constructed as a demographic fact, institutionalized as policy, and variously deployed as rhetoric. [...] Significantly a greater openness to a 'multicultural climate' coincides with the turn towards postmodernism and post-colonialism, traditionally seen as marked by the demise of unifying narratives of history; the

aesthetics of political mobilization of the oppressed peoples. As a discursive construct parallel to postmodernism, multiculturalism, too, is caught up in many contradictions and completing claims that have been played out in the shifting dialectic of resistance and celebration" (11).

3 These comments were collected from interviews conducted by student researchers, Isabel da Silva, Maki Nagisa and Melissa Buhler from interviews conducted with Teressa Oliinik, Palwasha Humayun, Slava Gottselig, and Neelu Sachdev. The specific dates and specific attribution of the comments is no longer available.

4 In October 2000, the Ontario Federation of Indian Friendship Centres (OFIFC) released a report titled *Urban Aboriginal Child Poverty Background.* The report cites some alarming statistics that reveal the extent of the problem: 52.1% of all Aboriginal children are poor; 12% of Aboriginal families are headed by parents under the age of 25 years; 27% of Aboriginal families are headed by single mothers; 40% of single Aboriginal mothers earn less than $12,000 per year; 47.2% of the Ontario Aboriginal population receives less than $10,000 per year; and, Aboriginal people have a disability rate that is more than twice the national average. The distinct nature of Aboriginal child and family poverty in Canada is rooted in cultural fragmentation, multi-generational effects of residential schools, wardship through the child welfare system, and socio-economic marginalization. For reasons none other than "being Aboriginal," Aboriginal people have, for generations, grown up poor.

5 Psychogeography can be broadly defined as the study of how physical surroundings affect mood and behaviour. It is documented on websites and blogs and described as a contemporary, site-specific practice that combines art and political activism with the agreeable pastime of walking, particularly for those who like to "stroll, drift and wander simply for the pleasure of turning the next corner" (Glowlab).

6 While this claim is speculative, it is a fair assumption that many STC clients do not participate in mainstream theatre where single-ticket prices at Regina's regional theatre, the Globe, range from $30–$35 and the season line-up generally appeals to a middle-class, white demographic. In the example of *The Bus Project*, no such barrier prohibited involvement in the event and the engagement level was observed to be high.

Works Cited

"Bus Project, The." 22 February 2009. http://uregina.ca/Bus_Project/busproject.html.

Friedman, Jonathan. *Cultural Identity and Global Process.* London: Sage, 1994.

Glowlab. *Shuffle – Psychogeography with a Deck of Cards and Your Own Two Feet.* 19 April 2005. www.glowlab.com./shuffle_about.html.

Hagebölling, Heide. *Interactive Dramaturgies: New Approaches in Multimedia Content and Design.* Berlin: Springer, 2004.

Hall, Stuart, "Old and New Identities, Old and New Ethnicities." *Culture, Globalization and World Systems: Contemporary Conditions for the Representation of Identity.* Ed. Anthony D. King. Binghamton, NY: Dept. of Art and Art History, State University of New York at Binghamton, 1991. 51–68.

Karpinski, Eva C. "Multi-cultural 'Gift(s)': Immigrant Women's Life Writing and the Politics of Anthologizing Difference." *Literary Pluralities.* Ed. Christl Verduyn. Peterborough: Broadview, 1998. 111–24.

Robert Lepage (KÀ Creator). *KÀ EXTREME* [DVD]. Quebec, Canada: Productions Conte Inc., 2005.

Lippard, R. Lucy. *The Lure of the Local: Senses of Place in a Multicentered Society.* New York: New Press, 1997.

Loveless, Richard. "Time Past … Time Present … Time Future: Re-Envisioning the Aesthetic in Research for Human Performance." *The Routledge Reader in Politics and Performance.* Ed. Lizbeth Goodman and Jane de Gay. London: Routledge, 2000. 283–87.

Massey, Doreen. *Space, Place and Gender.* Minneapolis, U of Minneapolis P, 1994.

Ontario Federation of Indian Friendship Centres. *Urban Aboriginal Child Poverty Background.* Report. October, 2000.

Plan (Pervasive and Locative Arts Network). "Context Weblog: Sampling New Cultural Context." 6 December 2007. http://straddle3.net/context/03/en/2005_01_28.html. April 10, 2005. http://www.open-plan.org.

Posner, Michael. "Reinventing the Cirque du Soleil Spectacular." *The Globe and Mail,* 5 February 2005, Western Edition: R12.

Wilson, Elizabeth. *The Sphinx in the City: Urban Life, the Control of Disorder, and Women.* Berkeley: U of California P, 1991.

Editorial Note

For photos of the kiosk, see illustrations 22–23 (74).

Michael Levine: Tracing the Moments of Scenographic Dramaturgy

by Natalie Rewa

Michael Levine is a production designer based in Toronto who has been designing set and costumes for opera and theatre in Canada and internationally since the late 1980s. He was the production designer for the *Ring* cycle mounted by the Canadian Opera Company (2004–06), collaborating with three different directors and making his own director-designer debut. He has worked at the Paris National Opera, the English National Opera, The Metropolitan Opera, Glyndebourne as well as with companies in Amsterdam, Vienna, Chicago, and Tokyo. He has collaborated with director Robert Carsen, a fellow Canadian, in over a dozen opera productions as well as with opera and theatre director Tim Albery and film and opera directors François Girard and Atom Egoyan. For Complicité, a movement company in London, he has contributed scenographies for two devised works—*Mnemonic* (1999) and *The Elephant Vanishes* (2003), inspired by the collection of short stories by the same name by Haruki Murakami. In Canada he has also designed productions for the Shaw Festival (1984–87), Tarragon (1985, 1987) and Soulpepper (1999, 2001) Theatres.

Striking in his design work is an attitude to stage space as an active and dynamic player in the performance. His organization of space and consciousness of lighting design are integral to the choreography of the performance and his disposition of individual elements provides a restrained and articulate visual vocabulary. His artistic process is marked by meticulous attention to the human presence on the stage and so his design substantially shapes the production. Initial discussions with a director progress to a scale model, and his presence at rehearsals as well as in the construction workshops crafts the visual narrative of the performance. It is of interest to the discussion of design and scenography how Michael Levine moves between the two foci—one on the specific object being designed, and the other how it will contribute to the overall narrative.

On September 24th, 2008 Michael Levine paused amid design commitments to discuss the specific form of dramaturgy that his work as designer takes. The conversation focused on identifying moments in the processes of collaboration with a director when his contribution becomes most specifically dramaturgical. The examples presented here are chosen from his recent work: *Candide* (Châtelet 2006), *The Elephant Vanishes* (Complicité 2003) and *Madame Butterfly* (English National Opera 2005), and *The Coronation of Poppea* (Glyndebourne 2008).

Natalie Rewa: Your process of framing the production often consists in doing so literally by selected elements which contribute to a gestural or choreographic expression so that the actors/singers perform in an environment that is itself articulate. Often you provide the audience with an opportunity to meditate upon the space and perceive it at another pace in relation to the progress of the production, as a total volumetric environment.

Candide

Michael Levine: I like to work inside the stage, and designers can't help that—they are spatially in charge. In *Candide* the imagery began with the 1950s television set, so the imagery collected on the side of the frame were knobs of an early television set. All this imagery of 1950s television was interpreted a little like a Las Vegas stage receding upstage. It was this very strong conceptual idea that shaped the project from the start.

In this case the production design shaped the essence of the production, because the story takes place all over the place—there is a voyage and travelling to several places. When Robert [Carsen] and I met we wanted the voyage to be much more: *Candide* is a satire, it would have been a satire when Voltaire wrote it originally, but now taken out of its context—it is very hard to write about the kings and the political situation in Voltaire's time. Why should we care about Voltaire's time? It holds resonances and we wanted to update it somehow, to make it about our time, and about optimism. Ultimately one thing that *Candide* is about is optimism. One of the things that we talked about, because it's set in many places, is the way in which we view TV now, the way we view cataclysmic events. In *Candide* there are cataclysmic events and people keep coming back to life. TV is one of the ways in which our society experiences such big events. The TV is the perfect example of how television was something that shaped the production.

The Elephant Vanishes

ML: In opera it is possible that a design shapes the production physically on some level; it's possible in opera where you work so far in advance because it has to be built; on other productions I do not take the lead, the lead is taken by the production and I follow that lead. For projects such as *The Elephant Vanishes* with Complicité the design comes out of rehearsals and what the actors are doing and my observation of that. This design was me responding to the needs of a production in a different way—physically trying to support what was taking place in the rehearsal room; it is not me trying to impose a physical sense.

With *The Elephant Vanishes* we started with nothing and the actors came up with something. There was a ten-day rehearsal period. The actors, out of their improvisations had worked out certain scenes, I observed these and saw the bits that they had worked out and the objects that they were working with. Then there was a day when, in the process of working out this project, we were able to set up in the theatre and I thought it would be interesting to use a couple of moving things that the actors were already working towards. Afterwards I made the physical things and we brought them into the rehearsal room. The actors were able to use them, to take them a step further. The objects in this production originated from within the rehearsal and I could take them and refine them.

The use of screens is a good example. The shoji screen[1] was an interesting object that we put on wheels in the rehearsal room, then the shoji screen developed into a moving glass door because it was more modern, and then we introduced the televisions, flying televisions screens, into the rehearsal room and these became an integral part of the show. The stage evolved out of our looking at Japan, trying to make a version of Japan that was related to modern Japan, and one derived from Haruki Murakami. We were borrowing little aspects without putting Japan on stage: Japan is full of fluorescent lighting everywhere and there are wires overhead, every street you go down there are wires running from building to building: these are physical aspects of Japan. For movement of the shoji screens, and the glass doors as well as the televisions, we used wires strung across the stage and this was all roughed together in the rehearsal room. From this work in the rehearsal room I then built a model and then they built the production based on that, and so, when the actors got on stage the transition was not extreme. This is a different process.

Madame Butterfly

ML: The design for *Madame Butterfly* was a reflection of the needs of the production plus, I would say, that the design shaped the production to a certain extent because by making a box of tricks it meant that the production acted in a certain way—behaved in a certain way. It is a good example of the melding of design and direction in an unusual way in that it was an overlap on both sides, in that the design was a reflection of the space without actually being the space, and then there were aspects of the design that shaped the production. Anthony Minghella was very interested in the mechanics of Japanese theatre and wanted somehow that *Madame Butterfly* reflect that. By mechanics, Minghella meant Bunraku theatre, where the operators are present on stage. He had done a little workshop just playing around with ideas that he was considering around the production. One which was central was to use a puppet instead of a child and he wanted to see if that worked. In a workshop production that I came to see, they were working with the child as a puppet, but were also able to manipulate other things on stage within the production. So then I went away with the understanding that he wanted to develop quite a lot of the production in rehearsal. Ultimately, he was directing his first opera and he had this idea that the production was going to come out of rehearsal but, in fact that is very difficult to do; you can't build the set overnight, there is a lot you have to preplan. So when I went back I thought it would be very interesting to create, to set up, an environment, where we could manifest, if we wanted to, an environment right away and take it away immediately, but that could also be manipulated by the players on the stage. So that you could make the house in Japan, but it could also disappear and so that was my brief. There is actually a cue in the libretto when Goro explains to Pinkerton that all the walls can move and disappear.

I thought it would be interesting where he could have an environment where he could play, where he could make the production come to life on stage: so that we could make the room, get rid of the room; a child could be a puppet, in this environment, (that's not so easy in a naturalistic environment where you can't have a puppet wandering around). In Bunraku theatre, there is realistic scenery, but you are always aware of the playing, so I thought we should take a page from that, and in the production there would be all these people moving the scenery.

In the end the actors did not move the scenery, but it was as if they were in this kind of environment, as if they were puppets. There were actual manipulators who were around and manipulating the set so we were able to get the environment with a minimal structure, and he was able to create whatever environment he wanted and it meant that it could change up to the last minute.

This design gave them the freedom not to be restricted by physical confines of a house on stage. So we could have a house one minute and the next it would be gone and we could be somewhere else or we could also put a smaller house on stage, just by bringing on fewer screens—which we did in the second act, when she is abandoned—just a few screens, just a corner of a house. It gave him a lot of freedom to play with everything and the production came together in a similar way. The lighting designer Peter Mumford had lights that moved up and down on flybars on the sides and these became another character, another manipulator in the piece. The lights would move with the action—higher or lower. The stage became a kind of black box with doors that opened to let the light come in. So this work was a reflection of what came out of the workshop and a desire to satisfy the needs of the director plus this hybrid idea of a Japanese theatre telling of this Western opera.

In performance it is the manipulators who signify the production. At the beginning the mirror comes into play. It starts off when two manipulators come out and pull on the cords that raise a big mirror. The mirror opens in silence and Butterfly comes in over a mirrored rise upstage and then the music starts. With the mirror suspended up above, it became a way of extending the scenes behind the screens. So if someone was asleep on the floor in the house, you could see her while downstage people were talking about her. It gave a sense of what was happening around there.

NR: When did the dramaturgy begin and end?

ML: It started off in a different way from other productions. I started off with the idea of making something that was a kind of magic box, that came directly from his workshop. I made a little model and Anthony came to discuss it and we played around with the idea of the rooms, and different shoji mats rooms. I started looking at floors, screens moving in floors, and then Anthony took the floor and tilted it, and I took the floor and curled it and these were the different things that came from those meetings. He wanted to get a sense of height, somehow of her coming over the mountain (as it says in the opera), and we originally did not have a slope, and he wanted to get a sense of coming down into a higher plane. Originally the mirror did not open and there was no staircase and then we built these in and things started to develop in that way.

In the rehearsal room they also worked with the shoji screens. In one scene a screen is brought in front of Butterfly and actually behind the screen is Pinkerton, whom we don't see as he walks on the stage, but once Butterfly leaves, Pinkerton is left on the stage. The moment is like the memory of her. This scene came directly out of providing the screen to the rehearsal room. Other scenes developed in rehearsals too. There was a scene with birds, and we developed bird puppets. The mirror on the floor became very important when it comes into play. At first the mirror opens in silence as Butterfly comes over the top of it, then the music starts, and then there is a whole scene about preparing Butterfly for her wedding. This Butterfly is a dancer, and as she comes over the mirror she has four long strips of silk in which she wrapped on stage—it is like a cocoon. It is a beautiful moment.

We also cut things. One of the things that we said early on would be really nice, would be a stage full of cherry blossoms, and we ended up not having them in the production. During rehearsals I continued sketching while they continued with their work on the production and then we would meet to play with these ideas.

The creation of these objects such as the shoji screens are an example of refining an object for the performers. We wanted the screens to stand up on their own and so had to devise how to engineer them. The first attempts to make them used plexiglass with paper stuck on it, then we tried canvas but that was still too heavy to achieve the effect we wanted. Finally we stretched cloth on a frame and glued paper to it so that we made this light structure that was so light that it could really glide well and the manipulators could push them and they would slide across the floor. It is never sufficient to hand in the designs, my work as a designer is carrying things through to performance—to make them work—in this case to give the screens lightness and movement. It gives joy to the audience of the object and its material qualities.

The Coronation of Poppea

ML: This production raises many technical questions and is an example of the gap that appears between the conceptual idea and carrying the production into the theatre. The design came through discussions with Robert Carsen, the director, and the sense of what we wanted the production of *The Coronation of Popea* to be—it was not that we wanted it to be set in Rome, but to be a reflection of what the opera is about. When we moved into the theatre we were confronted with the technical aspect of the production and in that sense it is a good example.

We had conceived the production around the idea that we were "in" Amore's theatre: the opera is about a battle of three gods: Virtù, Fortune and Amore and Amore wins in the end. The performance was going to start with (which it did) an argument between Virtù and Fortune in the auditorium; the two start fighting and make their way to the stage, as if they were two members of the Glyndebourne public who have an argument and end up on stage. Amore confronts the two of them and claims victory in the argument because love is what wins out in the day. As she does so she pulls down the front curtain and on the stage we find another audience—a representation of the Glyndebourne audience who are now watching the audience in the auditorium. The key to the production was that this onstage audience was going to be transfixed by Amore who was going to take them through the production and they were going to become Amore's slaves. So that was the idea that we discussed and it was to be based on a design idea in which the onstage audience would follow Amore off the stage. For this, I had designed chairs for the onstage audience that were going to slide off stage, so that this mechanism would free this audience to follow Amore. When we got to into the production, because of budgetary reasons, we had to cut the chairs sliding and that raised an interesting question…

When we got onto the stage, and into that week of rehearsals on the stage, we realized that without the possibility of the chairs sliding off stage there was an enormous problem since the conception had been that the audience would have a very clear understanding that the onstage audience was transfixed by Amore. So by not having the chairs slide away, it meant that the scene became about people moving chairs, rather than following Amore transfixed off the stage. That's a very good example of a conceptual idea that doesn't come to full realization because of the practicalities of working in a theatre and how a design is based in a dramaturgical idea, rather than a naturalistic idea or sense of some sort of portraying space.

(2009)

Note

1 A shoji screen is a translucent Oriental screen made of a wood frame and rice paper, often used as a room divider.

Work Cited

Murakami, Haruki. *The Elephant Vanishes.* Trans. Alfred Birnbaum and Jay Rubin. New York; Vintage, 1994.

Editorial Note

For photos of *Candide* and *Madame Butterfly*, and a drawing from Levine's sketchbook for *Candide*, see illustrations 24–26 (74–76).

Suggested Further Reading

Adams, Stephen. "An Audience of the Trees: R. Murray Schafer's *The Princess of the Stars*." *Canadian Theatre Review* 96 (1998): 44–49.

Armstrong, Robert. "Designers by Design." *Theatrum* 30 (1992): 10–11.

———. "The Levine/Lepage Connection." *Theatrum* 32 (1993): 8–9.

Arnott, Brian. "Scene from All Sides – on the Liberation of Scene Design." *Scene Changes* 6 (1978): 4–5.

———. "Artists not Craftspeople: Interview with Susan Benson." *Canadian Theatre Review* 33 (1982): 30–39.

Aronson, Arnold. *Looking into the Abyss*. Ann Arbor: U of Michigan P, 2005.

Bachelard, Gaston. *The Poetics of Space*. Trans. Maria Jolas. Boston: Beacon, 1969.

Baugh, Christopher. *Theatre Performance and Technology: The Development of Scenography in the Twentieth Century*. Basingstoke: Palgrave Macmillan, 2005.

Beauchamp, Hélène. "Theatre Production for Young Audiences in Quebec." *Canadian Theatre Review* 70 (1992): 15–19.

———. "Scenography as it Stands/The Stands of Scenography." *Canadian Theatre Review* 71 (1992): 37–41.

Beaupre, Therese. *Theatre Design Explorations/Scénographie au Canada*. Toronto: Associated Designers of Canada, 1979.

———. "VideoCabaret: form of Protest." *Canadian Theatre Review* 26 (1980): 44–57.

Black, Jean Charles. *Plain and Fancy: A Manual on Costume Design*. Toronto: Theatre Ontario, 1980.

Bleeker, Maaike. *Visuality in the Theatre: The Locus of Looking*. Basingstoke: Palgrave Macmillan, 2008.

Borboën, Véronique and Natalie Rewa, eds. *Quadriennale de Prague 2007, De L'Idée au dessin: Les Traces au processus créateur/Prague Quadrennial 2007: Imprints of Process*. Montréal: Association des professionnels des arts de la scène du Québec (APASQ), 2008.

Bourriaud, Nicolas. *Relational Aesthetics*. Dijon-Quetigny: Les Presses du Réel, 2002.

Bouzek, Don. "Industrials for the Social Services." *Canadian Theatre Review* 99 (1999): 10–15.

Brown, Ross. "The Art of Sound Design: Real and Imaginary Soundscapes." *TD&T* 37.3 (2001): 38–43.

———. "The Theatre Soundscape and the End of Noise." *Performance Research* 10.4 (2005): 105–19.

Burgess, David. "The Greatest Show: Schafer's Patria Three: The Cycle Continues." *Canadian Theatre Review* 55 (1988): 34–42.

Burrows, Malcolm. "Tectonic Plates. Bridging the Continental Drift." *Canadian Theatre Review* 55 (1988): 43–47.

Burton, Rebecca. *Adding it Up: The Status of Women in Canadian Theatre.* Canada Council for the Arts, 2006.

Carpenter, Edmund and Marshall McLuhan. "Acoustic Space." *Canadian Theatre Review* 6 (1975); 46–49.

Christianson, Jonathan and Bretta Gerecke. "Destination Unknown: A Director Designer Dialogue." *Canadian Theatre Review* 119 (2004); 24–29.

Christilles, Dennis and Delbert Unruh, "The Semiotics of Action Design." *Theatre Topics* 6.2 (1996): 121–41.

Chua, Derek, "The Spirit of China Lives in Canadian Theatre." *Canadian Theatre Review* 110 (2002): 16–19.

Clunes, Amaya. "Spaces of Scenography." *Canadian Theatre Review* 91 (1997): 25–32.

Copeland, Darren. "Associative Listening." *Soundsacpe: The Journal of Acoustic Ecology* 1.1 (2000): 23–26.

———. "Outside the Black Box: Sound Design in Non-theatre Contexts." *Canadian Theatre Review* 129 (2007): 48–50.

Cooper, John, "When the Canvas Isn't Blank: An Interview with Marsha Sibthorpe." *Canadian Theatre Review* 107 (2001): 26–31.

Court, Paul. "New Technology, New Technicians and an Ancient Art." *Canadian Theatre Review* 131 (2007): 40–44.

Dean, Anthony. "Of Speaking Pictures and Mute Poetry: Intersection of Dramaturgy and Scenography." *Theatre Design Research* 1 (2002): 37–44.

Doherty, Tom. "Recognizing the Designer." *Canadian Theatre Review* 33 (1982): 40–43.

Dolgoy, Sholem. "Lighting: Untapped Potential." *Canadian Theatre Review* 33 (1982): 26–29.

Doolitle, Joyce. "Ronnie Burkett: Bad Boy: *Awful Manors*." *Theatrum* 28 (1992): 21–22.

Eagan, Michael. "Defining a National Scenographic Style at the National Theatre School of Canada." *Canadian Theatre Review* 91 (1997): 22–24.

Eynat-Confino and Eva Soromova. *Space and the Postmodern Stage.* Prague; Ekon, 2000.

Feheley, David. "The Canadian Opera Company's *Wozzeck* Fourteen Years Later." *Canadian Theatre Review* 131 (2007): 45–48.

Ferrington, Gary. "Keep Your Ear Lids Open." *Journal of the International Visual Literacy Association* 14.2 (1994): 51–61.

Filewod, Alan. "The Face of Re-enactment." *Canadian Theatre Review* 121 (2005): 9–15.

Foreman, Kathleen. "Transforming Traditions: *Commedia dell'arte* and masQuirx (Contemporary Mask Performance)." *Canadian Theatre Review* 104 (2000): 93–97.

Gallery Stratford. *Susan Benson Artist/Designer.* Stratford: The Gallery Stratford, 1989.

Garebian, Keith. "Casting Light on Stage Narrative." *Theatrum* 39 (1994):13–17.

Gravestock, Steve. "Notes from the Underground: Music and Theatre in New Combinations." *Theatrum* 42 (1995): 18–21.

Grey, Susan. "Set Up: How Quebec Scenographers Have Caught Our Eye." *Theatrum* 32 (1993): 17–20.

Hogg, David, A. "Theatre of Actualities." *Masses* 1.1 (1932): np.

Holdar, Magdalena. *Scenography in Action: Space Time and Movement in Theatre Productions by Ingmar Bergman.* Stockholm: Konsvetenskapliga institutionen vid Stockholms universitet, 2006.

Hood, Hugh. "Murray Laufer and the Art of Scenic Design." *Artscanada* 29 (1972–73): 59–64.

Hood, Sarah B. "Mas Appeal: The Influence of Carnival on Toronto Theatre." *Theatrum* 24 (1991): 20–24.

———. "Ritual ABUSE: The Urge for and the Effects of Re-ritualizing the Theatre." *Theatrum* 30 (1992): 18–23.

Howard, Pamela. *What is Scenography?* London: Routledge, 2002.

———. "Locked Doors and Hidden Secrets: Exploring Cultural Identities through Fernande de Rojas' *La Celestina.*" *Theatre Design Research* 1 (2002): 7–16.

Howard, Ruth. "Holding On and Letting Go: Designing the Community Play." *Canadian Theatre Review* 90 (1997): 15–19.

———. "The Aesthetics of Including Everyone: Use of Multiple Languages and South Riverdale Lives and Legends." *alt.theatre* 2.2 (2002): 12–13.

Hume, Charles. "The Apprenticeship Program of Associated Designers of Canada: Charles Hume in Conversation with Bill Corcoran, Laura Lisowsky, and Arun, Srinivasan." *Canadian Theatre Review* 91 (1997): 37–40.

Hunt, Nigel. "Taking Note: Making Music for New Drama: A Forum with David Akal Jaggs, Allen Cole and Lesley Barber." *Theatrum* 22(1991): 10–15.

Irwin, Kathleen and Mark Kristmanson. "Uses and Abuses of Cultural Diplomacy." *Canadian Theatre Review* 85 (1995): 71–74.

Irwin, Kathleen and John Poulson. "The Site's The Thing: The Shifting and Expanding Role of the Site Specific Designer." *Canadian Theatre Review* 126 (2006): 38–41.

Johnson, Denis. "Cybershaw: A Nineteenth Century Mandate Meets Twentieth Century Technology." *Canadian Theatre Review* 81 (1994): 32–35.

Jones, Mark J. "Through the Looking Screen: Performance Technology Comes of Age." *Theatrum* 41 (1995): 19–24.

Kareda, Urjo. "Architect of Dreams." *Canadian Art* 11.3 (1994); 100–07.

Kerr, Mary. "*Mandragola*: A Designer's Portfolio." *Canadian Theatre Review* 2 (1974): 34–39.

Knowles, Ric[hard Paul]. "Robin Phillips' Strange and Wondrous Dream." *Theatre History in Canada/Histoire du théâtre au Canada* 9.1 (1988): 35–58.

———. "The Legacy of the Festival Stage." *Canadian Theatre Review* 54 (1988): 39–45.

———. "Survival Spaces: Space and the Politics of Dislocation." *Canadian Theatre Review* 88 (1996): 31–34.

———. "Looking for Enlightened Lighting: The Discourses of Lighting Design, Training and Practice." *Canadian Theatre Review* 107 (2001): 5–10.

———. *Reading the Material Theatre.* Cambridge; Cambridge University Press, 2004.

Laufer, Murray. "Designing at the Centre." *Canadian Theatre Review* 3 (1974): 42–45.

Lehman, Hans-Thies. *Postdramatic Theatre.* Trans. Karen Jürs-Munby. New York: Routledge, 2006.

Litzenberger, David. "Of Puppets and Dream Plays." *Canadian Theatre Review* 17 (1978): 21–26.

Malina, Jaroslav. "The Outer and Inner Spaces of Scenography: A Conflict Between Geometry and Emotion." *Theatre Design Research* 1 (2002): 73–78.

Mark, Lisa Gabrielle. "Confessions of Disguise/Disguises of Confession: Looking at Primus Theatre's *The Night Room.*" *Canadian Theatre Review* 82 (1995): 26–28.

McAuley, Gay. *Space in Performance: Making Meaning in the Theatre.* Ann Arbor: U of Michigan P, 1999.

Mendes, Tanit and Janet Tulloch. "Set Design as Cosmic Metaphor: Religious Seeing and Theatre Space." *Theatre Research in Canada/Recherches théâtrales au Canada* 27.2 (2006): 260–88.

Mirzoeff, Nicholas. "On Visuality." *Journal of Visual Culture* 5.1 (2006): 53–79.

Mitchell, Elizabeth. "Only the Hairdresser Knows For Sure! Martha Gleeson's Adventures in Wigland." *Theatrum* 31 (1992/3): 7–8.

Mitchell, W.J.T. *What Do Pictures Want?* Chicago; U of Chicago P, 2005.

Nicholls, Liz. "World on a String." *Canadian Theatre Review* 95 (1998): 31–37.

Noiseux-Gurik, Renée. "French Language Studies in Scenography and Stagecraft in Quebec." *Canadian Theatre Review* 91 (1997): 13–18.

Oddey, Alison and Christine White, eds. *The Potentials of Spaces: The Theory and Practice of Scenography & Performance.* Bristol: Intellect Books, 2006.

Page, Malcolm. "Setting the Stage: The Director/Designer Relationship." *Theatrum* 38 (1994): 14–18.

Perkins, Don. "From Megaworlds to Minimagic: Catalyst Theatre's Process for Small Scale Spectacle." *Canadian Theatre Review* 97 (1998): 12–17.

Porter, Deborah and Nigel Hunt. "Staging Spectacle: The Phantoms behind the Phantom and Other Backstage Magic." *Theatrum* 17 (1990): 11–15.

Rewa, Natalie. "Perspective on Scenography: Scenes, Seen, Unseen." *Canadian Theatre Review* 79/80 (1994): 28–32.

———. *Scenography in Canada: Selected Designers.* Toronto: U of Toronto P, 2004.

Reid, Gilbert. "Perspectives on Recent Set Design by Ken MacDonald." *Canadian Theatre Review* 91 (1997): 67–70.

Rickerd, Julie Rekai. "A Unified Vision." *Lighting Dimensions* 23.2 (1999): 56–60, 79, 80.

Rogalsky, Matt. "Audience is a verb: A conversation with Darren Copeland." *Canadian Theatre Review* 129 (2007): 51–53

Shaw Festival. *The Pictorial Stage: Twenty-Five Years of Vision and Design at the Shaw Festival.* Exhibition catalogue. Stratford: Beacon Herald Fine Printing Division, 1986.

Sofer, Andrew. *The Stage Life of Props.* Ann Arbor: U of Michigan P, 2003.

Souchotte, Sandra. "Designing Women: Four Young Designers Colour Their Theatrical World." *Scene Changes* 8.1 (1980): 8–15.

Stratford Festival. *A 10th Season Souvenir Collection of Costume Designs from the Stratford Festival.* Stratford; Stratford Festival, 1962.

Strike, Maurice. "The Designer's Dilemma." *Canadian Theatre Review* 1 (1974): 45–48.

Svoboda, Joseph. *The Secret of Theatrical Space: Memoir of Joseph Svoboda.* Trans. and ed. J.M. Burian. New York: Applause, 1993.

Thomson, Graeme S. "Imagining New Places." *Theatrum* 12 (1989): 23–26.

Tubridy, Derval. "Sound Spaces: Aurality in Samuel Beckett, Janet Cardiff, and Bruce Nauman." *Performance Research* 12.1 (2007): 5–11.

Souvenir Costume Designs from the Stratford Festival. Stratford, Stratford Festival 1967.

Wallace, Robert. "The Theatrical Designs of Michael Levine." *Insite* 3.1 (1993): 42–43.

Watts, Allan. "Sculptured Spaces: Jim Plaxton in Conversation with Allan Watts." *Canadian Theatre Review* 70 (1992): 54–59.

———. "De/Sign/ificant Assumptions." *Canadian Theatre Review* 71 (1992): 32–36.

———. "Learning to be Bold with Lighting: A Conversation with Andrea Lundy." *Canadian Theatre Review* 107 (2001): 11–15.

West, Nigel. "Visual Directories for Invented Worlds: Costuming Shakespeare." *Theatre Design Research* 1 (2002): 45–56.

Special Issues

Playing Space and Spaces. Canadian Theatre Review 6 (1975).

Scenography. Canadian Theatre Review 70 (1992).

Designer Training in Canada. Canadian Theatre Review 91 (1997).

Stage Lighting in Canada. Canadian Theatre Review 107 (2001).

Sound Design. Canadian Theatre Review 129 (2007).

Web Addresses for Projects Discussed in the Volume

Herman Voaden
www.lib.unb.ca/Texts/Theatre/voaden/default.htm

Ken MacDonald and Morris Panych
www.2x2ltd.com/2x2.html

Astrid Janson
www.astridjanson.blogspot.com

Axel Morgenthaler
www.photonicdreams.com
www.axelmorgenthaler.com

Michael Whitfield
www.theatremuseumcanada.ca/legendlibrary.asp#WhitfieldBenson

Camellia Koo
www.nightswimmingtheatre.com

Kathleen Irwin
uregina.ca/Bus_Project/busproject.html

Dany Lyne
www.siminovitchprize.com

Nancy Tobin
www.mmebutterfly.com/restarea/

Notes on Contributors

Ana Cappelluto is an Associate Professor in the Department of Theatre at Concordia University where she teaches design for the theatre. Her research focuses on the development of new scenographic tools. In 2000 she completed a two-year project entitled Capturing Costume History: Assessing the contribution of three major modern Quebec costume designers, François Barbeau, Louise Jobin and François Laplante (http://collections.ic.gc.ca/costume). Ana Cappelluto is also an award-winning scenographer. She has designed shows that have been produced in Montreal, Toronto, New York, Switzerland, Italy and Paris. Her designs have travelled to numerous national and international festivals.

Michael Devine is a theatre director who has created and directed productions in Hungary, Romania, Finland, Greece, Bulgaria, and Serbia and Montenegro, as well as in his native Canada. His workshop for actors, BOXWHATBOX, incorporates his own approach to "an open heart in an open body." A Professor of Theatre Studies at Acadia University in Wolfville, Nova Scotia, he regularly publishes articles on aspects of Canadian and international drama.

Ron Fedoruk has been teaching scenography in the Theatre Program at UBC since 1989. His career as a designer spans more than thirty-five years, and he has created designs for many Canadian theatres. For six years he was the Scenographer for Bard on the Beach Shakespeare Festival, for which he designed a dozen productions. From 1993 to 2000, Fedoruk was a Canadian representative to the International Theatre Design Organization (OISTAT). His work was exhibited in the prestigious Prague Quadrennial Scenographic Exposition in 1995.

Anna Friz is a sound and radio artist living in Montreal. She has produced numerous original works for campus and community radio, CBC's Brave New Waves, and national radio in Austria, Denmark and Germany. She has presented installation and performance work in Vancouver, Winnipeg, Toronto, and Montreal, as well as Chicago, Vienna, and Berlin. She is currently creating a mechanized puppet theatre in functioning tube radios from the 1940s. Her article on Montreal's Silophone Project appeared in *Musicworks* 83.

Reid Gilbert is Adjunct Professor at the University of British Columbia, having recently retired from Capilano University in Vancouver. He is a co-editor of *Canadian Theatre Review* and a member of the Editorial Advisory Board of *Theatre Research in Canada.* He has written a play (produced ten times), and is widely published in Canadian and international journals and collections on drama (including five articles in volumes of this series). He has co-written (with Sylvan Barnet) *A Short Guide to Writing about Literature*, now in a second Canadian edition.

Kathleen Irwin is Associate Professor, teaching scenography in the Theatre Department, University of Regina. She is Co-Artistic Director of Knowhere Productions Inc. a performance company that explores the relationship of a local population to a particular place, time, and community and produces distinctive site-specific events that draw upon the particular and discrete cultural and geographical resources of found performance sites. She is also Co-chair of ArtsAction Inc., an arts-based research organization that investigates the arts as a driver and measurement of urban renewal. Recent research in media and cyberspace proposes the internet as a performance platform that encourages ethical cosmopolitanism.

Camellia Koo is a set and costume designer and installation artist. Recent designs include the set for *The Stepmother* (Shaw Festival) and sets and costumes for *East of Berlin* (Tarragon). Other collaborations include fu-Gen Asian Canadian Theatre Company (Resident Designer and Artistic Associate), Cahoots Theatre Projects, b current, Modern Times Theatre, Nightwood, Native Earth Performing Arts, Lorraine Kimsa Theatre for Young People, Fujiwara Dance Inventions, Great Canadian Theatre Company, The Shaw Festival, The Second City (Toronto and Chicago), Soulpepper and Tarragon Theatre. She is the recipient of four Dora Awards and shared the 2006 Siminovitch Protegé Prize. Camellia holds an MA from Central Saint Martins College of Art & Design (UK).

Edward (Ted) Little is Professor and Chair of the Department of Theatre at Concordia University, Associate Artistic Director of Montreal's Teesri Duniya Theatre, and Editor-in-Chief of *alt.theatre: cultural diversity and the stage*—Canada's only professional journal examining intersections between politics, cultural plurality and the stage. His areas of specialization include Intercultural, Community-engaged, and Popular Theatre forms. He is currently heading the Oral History and Performance Group, one of seven research clusters comprising Life Stories of Montrealers Displaced by War, Genocide, and Other Human Rights Violations project (www.histoiresdeviemontreal.ca).

Dany Lyne has been involved in over eighty productions in Canada, the United States and Europe, from new plays, to opera, from small independent theatres to large international theatres. Her work has been seen at the Stratford Festival of Canada, the Canadian Opera Company, Théâtre Français de Toronto, Necessary Angel Theatre Company, Soulpepper, the National Arts Centre, Tarragon Theatre, Elgin Theatre, Tapestry New Opera Works, Pacific Opera, Cincinnati Opera, Central City Opera (Denver), Nationale Reisopera (Netherlands), Opera North (England), and De Vlaamse Opera (Belgium), among others.

Natalie Rewa is the author of *Scenography in Canada: Selected Designers* (University of Toronto Press, 2004). She was an editor of *Canadian Theatre Review* from 1987 to 1995. Her current research focuses on Michael Levine's production design for opera. She was the co-curator of the Canadian exhibit for the Prague Quadrennial 2007. She is Professor of Drama at Queen's University in Kingston.

Jerrard Smith has created set and costume, mask and puppet design for dance and theatre since 1980. He has closely collaborated with R. Murray Schafer on the works of the Patria cycle. Past works include set and costume designs for Robert Desrosiers's *Corridors, Blue Snake* and *UltraCity* and Debra Brown's *Apogée*, costume design for Walt Disney's World on Ice productions and the creation of a visual spectacle for the New Year's Eve Millennium celebration on Parliament Hill in Ottawa. His theatre design work for Ann-Marie MacDonald's *Nigredo Hotel* and for Phyzikal Theatre Company's *Flesh and Clay* have earned him nominations for the Dora Mavor Moore Award. Jerrard and his wife Diana were among the Canadian exhibitors at the 2007 Prague Quadrennial of Scenography and received "Honourable Scenographer" awards from OISTAT. Jerrard currently teaches in the Drama department at the University of Guelph.

Rahul Varma is a playwright, essayist and an activist who migrated to Canada from his birth country India in 1976. He is currently the artistic director of Teesri Duniya Theatre which he co-founded in 1981. The company is dedicated to producing politically relevant theatre examining issues of cultural representation and diversity in Canada. Some of his plays are *No Man's Land, Trading Injuries* (radio drama), *Counter Offence* and *Bhopal.*

Herman Voaden (1903–1991) was a playwright, director, educator and editor. He developed a unique nonrealist multimedia playwrighting and production style, which he termed "symphonic expressionism" during the 1930s. Influenced by the paintings and cultural nationalism of the Group of Seven, his "symphonic theatre," a fusion of realistic and poetic choral speech, music and dance and non-realistic lighting and setting, was the primary stylistic alternative to the prevailing realism in Canadian theatre production. Following the suspension of regular theatre production because of WW II, Voaden began a second career as an arts lobbyist. He was the president of the Canadian Arts Council (1945–48), the national director of the Canadian Conference of the Arts (1966–68), and the president of the Canadian Guild of Crafts (1968–70). The Estate of Herman Voaden endows the Herman Voaden National Playwriting Competition at Queen's University. His plays are collected in *A Vision of Canada: Herman Voaden's Dramatic Works 1928–1945*, edited by Anton Wagner (Toronto: Simon and Pierre, 1993). The Herman Voaden Papers are located at York University. There is a detailed inventory of these papers, as well as biographical information available on the York University website:
http://info.library.yorku.ca/de pts/asc/Finding_aids/Voaden_webpage/hvindex.htm.
Electronic copies of his plays, essays and criticism are available on the following website: http://www.lib.unb.ca/Texts/Theatre/voaden/index.htm.

Lowrie Warrener (1900–1983) was a painter and sculptor. He was influenced by the Group of Seven. He graduated from the Ontario College of Art in 1924 and worked and studied in Antwerp and Paris. Upon his return to Canada he designed the set for *Antony and Cleopatra* produced in Hart House in 1928 by Carol Aikens. He designed sets for several other productions in Toronto and began his collaboration with Herman Voaden after winning a theatre design competition convened by Voaden. The four one act plays for which he proposed designs were produced in April 1929. During the summer of 1929 Warrener and Voaden travelled to California and in 1930 across Canada by train. It was during this trip that they composed *Symphony*. The artistic partnership dissolved in 1930, but continued with Voaden purchasing Warrener paintings.

Allan Watts is a retired professor and scenographer (School of English and Theatre Studies, University of Guelph) who is currently enjoying his new avocation as an studio painter.

Michèle White is a painter and a Professor of Drawing & Painting in the Faculty of Art at the Ontario College of Art & Design. She is represented by the David Kaye Gallery and has participated in solo, group and collective exhibitions since 1975 in public and private galleries throughout the province.